T0331045

Digging Deeper

How Purpose-Driven Enterprises
Create Real Value

A shift is taking place in the narrative about the role of business – from a profit-maximization, shareholder supremacy orientation to a commitment to a deeper purpose, one that resonates with a broad array of stakeholders, producing multifaceted value well beyond financial returns and profit, creating true meaning in our lives. *Digging Deeper* aptly captures this transformation, with myriad inspirational examples that captivate the reader, providing insight into how businesses can develop deeper roots – with a long-term orientation, lasting relationships, a strong local presence, commitment to a learning community, and leadership focused on creating a better life for all stakeholders. As the authors convincingly argue, the resulting real value – for companies, communities, society, and the environment – can take us from purpose to prosperity.

Anthony F. Buono, Professor of Management & Sociology, Bentley University

The authors of *Digging Deeper* describe writing the book as a "wonderful journey." Reading *Digging Deeper* enables you to embark on that journey to all the fascinating places described, including the Benedictine monastery of Admont in the Austrian Alps, Mondragón in the Basque region of Spain, or the island Inis Meáin off the west coast of Ireland. As well as encountering inspiring entrepreneurs and business leaders portrayed in the book, the readers also embark on a journey to the spiritual backbone of sustainable business.

Katharina Spraul, Professor of Sustainability Management,
University of Kaiserslautern (Germany)

Business should not just be about making money. But where are the examples that show me what business should be? They are all gathered in this book. Like a documentary, it tracks down some of the most fascinating and unusual species out there in the business world. Companies that have a purpose, thrive based on principles, and make money in ways that lift others up. They really exist, and learning about those companies is a great eye-opener. The book supplies fascinating topics for discussion, deep inspiration for business people, and hope for everyone. A beautiful and important book!

Julian Kölbel, Postdoctoral Fellow, MIT Sloan School of Management

In the Anthropocene when human organizations and activities are the biggest source of changes in nature, we need to conceptualize successful organizations creating enduring value with purpose through cooperation, with long-term orientation, and grounding in place. *Digging Deeper* digs deep and wide, to tell the much-needed stories of just such organizations. A must-read book for managers and students of management.

Paul Shrivastava, Executive Director, Future Earth, David O'Brien
Distinguished Professor of Sustainable Enterprise, John Molson School of
Business, Concordia University

DIGGING DEEPER

How **Purpose-Driven Enterprises**
Create **Real Value**

Dietmar Sternad,
James J. Kennelly
and Finbarr Bradley

Routledge
Taylor & Francis Group

LONDON AND NEW YORK

First published 2016 by Greenleaf Publishing Limited

Published 2017 by Routledge
2 Park Square, Milton Park, Abingdon, Oxon OX14 4RN
711 Third Avenue, New York, NY 10017, USA

Routledge is an imprint of the Taylor & Francis Group, an informa business

Cover by Sadie Gornall-Jones.

British Library Cataloguing in Publication Data:
    A catalogue record for this book is available from the British Library.

    ISBN-13: 978-1-78353-539-2 [pbk]
    ISBN-13: 978-1-78353-538-5 [hbk]

Contents

Figures

Figures

Foreword

Michael V. Russo

Digging Deeper will challenge your assumptions, lift your spirits, and leave you wondering why purpose-driven enterprises are not the subject of greater praise – and emulation. Dietmar Sternad, James Kennelly, and Finbarr Bradley have written a book that is at once scholarly and highly accessible. Like a fine sweater of the variety made on the Irish island of Inis Meáin, it deserves to be appreciated for its craftsmanship and authenticity.

Evidence of renewed interest in the purpose of enterprises is everywhere. This is the result of a confluence of forces that had its latest peak in the Great Recession, which left citizens reassessing the trust they placed in private enterprise. At the same time, consumers began demanding greater transparency on the part of enterprises, and used emerging technologies to broadcast resulting discoveries through social networks. But it is the content of what they share that is critical and underscores the thesis of this marvelous book: A company's financial performance depends as much on the company itself as it does on the products it sells.

Against this backdrop, many established enterprises are engaged in rear-guard actions to shield their reputations by erecting façades of respectability. But claiming a purpose in this way is a sham. Instead, Sternad, Kennelly, and Bradley show that purpose is compelling only when it is an authentic, foundational organizing principle. In fact, when an enterprise's core purpose strengthens over the long run, it infuses social relevance and identity in enterprises that have always been about more than profit. The case studies in this book, covering enterprises from pencil makers to coffee roasters, illustrate that longevity demands what you might call "radically old" thinking.

This thinking, dating back to the inception of communities and organizations themselves, gives voice and value to a broad constellation of stakeholders. Many professionals and academics stubbornly assert that a focus on more than money confounds management by shifting focus away from the unitary goal of profits. This is surely true in one respect. By undermining the utilitarian approach of neoclassical economics, which relies on the use of a single metric – money – to evaluate alternatives, life does become more complicated for managers. But that does not mean that trying to balance economic, social, and environmental imperatives is wrongheaded. In fact, it is precisely what was expected of organizations for centuries!

If an organization is to be an embedded member of society, driven by its core purpose and creating real value for a range of stakeholders, it must transfigure its strategic principles. The beauty of this book is its insightful and comprehensive approach to working through those principles. In so doing, the authors directly attack many of the fundamentals of the single-bottom-line business. Purpose-driven enterprises live in a world of long-term relationships, not a world of episodic and faceless arm's-length transactions. For them, the depth, longevity, and character of relationships create a strong sense of mutuality and equifinality that draws partners together to advance common goals. Purpose-driven enterprises also reflect and leverage their local roots rather than operate as immaterial nomads in search of tax havens and cheap labor. An unwavering sense of place is fundamental to the identity of purpose-driven enterprises and enriches their most treasured relationships.

Sternad, Kennelly, and Bradley weave these and other characteristics of successful purpose-driven organizations into a set of six practices that define their attractiveness and utility in the modern economy. Copious research in the organization sciences has established that enterprises with leading environmental and social programs also can be profitable. This book brings the level of analysis down to earth by providing a framework to appreciate how exactly this is done. Thus, it would behoove managers of larger, more conventional enterprises to read this book. In the same way that executives look for smaller technology-oriented enterprises to provide "proof of concept" for innovative new products, an analogous effect is in evidence here. Executives are scrutinizing small, purpose-driven organizations to appreciate innovative social and environmental programs that they might integrate into their own organizations. As those purpose-driven organizations then push farther into the social and environmental space, this creates a virtuous cycle with tangible and expansive benefits for society.

Any scholarly book can be judged by the extent to which it elicits more ideas, conjecture, and debates than it puts to rest. I am happy to report that based on these criteria, *Digging Deeper* is an outstanding book! I look forward to recommending it to students, professionals, and anyone exploring how an organization can maximize its potential on truly meaningful dimensions. When the values of an enterprise match those of its local citizenry, it can realize its full potential. As this book illustrates, an organization's purpose then becomes not a utopian vision but a manifestly practical credo.

Michael V. Russo, Lundquist Professor of Sustainable
Management, University of Oregon
Author, *Companies on a Mission: Entrepreneurial Strategies
for Growing Sustainably, Responsibly, and Profitably*

Preface

> "What's optimism?" . . .
> "Alas," said Candide, "it is the madness of
>   maintaining
> that everything is right when it is wrong."
>   Voltaire, Candide

Indeed, much seems to be going wrong in today's business world. Myopic executives and detached financial analysts view corporations as short-term profit maximization machines. Disciples of the share price God, they set ever-increasing profit goals, reach new heights of creativity in devising sophisticated control systems that resemble the drummer of slave galleys, and celebrate lay-offs as "successful restructuring measures." We see executives who are convinced that shareholder value is the highest value of all, regardless of any detrimental effects that their decisions and their corporations' actions have on our society and environment. We can observe rootlessness, excessive individualism and rivalry, a wide array of irresponsible managerial behaviors and a general lack of sustainability. Sad to say, these views also seem to hold sway among policy-makers and media commentators. Many seem to have for-gotten that business should actually fulfill a key role in society, the provision of goods and services that make life easier or better. They do so in exchange for money, of course, but it used to be an *exchange*, not the single-minded money-orientation that is so common in many of today's C-suites.

But despite this rather bleak picture, and perhaps because we teach in institutions of higher education, we are optimists. How could we not be? As educators, we see our role as helping students to develop the knowledge, skills, and values that will enable them to positively contribute to society, find a place where they can make a difference, and find meaning in their professional lives. We are quite certain that this is what many of today's younger generation hanker after and aspire to. We further believe that we and they can learn a lot from good examples, following the dictum often attributed to Albert Schweitzer: "The good example is not just one possibility to influence other people, it is the only one." Each of us individually has long been interested in finding examples of an alternative approach to business. We are interested in people who refuse to give all their devotion to increasing share prices, in entrepreneurs and managers who take their societal responsibility seriously and build businesses with a long-term orientation, a strong sense of place, respect for people and the environment, fair and co-operative relationships with all stakeholders, and a deeper purpose that is related to improving other people's lives.

We consider ourselves fortunate to have made contact with each other to share some stories about these purpose-driven businesses, stories that we had written in the form of case studies for our students. We soon recognized that the businesses that we were studying, albeit in very different corners of the world, nevertheless share a common orientation: They are focused on creating value that goes far beyond "money value," and follow very similar patterns in both their value bases and actions. So we decided to join forces to dig deeper and identify other people who also ran their companies with a deeper purpose and a high level of societal responsibility. For months, we exchanged newspaper stories, researched databases and lists of sustainable and responsible businesses, and used our personal and professional networks to find the most positive examples from all over the world. Out of the hundreds of companies that we scanned, we carefully selected a few inspiring stories of entrepreneurs and leaders for whom making meaning is at least as important as making money. We discovered them on different continents, in various industries, and in sizes from small and medium-sized enterprises to large corporations – some already well known to the public, others hidden gems – showing that the creation of real value is not bound to a certain niche, but can be implemented everywhere people deliberately decide to follow a deeper purpose.

Every example in this book offers a good reason for optimism. If these companies and their leaders can make a difference, each one of us – whether engaged in the cut and thrust of business itself or in educating future business leaders – can do so, too. We do not claim that everything is right, even in the companies that we portray in this book. But we believe that all of us can learn from exceptional business leaders who follow a deeper purpose. These exceptional people help us realize that business is about far more than just making money. It is fundamentally about meaning.

Writing this book has been a wonderful journey for all three of us. Since that fortuitous day we first made contact, we have become fast and trusted friends. We explored new terrain and met business leaders who are quite literally awe-inspiring. These pages are full of their stories.

We would like to thank all these entrepreneurs, leaders and organizational professionals who shared their time and experience with us. In particular, we would like to thank Christine Arlt, Rudi Daelmans, Marie-Thérèse de Blacam, Ruairí de Blacam, Tarlach de Blacam, Michael Elsas, Johannes Gutmann, Helianti Hilman, Andrea Illy, Ernst Kronawitter, Helmuth Neuner, Christine Pascolo, and Sandra Suppa. We are also grateful to Michael Russo, the Lundquist Professor of Sustainable Management at the University of Oregon, for so generously and graciously contributing the wonderful Foreword to this book.

Dietmar Sternad would like to thank his family, Katja, Jakob, and Elisabeth, and his parents Edith and Peter for all their love and understanding. He would also like to thank his colleagues at Carinthia University of Applied Sciences for their collegiality and support, and his students, a source of constant inspiration. One former student, Kristina Erlacher, also contributed to this work directly by interviewing one of the protagonists in this book. A very special thanks goes to his co-authors James J. Kennelly and Finbarr Bradley. It is a wonderful experience to collaborate with friends who share the same values, an incredible degree of enthusiasm, and good humor.

James Kennelly thanks his wife Linda, and his sons Brendan and Terence for their love and support and for their reminders of what is truly important in life, and in business. He would also like to gratefully acknowledge the support of Courtney Sale Ross and the Courtney and Steven Ross Chair in Interdisciplinary Studies, who helped to make this project possible, and the collegiality and support of his colleagues at Skidmore College. He has greatly enjoyed this transatlantic collaboration with like-minded colleagues Dietmar and Finbarr, and will value their friendship long after the last copy of this book (and there will hopefully be many) is sold.

Finbarr Bradley wishes to express his gratitude and thanks to his late parents, family and close friends for their encouragement and support over the years. He considers himself blessed to have been given the opportunity to work on this book with wonderful colleagues and now special friends, Dietmar Sternad and James J. Kennelly. He has learned so much from them both, not just about the theory and practice of business but also about how to combine a commitment to ideals with attractive writing and academic rigor.

Last, but by no means least, we would like to thank Rebecca Marsh and Anna Comerford at Greenleaf Publishing for their belief in this project and their thoughtful help and advice, Sadie Gornall-Jones for the outstanding cover design, Dean Bargh for so ably managing production, and everyone in the Greenleaf sales and marketing team for all their efforts to make our book available to a wide audience.

Dietmar Sternad, Villach, Austria
James J. Kennelly, Saratoga Springs, USA
Finbarr Bradley, Dublin, Ireland
August 2016

1

In search of real value

What is a cynic?
A man who knows the price of everything,
and the value of nothing.
    Oscar Wilde, *Lady Windermere's Fan* (1892), Act III

Ask anyone on Wall Street about the value of a particular business. They will likely launch into a lecture on market capitalization, discounted cash flows, capital asset pricing models, mark-to-market accounting or price-to-earnings ratios. But, whatever we call these sophisticated methods, they fundamentally boil down to the proverbial bottom line: how much cash and profit does a company throw off, and what are its stock price and market valuation?

Though the primacy of shareholder value has dominated the mainstream business mindset for decades, and still does even after the latest global financial crisis, it is no longer uncontested. The myopic focus of the business world on maximizing shareholder wealth is now fair game for critics, given its short-termism and lack of sustainability, its neglect of social or environmental impacts, its fostering of economic inequality, and its tendency to incentivize unethical and unprincipled behavior. The call for a broader notion of business and its value-creation imperative is getting louder.

This call is even coming from companies themselves. Take the refreshing example of Apple, where at its 2014 Annual Meeting, the usually calm and collected CEO, Tim Cook, rebuffed a shareholder asking him to commit to only making moves that were profitable for the company. "When we work on making our devices accessible by the blind, I don't consider the bloody ROI," Cook told the questioner, a climate change denier complaining about Apple devoting funds to renewable energy and sustainable projects. A clearly incensed Cook added: "If you want me to do things only for ROI reasons, you should get out of this stock" (*Business Insider*, 2014).

This is a book about businesses that create value. At first blush, this is hardly a novel topic. After all, isn't value creation the ultimate goal of all businesses? We believe it is. We also believe that profit-making firms are central to the modern economy. But profit-making is not the same as value creation. Clearly, the concept of value means many things to many people. Therefore, before we rush to conclusions too fast, we need to explore a seemingly simple question: What is value? Or, more to the point: What is *real value*?

Let's begin this exploration in a metaphorical vein by imagining a garden. A garden is a patch of cultivated earth, tilled and tended by human beings to yield flora of all types – flowers and herbs and vegetables and fruit. Depending on the season, the garden may blaze with bright colors, or scent the air with subtle fragrance, or yield an abundance of fresh produce, or lie dormant and somnolent as it recharges itself. A garden conjures visions of fertility, beauty and utility – co-existing within its ordered confines.

What is the value of a garden? Is it the monetary value of the land on which the garden was cultivated? Or the exchange value of the produce of the garden when it is sold at market? Or are there other, deeper, maybe even hidden sources of value in a garden?

For visitors, a garden might offer a sensory and aesthetic experience, as they admire its order, tranquility, and beauty. Those with a more meditative bent may have a spiritual experience when they contemplate the unique and complex relationship between nature and culture. (It is interesting that the words *cultivate* and *culture* both share a similar etymology.) A garden might even offer a healing experience – for the body, with the use of medical herbs that grow in a garden, as well as for the mind, when the outer tranquility releases calmness inside. For those who own a garden, it can represent an artistic creation, a means of self-expression and a level of self-reliance. It can be a work of art because it achieves harmony so that all forms of life are given the opportunity to flourish and reach their potential.

Even for professional gardeners who do not own the garden, the act of cultivation itself can lead to pride in having brought more beauty into our world. They assess a garden's merit not through growth of its plants but through their beauty and overall harmony. Gardens are also good for the community. They offer a peaceful environment where people can meet, refresh, and relax. They strengthen our relationship with and stewardship of nature. And they can promote physical activities and mental well-being. Last but not least, gardens can have a positive effect on our natural environment, and produce many positive externalities like soaking up carbon dioxide, reducing air pollution and offering a nurturing habitat for insects, birds, and other creatures. In short, gardens are good for us – as individuals and as a community.

The *real value* of a garden thus goes far beyond its mere monetary value. It lies much deeper, in improving the quality of life of the people who own, cultivate, and visit the garden and of the natural environment that sustains it. Studies have confirmed that gardens have decidedly positive effects on people's happiness and health (Pretty, 2004; *Gardener's World*, 2013; Balch, 2015). And, even if this does not all translate directly into money, the deeper value is there, and it is real.

"Our perception of value is dramatically subjective," says Dan Ariely, professor of psychology and behavioral economics at Duke University. "It comes from lots of things from the environment," he explains in the award-winning documentary *Real Value*. "Neoclassical economics has a very simple answer to it; something's value is whatever people are willing to pay for it. But the deeper question of what is value is much more complex."[1] Ariely conducted experiments in which people bought coffee. The coffee was surrounded by condiments that were usually never used with coffee. For one sample, these condiments were put into beautiful glass and metal containers, for another sample in non-descript Styrofoam cups. None of these containers had any influence on the taste and use value of the coffee. Yet people were willing to pay a lot more – actually around twice as much – for the coffee that was surrounded by beautiful things. The perceived value of the product dramatically changed with the feelings that the surroundings conveyed.

To explore this more expansive notion of value, let us consider a very special type of garden, one that is mostly used for economic purposes – a vineyard. What is the value of an acre of vineyard? It depends, the connoisseur would say, on many factors – for example, on the *terroir*, the location of the land and its interaction with the climate, terrain, and soil, on the knowledge and passion of the people who tend the vines, on the tradition and reputation of the wine-growing region and of the estate, and on the age of the vines. It also depends on the "character" of the vines: how have the vines been treated? Have they been exploited for maximum short-term yield, or grown and maintained with care? Has the wine-grower recognized the limits of the plants – for example, regarding their number per acre and the amount of chemical pesticides that they can absorb? Was the focus of the winery itself on the quality or on the mere quantity of the wine? No wine expert would ever assess the value of a vineyard solely on the number of grapes that it yields. Such reductionism, however, is exactly the dominant tendency when we discuss "success" in business. All too often, the value of a business is reduced to one dimension that must be maximized – its financial value.

We think it's time to liberate the notion of value from the chains with which the financial world has imprisoned it. We believe that *real value* goes well beyond the more common conception of value bandied about by the general business community. Of course, business value *is* linked to money and profits: businesses without positive cash flows and profits – at least over time – will simply cease to exist. We are, however, convinced that the real value of a business is far broader than a narrow, financially dominated definition would suggest. As in a garden, the real value of a business lies at least as much in its emotional value and in its contribution to improving the quality of people's lives as in its financial metrics.

"The world's dumbest idea"

The English word *value* stems from the Old French *valoir*, meaning "to be worth." A quick look into the dictionary tells us that the term *value* is used for "the material and monetary worth of something."[2] But this definition, in fact, is ranked second in the dictionary to another, more encompassing definition of value: "the regard that something is held to deserve; the importance, worth, or usefulness of something."[3]

What is the value – in its wider meaning of the *importance, worth,* or *usefulness* – of a business, then? Of course, the answer depends on who is asking. A business owner may answer differently from an employee, a customer, or a neighbor who is affected, for better or worse, by the activities of the enterprise.

It has been decades since R. Edward Freeman's seminal work in the 1980s first challenged the predominant shareholder value approach with a different, even revolutionary, perspective. His idea was that regardless of their ultimate purpose – which may well remain making money for the owners – businesses needed to pay attention to the effects of their actions on others (Freeman, 1984). Freeman made a case for balancing the interests of all *stakeholders,* whether employees, suppliers, customers, communities, the environment, or anyone else who could affect or be affected by a business (Freeman *et al.*, 2010). Although stakeholder theory, as it was called, experienced a lot of pushback from both mainstream business gurus who saw it as making unreasonable demands on business and some theorists who asserted that following multiple objectives in the end leaves managers with no objective at all (Jensen, 2001), many businesses have since begun to move toward creating "stakeholder value." This represented a first, tentative step toward a more comprehensive understanding of value.

Harvard Professor Michael Porter and his colleague Mark Kramer took another step forward in their 2011 *Harvard Business Review* article "Creating Shared Value" in which they questioned the "outdated approach to value creation that has emerged over the past few decades" (Porter and Kramer, 2011, p. 64). They complained that companies "continue to view value creation narrowly, optimizing short-term financial performance in a bubble while missing the most important customer needs and ignoring the broader influences that determine their longer-term success" (Porter and Kramer, 2011, p. 64). To their mind, it is time for companies to reorient themselves toward focusing on both creating monetary value for their owners and societal value by addressing the real needs of people and communities. They see an urgent need for capitalism to "reinvent itself" around the concept that they call "shared value," and are convinced that this new approach of combined monetary and societal value creation will spark a new wave of innovation and prosperity.

Now even Jack Welch, former GE Chief Executive and one of the fathers of the shareholder value movement, has changed his mind. Welch calls the singular goal of maximizing shareholder value the "world's dumbest idea" (*Financial Times*, 2009). The apparent limitations of shareholder value thinking are also openly discussed in the business press as well as in leading newspapers such as the *New York Times* and the *Washington Post*.[4] In the UK, leading economist John Kay, who writes a column for the *Financial Times*, disagrees that the only purpose of a for-profit business is to make a profit: "we must breathe to live but breathing is not the purpose of life."[5] Commentators argue that nothing in the law compels business to put shareholders ahead of other stakeholders. What the law does require is that directors promote the success of the company, which usually means balancing competing pressures and interests.

The idea of shareholder primacy was strongly promoted by ideologically driven economists like Milton Friedman, who argued that the *only* goal of the firm was to maximize profits for shareholders (Friedman, 1970). This view has led, as a recent *Harvard Business Review* article puts it, "to the election of directors who, frankly, don't know what their legal duties are" (Heracleous and Lan, 2010, p. 24). The article cites a study in which 31 out of 34 directors of

Fortune 200 companies said that they would cut down a forest or release unregulated toxic substances to the environment if it had a positive impact on profits (Rose, 2007). They believed that it was their duty to do whatever they could, within the boundaries of the law, to maximize shareholder wealth.

Cornell Law School professor Lynn Stout debunks the idea that shareholders can actually own a public corporation, which she holds is actually an autonomous legal entity; in effect, corporations own themselves (Stout, 2013). What shareholders own, she says, are shares, a contract that gives shareholders limited legal rights. Thus, shareholders need not take precedence over other stakeholders such as bondholders, suppliers, and employees. Contrary to popular belief, says Stout (2013), "the managers of public companies have no enforceable legal duty to maximize shareholder value." Sure, they can follow a profit maximization principle. But they are also free to choose other objectives: for example, to take care of employees, the local community or society at large. Stout goes even further, arguing that a policy of always putting shareholders first can actually backfire, harming the corporation and even shareholders themselves, particularly when viewed from a long-term value-creation perspective. Stout suggests a better alternative to maximizing shareholder value: "satisficing." Here, firms try to reach certain threshold levels – or do "well enough" – on several objectives rather than maximizing only one to the detriment of all others. Without doubt, firms cannot survive in the long term without making profits; but by no means does that automatically imply that profit maximization must be the sole and superordinate corporate objective.

Clearly, more companies than ever are questioning the conventional ideology, going beyond the issue of how a business operates to ask why it exists and in what kind of society it is embedded (Markevich, 2009). They ask, do their products or services truly serve deep human needs or is mere consumption the ultimate goal of human existence? Such companies regard profit as important and necessary – but not at the expense of everything else! (Canals, 2010). They realize there is often a mismatch between the two things people genuinely desire: material prosperity and spiritual fulfillment. Progressive companies capitalize on this emerging trend by enabling people, employees, and customers to understand and fulfill their real needs. They know that in the emerging "experience" age, value is increasingly determined by intangible resources such as emotions, meaning, identity, memory, belonging, and community. They clearly understand that the *real value* of a business reaches far beyond the ubiquitous money-making imperative.

The real meaning of value

Judgments about real value will always be made by human beings – and human beings make judgments with their brains. Neuroscience tells us that human brains make judgments not solely in their prefrontal cortex, the brain region which is associated with rational decision-making, but also in the limbic system. This very old part of the brain (in an evolutionary sense) is also called the "emotional brain." All stimuli that our senses send to our brain pass through the limbic system, where they are checked for their emotional value, arousing either positive or negative emotions. Human judgment and human decision-making are thus inextricably tied to our emotional lives. In our brains, rationality depends critically on sophisticated emotionality, and both must work well together to create intelligent behavior. But as psychology professor Jonathan Haidt points out in his book *The Happiness Hypothesis* (2006, p. 13) emotion does most of the work.

This means that when we judge what something is worth, we do not confine ourselves solely to a rational assessment of its utility or "price tag." We also have *feelings* about it, triggered by the emotional centers of our brain. We determine *real value* by combining the assessments – consciously or unconsciously – of both rational-functional value and emotional value. This is the reality of how human beings value things! Clearly, it is a far different way of determining value than that employed by the all too fictional *Homo economicus*.

Debate about the real meaning of value is not some recent fad. Around 360 BC, in *The Republic*, Plato distinguished between a class of goods that included "various ways of money-making," which "no one would choose . . . for their own sakes, but only for the sake of some reward or result which flows from them" on the one hand and goods "which we welcome for their own sakes, and independently of their consequences" on the other hand. Today, we would make the distinction between *instrumental value* as a means to obtain something else and *intrinsic value* of something that is valuable "as such." Money, whether it comes in the form of profits or stock prices, only has instrumental value, as we can use it to buy other things that we really value. It is functional for getting something else, but it still remains on the surface of what real value is about. *Deeper value* – the intrinsic-emotional side of real value, for example in the form of an aesthetic experience, affection for someone or something, happiness, freedom, self-expression, or positive feelings of having contributed to a good cause – is an end in itself. It is something that is simply good to have, even if it cannot be exchanged for something else.

The primary way of creating deeper value is through creating *meaning*. Meaning, as we use it in this book, is mainly about purpose or ends. Yet nothing is meaningful in itself. According to Viktor Frankl, the world-renowned psychiatrist and a concentration camp survivor, meaning is strongly related to engaging oneself in something that reaches beyond the boundaries of the self. He held that human beings are mainly concerned not with gaining pleasure or avoiding pain, but seeking meaning in their lives. Frankl, who argued that meaning is different and unique to each individual, was convinced that human beings fulfill themselves in "self-transcendence," through "the service to a cause or the love of a person" (Frankl, 2001, p. 147). In other words: in doing something good for others, we feel better ourselves.

Meaning, value, and money are related. If an experience, an idea or a physical object conveys meaning, it tends to be more valuable, so a person or society is willing to pay a higher price for it. Human beings always long for meaning in their lives. "People have enough stuff, but they don't have enough meaning," is how marketing expert Seth Godin (Tracy, 2014) expresses it.

The deeper value that we obtain from meaning, from having a positive impact on others, is what makes life worth living. If meaning and deeper, emotional value play such a pivotal role in our lives, why do we so often neglect them when we talk about the value that a business – which is after all a collection, and a creation, of people itself – creates? Why don't we talk about the *real value* of a business?

A tree full of value

To return to our garden metaphor: gardens need trees. Trees provide shelter, improve the quality of the air, and prevent the erosion of soil. Further, they also have a spiritual value as we admire their majesty and beauty. Trees also nurture us with their fruit. In order to abundantly bear fruit, however, trees must first have deep roots. The roots firmly anchor a tree and support it with life-sustaining water and nutrients.

Some trees have shallow roots, some deeper ones. So it is with enterprises. Those that focus solely on shareholder value are only shallowly rooted in their narrow-minded money-making focus. Thus, they also limit their potential to bear fruit. Their major fruit is the very limited and solely financial value that accrues more or less exclusively to the shareholders. They combine this with the "by-products" of jobs and salaries for employees, products and services for customers, and taxes for the community (when they are not opting to move their headquarters to tax havens). But such businesses are limited, even stunted. And their shallow roots make them susceptible to environmental influences. In a heavy storm, the tree falls. The fates of Enron and Lehman Brothers offer cautionary examples.

However, we believe that businesses can create much more than just *money value* if they are willing to sink deep roots, draw upon their unique attributes and adopt a principled approach to their operations and strategies. By *digging deeper*, their leaders create an awareness of the larger whole, leading to actions that help shape the future of their businesses in a way that bears fruits for many rather than for a few – for owners, employees, customers, partners, the community, and the environment alike. These are the enterprises that create *real value* (see Figure 1.1).

There *are* such exceptional enterprises – and we will visit some outstanding examples in this book – that have already begun to dig deeper, having planted seeds and nourished trees that create real value. What these enterprises have in common is that they usually have a deeper purpose that is much more than just profit maximization. They have a clear mission or ultimate *raison d'être* that goes far beyond making money; it is also concerned with improving the quality of life of people. With this sort of clear purpose, these enterprises also provide meaning and identity for their employees, their customers, their owners, and the communities in which they

are based. They create emotional value through creating meaning
– having a "cause" that positively affects the lives of others.

FIGURE I.I   **The difference between "money value" and "real
value"**

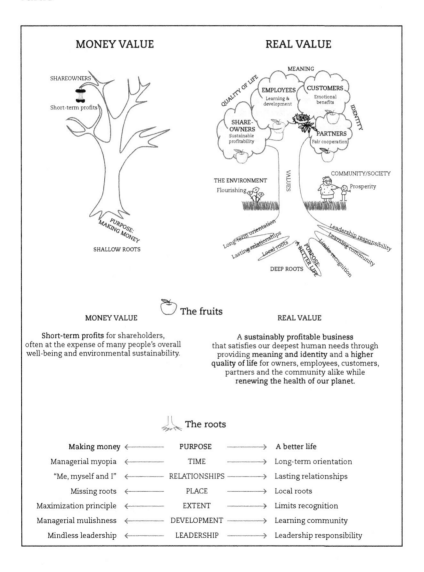

Employees get more than just a "job" and a paycheck from enterprises that focus on the creation of real value. They know *why* they work rather than just what they need to work on. Their jobs are meaningful because they contribute to something greater than just their own self-interest. And they generate learning and development possibilities for employees to grow themselves along the way. Customers, in turn, feel good when they buy the products or services of enterprises that are positively contributing to their own well-being as well as to society and the environment. Customers get emotional value in addition to the purely functional value of a product. It also offers them a way to express not only who they are but also what kind of world they want to live in. It gives them meaning and identity. It is not only employees and customers, however, who get more value out of real value-oriented enterprises. The shareholders will also reap more emotional benefits from their companies. They know that by owning and supporting such enterprises, they can contribute to improving other people's lives, which in turn can bring more meaning and identity to their *own* lives. Moreover, the deep-rooted businesses that they own will also be able to withstand stronger storms, thus making them more sustainably profitable from a business perspective.

These exceptional enterprises also create shared value in Porter and Kramer's sense as they contribute to thriving communities and a prospering society with their focus on improving people's quality of life. Not least, they also practice stewardship and respect for our over-stressed natural environment. Thus, they yield fruits that greatly exceed the *money value* of corporations that blindly follow the conventional shareholder primacy perspective.

These enterprises are able to create real value because of their deep roots. They tend to engage in general approaches and practices (the "6Ls" – see the roots in Figure 1.1) that sometimes go against conventional business wisdom. They focus on improving people's lives at least as much as on making money. They prefer to take the long-term view over "making the numbers" on a quarterly basis. They build and maintain fruitful long-term relationships instead of making the "best deals" through narrowly following their self-interest in every business interaction. They are deeply rooted in a place rather than seeing themselves as opportunity-exploiting global players. They recognize the limits of people, of communities, and of the environment instead of stubbornly following a short-term profit maximization principle in all they are doing. They see themselves as open learning communities instead of omniscient know-it-alls. And not least, they have leaders who take their responsibility seriously.

Instead of acting in a spiritual void, the people who develop and lead real value-oriented enterprises put *values* at the center of what they are doing. They know what is important to them, and care about what matters to the people around them, their community, and society at large. They both plant and water the seeds of the trees that create real value. Just like an enormous oak that grows from a tiny acorn seed, transformational change in any business emerges from those in charge possessing the ability to see, sense, and realize a range of possibilities by drawing on all the life-enhancing resources at their disposal. As Peter Senge and his colleagues noted in their book on a new theory of change and learning:

> Seeds do not contain the resources needed to grow a tree. These must come from the medium or environment within which the tree grows. But the seed does provide something that is crucial: a place where the whole of the tree starts to form. (Senge *et al.*, 2004, p. 2)

The business case for creating real value

When we talk about creating real value, we are not advocating that enterprises turn their backs on making money! Rather, we are thinking of those who want *more* than just making money. Although the people behind these enterprises are highly values-driven and tend to cherish the intrinsic emotional benefits that they derive from their businesses, they also understand that creating real value can contribute to creating more financial wealth.

How does that work? Business success in financial terms starts with a customer paying a bill. Let us therefore take a look at the customer perspective first. According to brand strategy expert David Aaker, the value proposition of any product or service offered to customers includes three types of benefits: functional, emotional and self-expressive (Aaker, 1996).

There are also three categories of product and service offers on the market (see Figure 1.2). The first category includes commodities without a brand identity. They provide purely functional benefits to customers. On the money value level, their economic added value is usually small, as it covers only the difference between the functional benefits and the production costs of the product or service. Offers that belong to the second category rely on heavy advertising to build brands. Successful brands do provide some deeper value in the form of emotional and self-expressive benefits to customers, but need to incur constant promotional costs to uphold this brand identity. These conventional brands also carry an authenticity risk. The emotional and self-expressive benefits can evaporate when the advertising messages do not match a company's real character; that is, when the brand promise is simply not kept. The third category of products and services includes those offered by enterprises that create real value. They naturally provide deeper value through their innate meaning and identity. They do not need heavy advertising to

FIGURE 1.2   How real value creation for customers translates into added value for the enterprise

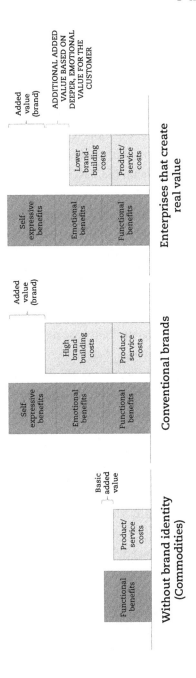

build an "artificial" brand image. The deeper, emotional value that they create is authentic, unique, and inimitable.

As marketing guru Philip Kotler and his colleagues point out in their book *Marketing 3.0* (2010), companies now realize they must offer products and services that inspire and reflect their customer's values. Ulrik Nehammer, CEO of Coca Cola Germany, agrees: "Consumers will choose your products neither on the basis of taste nor because of advertising, but mainly on the basis of the character of your company."[6] Savvy enterprises target the whole person, or mind, heart, and spirit, to satisfy the desire of consumers to contribute to making our world a better place (Kotler *et al.*, 2010). It's an argument consistent with that of Daniel Pink who writes in his provocative book, *A Whole New Mind*, that the future belongs to a very different person with a different kind of mind. The era of "left brain" dominance and the Information Age, he says, is giving way to a world in which empathy, meaning, and purpose dominate.[7]

Consider again the example of wine. Scientific research has repeatedly shown that ordinary people "can't tell plonk from grand cru" (Derbyshire, 2013) in blind wine tastings. Even expert wine tasters were found to be surprisingly inconsistent in their judgments. Frédéric Brochet, a French cognitive psychologist, made a revealing experiment in 2001 (Brochet, 2001). He served the same average quality wine to 57 tasters twice – with different labels, first as a simple table wine, and a week later as a grand cru. The terms used to describe the wine were totally different in the first and second tasting, although the wine was exactly the same. The "table wine" was seen as "simple", "unbalanced," and "volatile," and the alleged grand cru as "complex," "balanced," and "round". The perception of the value of a wine radically changes when it is served from a beautiful carafe rather than from a cardboard box or when you know it comes from a famous Château in Bordeaux rather than from a no-name vineyard. The emotional perception of the product, the deeper and *real value* that stems from what we associate with the *terroir*, the reputation of the wine-grower and the age of the wine, will highly affect the price we are willing to pay for it. Real value is not an illusion; it is very real in material as well as emotional terms.

This is true not only for customers who are willing to pay a lot more for products and services in which they see authentic emotional and self-expressive benefits. Enterprises that create real value also provide meaning and identity for their employees. Being able to contribute to a positive cause and to improve the quality of the lives of others can be a strong driving force for employees. With their innate care for the well-being of their customers, for the prosperity of society, and the protection of the environment, these enterprises are also highly attractive employers. Thus, they have a competitive edge in getting the best talent while saving recruitment and employee retention costs.

The creation of real value for communities, society, and the environment – in the form of providing meaningful jobs, helping to solve societal problems, and contributing to renewing the health of our planet – also pays back. A favorable attitude of public authorities toward businesses that create more expansive value and a positive public opinion can help these enterprises to survive difficult commercial conditions and the vagaries of economic cycles. The loyalty of employees, public policy-makers, and supporters in the community can act in an insurance-like way in adverse situations. Enterprises that are well embedded and supported by other societal forces are more resilient, and more likely to thrive over the long term. In this way, deeper emotional value can become very "real" and tangible again.

The roots of creating real value

Let us return to the "root" part of our tree diagram in Figure 1.1 to explore how enterprises that create real value in practice produce a good crop for everyone associated with them. In essence, what these enterprises do is to *dig deeper* in order to develop stronger roots. One of these roots – the strongest of all, we believe – is about the ultimate purpose – the *why* – of the business. Rather than solely focusing on making profits, some enterprises have a superordinate goal that is deeply connected to improving people's quality of life.

A deeper purpose: A better life

In its literal sense, *real value* is related to what people *really* value in life rather than what can be expressed in monetary terms alone. There is much more to life than just money. Quality of life also includes factors such as happiness, health, intact nature, love, beauty, peace, freedom, dignity, and the opportunity to fulfill one's potential. While many companies narrowly follow the goal of profit maximization, there are some that have a deeper purpose that is related to improving quality of life. In this book, we will encounter enterprises with such diverse purposes as creating high-quality jobs, preserving and reviving local traditions, providing education, improving soil quality and biodiversity, or simply making the world more beautiful. Although they know that they need to be sustainably profitable to be able to fulfill these deeper purposes, they do not see profits as their sole reason for existence.

Having a deeper purpose of improving the quality of life of people is the foundation stone to creating real value. Following a deeper purpose creates meaning for owners and employees alike. It will arouse positive emotions in customers who may be willing to go the extra mile (or, in many cases, pay the extra dollar) to buy the products and services from those who contribute to the well-being of others. Enterprises with a deeper purpose will also – more or less by definition – benefit our communities, society, and the environment, thus creating real value in a wider context. In short, deeper purpose and real value are closely intertwined.

Following a deeper purpose is what all the enterprises profiled in this book have in common. Consequently, we do not devote a separate chapter to purpose-driven businesses, as all the enterprises that we portray are such businesses. The six roots (or "6Ls") that we will focus on in the remaining chapters of this book are *long-term orientation*, building and maintaining *lasting relationships*, *limits recognition*, having *local roots*, developing *learning communities*, and having *leadership responsibility* to create real value. The "6Ls" are the fundamental practices that distinguish real value-oriented enterprises from those more narrowly oriented toward creating "money value." Through these practices, purpose-driven enterprises achieve performance – not in a narrow sense that is measured in terms of quarterly financial results, but in a more holistic way. They improve the quality of life of customers, employees, owners, and partners alike, and create meaning and identity for them. On this solid basis, they are able to weather market cycles and achieve sustainable profitability. Through this performance in a more encompassing sense, they also strongly contribute to the prosperity of society while assuming responsibility for renewing the health of our long-suffering natural environment (see Figure 1.3).

Unlike other business books, we do not see these seven roots– having a deeper purpose and following the "6L" practices of real value creation – as an absolute formula for success. They are tendencies, or characteristics, of enterprises that in our view have been able to create real value by firmly anchoring their strategies and operations in these roots. We also do not claim that these enterprises are the perfect "real value creators," nor do we wish to posit them as

FIGURE 1.3   From purpose to prosperity: The "6Ls" of enterprises that create real value

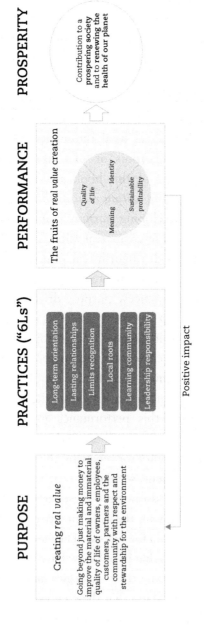

saintly or beyond reproach. Even though we see the creation of real value as an ideal, we are not even sure if such "perfect" companies really exist. What we do see, however, is that there are some enterprises that have made good progress in digging deeper, and have been able to harvest more fruits from the tree of real value. These enterprises are pioneers, we believe, of a new way of doing business and a new way of creating the sort of value that the world needs. Given the challenges that we face, as participants in the 21st-century global economy and as responsible members of our own communities and societies, such a new way of focusing on the creation of real value cannot come a moment too soon.

Let us now take a first look at the six practices of enterprises that create real value – practices that we will explore in more depth in the following chapters.

Real value creation practice #1: Long-term orientation

A beautiful garden is the result of many years of careful cultivation. Plants need both time and nurturing to grow and thrive. Just like cultivating a garden, creating real value is a long-term endeavor. Short-termism and managerial myopia are the main enemies of the creation of real value. Where quarterly results rule, real value creation falls by the wayside. Developing an enterprise that has a positive impact on the quality of life of many takes time. It also needs leaders with the wisdom to build potential for the future and concern for the long-term consequences of their actions. In our search for role models of long-term oriented management, we found two enterprises that have stood the test of time.

The first example, the more than 250-year-old German pencil manufacturer Faber-Castell, was already around before the French Revolution started and the United States of America was founded. With their long-term oriented approach, Faber-Castell's aristocratic owners have managed to maneuver the company through many challenges over the centuries, from wars and expropriation to the general threat to handwriting with the rise of the Internet. The other example of an extreme long-term orientation is the collection of business enterprises of the almost 1,000-year-old Benedictine monastery of Admont in the Austrian Alps. Managed in accordance with the ancient rule of the monastic order's founder, these businesses with their almost 600 employees create economic substance and real value with an eye to centuries rather than quarterly results.

Real value creation practice #2: Lasting relationships

Most businesses that are narrowly focused on the creation of money value are transaction-based, which means that all exchanges are a matter of buying and selling, and money is the medium of every exchange. If you are such a firm, you find and combine resources that will help you to produce a product or service, and compensate each of the resource holders (a supplier, an employee, a community) monetarily through purchases, salaries, benefits, taxes, or instrumental philanthropy. Business is done through a series of transactions, which are simple, mercenary exchanges. When the exchange is over, it is over. It is a "one-night stand," and no one looks back.

Businesses with a long-term orientation, on the other hand, know that success in the long-term (and creation of real value) is associated with the cultivation of productive and enduring positive relationships with customers, employees, suppliers, communities, and other stakeholders. These relationships flourish because of the connection that is felt among all of them – relationships that are deep and emotional. Put all of these relationships together, and you have an organizational culture that is thick, emotionally deep, trusting, caring, and likely to produce real value. In a lasting relationship, one *cares,* no matter the ups and downs that may challenge that relationship. Real value-oriented enterprises nurture such long-term relationships and foster a shared understanding of the deeper purpose of the company. They grow successful relationships that are the product of a culture that values, intrinsically, all stakeholders and treats them with respect, dignity, and simple appreciation. They also share more fully the fruits of their success, and are not afraid to grapple with notions of equity and fairness that other, more narrowly focused organizations avoid. And like a garden with many varieties of flowers and plants, trees and vines, these long-lasting relationships can be cultivated in many ways, particularly and most evocatively in certain "alternative" organizations.

One organizational form is fundamentally based on the principle of cooperation: the cooperative enterprise. Designed for the benefit and welfare of many instead of the financial wealth of a few, these enterprises put lasting relationships with their customers, suppliers, and employees at the center of their business mission and purpose.

With the story of Mondragón, the Basque cooperative that has become one of the biggest enterprises in Spain, we show how cooperatives can stay true to their values even when they are comparable in size to large multinational corporations. A U.S. example, Equal Exchange, provides further evidence for the compatibility of close, mutually beneficial ties between a cooperative enterprise and its stakeholders and business success.

Real value creation practice #3: Limits recognition

The good gardener recognizes that the goal is not to grow every plant to the greatest size possible but to strive for a flourishing garden with many types, shapes, and sizes of plants, each of which makes a unique contribution to the whole setting. Gardens are about harmony, proportion, and the relationships of plants, not about one plant outgrowing the others. So it is with enterprises that are focused on creating real value. Their leaders do not blindly follow a profit maximization principle at any price but respect the limits of the environment and of human beings. They are also aware that there are limits to inequality and growth. Through striving for balance rather than short-term profit maximization, they ensure economic, social, and environmental sustainability.

Independently of each other, two global carpet tile manufacturers on either side of the Atlantic, Interface in the U.S. and Desso in the Netherlands, decided to redesign their business models toward achieving total environmental sustainability. In this book we accompany them on their journey toward reaching the goal of eliminating any negative impact of their operations on the natural environment.

Negative impacts on human beings abound in the shark pool of financial institutions that are driven by greed, bonus schemes, and relentless attempts to squeeze the most out of their customers. Two regional banks in Germany and Denmark, however, refuse to buy into the conventional logic of making money through putting pressure on people. They recognize the limits of their employees and help them grow personally instead of constantly subjecting them to stress. Needless to say their staff is among the happiest and most motivated and loyal on the whole continent, helping the banks' businesses to thrive.

Suma Wholefoods is a remarkable example of an enterprise that clearly recognizes that there are limits to inequality. This UK natural food co-operative is owned and run by some 100 workers who are all paid exactly the same, making it the largest organization in Europe operating an equal pay policy.

Finally, we also look at enterprises that are part of the "postgrowth" movement that is gaining more and more support in Germany. Enterprises such as the deckchair producer Richard

Henkel and the Clemens Haerle brewery in Baden-Wuerttemberg explicitly choose *not* to grow in size in order to preserve the values on which they built their businesses. They strive for a balanced and optimal size rather than for maximization – and they are highly successful in creating real value.

Real value creation practice #4: Local roots

Place matters. It is, of course, a simple term, and a ubiquitous one at that. We use it continually without a second thought in our everyday lives. But on some reflection, it is actually a complicated, deep, multidimensional concept. It is, most obviously, a location; it has a latitude and longitude and it can be found using those coordinates. But it is also a physical environment, composed of a natural environment and a built (man-made) environment. Most importantly, however, it is socially constructed. People create and shape places as much as places shape people and their organizations. We care about and value places, and we are attached to them. Sometimes places even define us and provide us with a piece of our own identity. And every place is different, unique, and inimitable. Just like any garden, the plants that tend to thrive are native species, those specially adapted to the particular climate, soil, and growing conditions of that place.

All life "takes place" in places; all business happens in places. The businesses that we profile are deeply connected to their places, which are their homes, and draw inspiration, identity, and powerful advantages from them. They also give back. Inis Meáin Knitting Company, based on a remote island off the west coast of Ireland, provides us with a powerful example of a firm that draws strength and inspiration from the landscape, culture, and traditions of its native place. And sometimes communities themselves value their business enterprises so much that they are willing to buy them to make certain that they, and the value that they provide to their places, can survive. The ongoing and very successful movement to "save the local" pubs in Great Britain serves as an example of this inner drive of communities to sustain real value creation on a local level.

Real value creation practice #5: Learning communities

Real value-oriented enterprises are devoted to helping their employees and partners develop and thrive by creating a working environment that fosters learning. Through establishing learning communities, these enterprises not only develop knowledge, but also positive emotional experiences, engagement and new opportunities. And like the wise gardener, their leaders are always aware that the journey takes them from the present to some envisioned future. On the way, they are continually nurturing so transformative change can emerge from the relationships in the garden of learning and personal growth.

In the chapter on learning communities, we visit illycaffè, a family-owned Italian premium coffee enterprise that fully focuses on quality in all aspects of its business and sees improving its stakeholders' quality of life and seeking beauty in everything it does as core elements of its business philosophy. To promote a pervasive learning culture, illycaffè established scientific research laboratories as well as a "University of Coffee" that provides learning experiences for coffee lovers and hospitality professionals as well as for suppliers who are trained in the most environmentally responsible cultivation, harvesting, and processing techniques. We also include the story of Cooperative Home Care Associates (CHCA), a worker-owned home care agency in the Bronx, New York, with more than 2,000 employees that is dedicated to providing quality home care and creating quality jobs. Offering learning and development opportunities for its employees is a core purpose of CHCA. Hundreds of low-income or unemployed women receive free training every year. Thus, CHCA creates real value in the form of providing both excellent care for clients and development opportunities for care workers.

Real value creation practice #6: Leadership responsibility

There is no garden without a gardener. And there are no enterprises that create real value without the visionary entrepreneurs and managers who have deliberately decided to devote their businesses to a purpose that goes far beyond making profits. It is these exceptional people who create "alternative organizations" that serve people and strive to improve the lives of employees (through establishing beneficial, developmental, and meaningful work environments), customers (through providing safe, environmentally friendly and high-quality products and services), suppliers (through being a fair and trusted partner), and the people living in the communities in which they are based (through creating environments in which people can flourish), thus benefiting society at least as much as the company's shareholders. These leaders take the sixth L, *leadership responsibility*, very seriously, and try to orient their organizations toward the other five Ls, long-term orientation, lasting relationships, local roots, limits recognition, and creating learning communities.

We follow with the story of Ibrahim Abouleish, an Egyptian entrepreneur and Alternative Nobel Prize winner who has established a network of hundreds of biodynamic farms that offer organic textiles, clothes, foods, beverages and medicines in Egypt, Europe, and the U.S. He did this by literally *digging deeper*, starting his business with a well that he sank in the Egyptian desert. His singular enterprise Sekem is based on a holistic concept that integrates business, societal and cultural life, and ecology. Besides providing work for 2,000 people, Sekem also restored the vitality of soil and food, established learning opportunities through establishing schools and a university, and brought quality healthcare and rich cultural offers to the local community. Though strongly rooted in the place around the original well that he dug, the impact of Abouleish and his initiatives goes far beyond the immediate environment. Abouleish convinced a whole country to ban pesticides and continues to act as a role model for creating a new type of business that is devoted to generating *real value* in the broadest sense.

Leaders who understand and create real value are still rare. A surprisingly high number of them can be found in the organic food movement (maybe because they understand more about gardening!). In addition to Ibrahim Abouleish, we also take a look at two exemplary leaders who founded organic food enterprises in Europe (Johannes Gutmann of Sonnentor) and Asia (Helianti Hilman of Javara), and explore how they turned their visions of a better life into reality. The gardener imagines the future but accepts that she cannot do the growing herself but must nurture the plants under her care so these reach their full potential. In much the same manner, the leaders of enterprises that are focused on creating real value know their deeper purpose, envisage a better future, and understand the importance of nurturing others.

From bottom line to betterment

This is a book of stories about enterprises that create *real value* for themselves and their stakeholders. They are extraordinary enterprises, to be sure; they march to a different drummer than those narrowly focused firms driven solely by the bottom line. But they are also exemplary, representing inspirational, salutary examples that capitalism and its businesses *can* be harnessed for the betterment of people, for the protection of communities, for stewardship of the natural environment and, in short, can create real, enduring value. If these enterprises can do it, others can do so as well. We hope our book will help them do so.

In brief: In search of real value

- The real meaning of value goes far beyond the narrow conception that the financial community would have us believe. Value is not just about making money. Instead, *real value* is about improving the material and immaterial quality of life of customers, employees, partners, owners, and the community with respect and stewardship for the environment.

- Real value is strongly determined by positive emotions, for example, in the form of meaning, identity, affection for someone or something, happiness, or aesthetic experiences.

- Customers are often willing to pay more for the additional emotional and self-expressive benefits that they get from enterprises that create real value. Being authentic in their real value-creation efforts, these enterprises also need to pay less for brand-building activities to create emotional added value for customers.

- Enterprises that create real value can also reap additional benefits from being attractive employers and from strong societal support that makes them more resilient in adverse situations.

- Enterprises can create real value through focusing on six attitudes or practices, which we call the six roots (or "6Ls") of real value creation: *long-term orientation*, building and maintaining *lasting relationships*, *limits recognition*, having *local roots*, developing *learning communities*, and *leadership responsibility*.

- Some entrepreneurs and managers are *digging deeper* than others, and lead their organizations to sink deeper "6L" roots than others that are narrowly focused on short-term profits. These exceptional people plant the seeds that will enable their enterprises to bear the fruits of the tree of real value: sustainable profitability in combination with the satisfaction of having contributed to a better life.

2

Long-term orientation: creating value for generations

What a Sincere and Righteous Merchant Must Have
  Within Himself.
Uprightness always fits him,
Long foresight suits him well.
And what he promises does not get lost;
And he shall be, if able, of beautiful and honest
  character
According to the intended trade or reason.

                  Francesco Balducci Pegolotti,
        La Pratica della Mercatura (around 1340 AD)
        (Pegolotti, 1766, p. XXIV, trans. by the authors)

Fulfilling a deeper purpose – striving to improve the lives of others while finding meaning in one's own – takes time. Creating real value, therefore, demands physical and emotional stamina coupled with a long-term orientation. But taking a long-term perspective is hardly the norm in today's "financialized" business world, where analysts' quarterly profit forecasts drive share prices and corporations that miss expectations pay a heavy price. "If you miss by a penny, the market knocks your stock down by 4% to 8% – for a penny, which is meaningless," says Sam Palmisano (2014, p. 82), the former CEO of IBM in an interview with the *Harvard Business Review*. "Not every quarter is going to be perfect. We all know that operationally, but you're still pressured to do things that aren't necessarily in the long-term interests of the entity in order to make your numbers" (Palmisano, 2014, p. 82).

No wonder that managerial myopia is pervasive. Surveys reveal that a majority of top managers would be willing to destroy a part of the economic value of their firm and forego important investments in order to reach their short-term earnings targets (Grinyer *et al.*, 1998; Graham *et al.*, 2006). Some executives unethically, and sometimes even illegally, manipulate the company accounts – a practice euphemistically known as 'earnings management' – in order to achieve unrealistic quarterly targets (Nevins *et al.*, 2006). In a *McKinsey Quarterly* study (2013) of more than 1,000 board members and executives, 86% were convinced that a longer time horizon would allow them to achieve much better business outcomes. If this is the case, why are so many managers willing to compromise the value and the future of their companies – not to mention their own personal integrity?

"I miss the target, I'm out of a job" (Graham *et al.*, 2006, p. 30) is the straightforward answer of one executive. Executives feel this pressure. Wall Street likes certainty and predictability, and demands a smooth, upward quarterly earnings curve. Meanwhile, short-term-oriented traders looking for fast profits buy and sell shares at a dizzying pace. Financial analysts forecast quarterly results and transient investors run away the moment these expectations are not met. Investment bankers make money on all these transactions, and the more frequent these are the better. If all the people and institutions around them are focusing on near-term expected earnings, managers of publicly listed companies can hardly escape, especially if they too are evaluated on short-term profitability and compensated with stock options. How can anyone create real value in an environment where next month's numbers will always have precedence over long-term impacts? Doesn't business inevitably have to follow the beat of Wall Street's metronome?

Maybe not. There is an alternative. In this chapter, we will introduce entrepreneurs and top managers who refuse to concede to short-term pressures; who think in decades or even centuries rather than quarters; and who plan, and care, for the future in a deeper, more considered manner. The purpose of their businesses goes far beyond making a quick buck, and their organizations' longevity far exceeds the average life expectancy of a typical Fortune 500 company (de Gues, 2002). The companies that we will visit in this chapter have survived and thrived over many generations, and their top management surveys a planning horizon of centuries rather than quarters.

Over 250 years of real value creation at Faber-Castell

As he finished up his university studies in the 1970s, a young German aristocrat decided that he had scant interest in pencils. This was hardly earth-shattering news, but for the fact that the young man was the potential heir of one of the world's best-known pencil manufacturers. Count Anton Wolfgang von Faber-Castell preferred the buzz of Wall Street and the City of London to the quiet surroundings of the family castle and historic pencil factory near Nuremberg in Germany. He decided to eschew the family firm and instead embark on a career as an investment banker.

The family-owned firm of Faber-Castell, founded in 1761, was older than the United States of America. In the 1800s, Anton Wolfgang's great-great grandfather Baron Lothar von Faber created the world's first branded pencil when he put the logo "A.W. Faber" on his company's products to distinguish them from low-grade competitors. Today, it is the oldest trademark still in existence in the United States. Baron Lothar had a clear vision: "From the start I was determined to raise myself to the highest position by making the best that can be made in the whole world" (Faber-Castell, 2014a, p. 2). Thinking on a global scale, he opened a subsidiary in New York followed by branch offices in Paris and London and agencies in Vienna and St. Petersburg.

Around a century later, after Baron Lothar's third successor, Count Roland von Faber-Castell, passed away in 1978, his son Anton's responsibility toward the family and its business heritage took precedence over his lack of interest in pencils. "I consider what I got from my father as a kind of fiduciary property, which in a way does not belong to me," said Count Anton in an interview with the *New York Times* (Ewing, 2013) He had learned a lot about numbers and strategies during his time as an investment banker, but had not been infected with the virus of managerial myopia. He rather appreciated the advice that Baron Lothar von Faber had given to his son when he handed over the company to him in 1877: "make yourself ever more useful, better developed and more beautifully crafted by means of steady work towards progress and steady adherence to incontrovertibly correct principles," do what is "right, good and beautiful" and respect the "individual freedom" of every employee (Faber-Castell, 2014a, p. 2). Count Anton – who headed the family enterprise for 38 years until he died in early 2016 – regarded his ancestor's principles as a "guiding light" for managing the family business: "For me, following the guiding light also means not focusing on short-term successes, but keeping in mind the long-term perspective" (Faber-Castell, 2014a, p. 2).

Faber-Castell, the world's leading manufacturer of wood-encased pencils with annual revenues of €564 million in the 2014 fiscal year, is a prime example of a company with exceptional resilience. It has survived devastating wars, seizure of its foreign subsidiaries, hyperinflation, the collapse of its slide rule business following the introduction of electronic calculators in the 1970s, and the decline of its manual technical drawing instruments business due to the advent of computer-aided design tools in the late 1980s. With approximately 7,000 employees, a production volume of over 2.4 billion pencils per year, manufacturing sites in 9 countries, 25 international subsidiaries and trade representatives in over 120 countries, Faber-Castell is still flourishing as a global player. When Count Anton was asked about his company's recipe for long-lasting success on the occasion of Faber-Castell's 250th anniversary, he answered: "It takes forward-thinking, a dose of good luck, a smart wife – but what really counts is the people who believe in and identify themselves with the brand" (Faber-Castell, 2011, p. 6).

Reputation-building

In making the brand the pivotal element of his strategy, Count Anton clearly understood the importance of reputation for sustainable business success. Building reputation takes time. And everything that takes time first requires a firm commitment to the long term. Reputation, usually expressed in a brand, is about what people think of a company. It consists of beliefs, opinions, and feelings – intangible ideas with very tangible effects. A reputation as a good employer will appeal to highly talented and creative people.

A reputation for offering quality products and value for money will attract and retain customers. A reputation for being a fair business partner will lead to long-lasting and mutually beneficial relationships. And a reputation for being a good citizen will result in support from authorities, media, and the general public. Highly reputable companies enjoy more trust, commitment, support, and cooperation from their stakeholders, in both good times and bad. "One can survive everything nowadays, except death, and live down anything except a good reputation," says Lord Illingworth in Oscar Wilde's *A Woman of No Importance* (1894).

Empirical research suggests that companies with a good reputation tend to be more innovative and profitable (Roberts and Dowling, 2002). "Good corporate reputations are critical because of their potential for value creation," write Peter Roberts and Grahame Dowling, the authors of a study that confirms the link between reputation and financial performance, "but also because their intangible character makes replication by competing firms considerably more difficult" (Roberts and Dowling, 2002, p. 1077). A good reputation helps them to create a unique, competition-free space in the minds of consumers. An excellent reputation is as hard to copy as it is time consuming to build.

Count Anton cared intensely about the reputation of the company that bears his name, and devoted considerable energy to developing Faber-Castell into a global premium brand. He added new product lines including decorative cosmetics pencils and a wide range of writing and drawing products for children, artists, and home and office use. He also managed to shift the perception of pencils from cheap writing tools to prestige or even luxury objects. Selected Faber-Castell fountain pens cost up to tens of thousands of dollars. Recently, Count Anton also opened several flagship stores to increase the visibility of Faber-Castell's premium collections. At the same time, however, he never lost sight of the mass market.

Significant investments in production sites in South America enable his company to offer reasonably priced quality products, leading to clear market leadership on that continent.

In any case, whether on the highest or on the lower end of the market, Faber-Castell has always emphasized quality, which the company defines as:

- a "point of difference" or a meaningful added value for the customer;

- distinguished product attributes; and

- a characteristic and timeless design (Faber-Castell, 2015a).

In addition to constantly buttressing its reputation as a high quality brand, Faber-Castell is also focusing on its reputation for being a socially responsible company. Faber-Castell had been one of the first German companies to open a company kindergarten as early as 1851. Count Anton followed in the footsteps of his ancestors and supported parents working at Faber-Castell with a new daycare center that he established close to the company's main factory site in Germany. On a global basis, the count, who once said he can't stand managers who misuse their power and treat employees badly (faz.net, 2006a), signed a social charter that guarantees all Faber-Castell employees around the world high employment standards and fair and decent working conditions. His Children's Fund Foundation supports charities and social projects in many different parts of the world.

In a family company, the reputation of the business is invariably linked with the reputation of the family. Count Anton therefore also regarded himself as the main ambassador of the brand. He used to have his picture taken in front of the magnificent family castle – always immaculately dressed in a pin-striped suit with a perfectly adjusted tie and a pocket handkerchief – to properly convey the long-standing Faber-Castell tradition. From the 25-meter tower of the castle, he once hurled more than a hundred pencils to the stone-paved courtyard below to prove how indestructible they were (not a single one was broken). He also drank a glass of yellow ink in front of journalists to prove the absence of unhealthy substances in felt pens for children. And he demonstratively carried Faber-Castell writing implements, most notably his favorite special edition "Perfect Pencil," which is sold at approximately 1,000 times the price of a typical supermarket pencil. Count Anton felt that his role was to "authentically communicate a long-standing value culture, both internally and externally" (Faber-Castell, 2014a, p. 3), and wanted to see the brand personality "reflected everywhere in the company – in the buildings, the fittings, in the internal and external communication materials and in the employees themselves – as an essential component of a fully realized corporate culture" (Faber-Castell, 2014a, p. 3). Ultimately, reputation is not built by marketing, but by who you are and what you do.

Resource-orientation

"I disapprove of short-term profit seeking" (Faber-Castell, 2015b), said Count Anton. Of course, every company needs to be sustainably profitable to stay alive. A narrow focus on short-term profits, however, can lead to underinvesting in the future. Long-term oriented managers do not solely focus on profits, which after all are only a measure of past performance. Instead, they concentrate their attention on creating and maintaining the potential for future performance and on building and preserving valuable and inimitable resources for their company.

Resources can be tangible – like the equipment and machines in Faber-Castell's production plants, the fittings of its flagship stores, or the wood supply for the pencils. However, they can also be intangible, for example in the form of customer trust or the knowledge and capabilities of employees. Count Anton particularly highlighted the value of his long-time employees. He recognized that "while it is essential to set the right entrepreneurial agenda, it is equally important to find the right people who back and implement these decisions and are committed to the brand with dedication and passion."[8] Retaining employees during difficult economic time avoids knowledge drain, ensures continuity, and generates loyalty and engagement. Count Anton loathed lay-offs, "just as my father, who hated them, regarding them as a personal defeat," he said (faz. net, 2006b).

The count not only kept an eye on maintaining the resource base of his own company, but was also strongly concerned about securing natural resources for future generations (Braun, 2013). For a pencil producer, this means identifying sustainable sources of its major raw material – wood. In a flood- and drought-plagued region in Colombia, Faber-Castell initiated a unique reforestation project. The area had been completely overgrazed. Milk from zebu cattle had provided the local farmers with only minimal incomes. Many therefore decided to enter into a cooperative agreement with Faber-Castell, in which they would plant trees on their land and receive 30% of the revenues for the wood that was used for pencil production plus a third of the proceeds of United Nations carbon credits for projects that help to constrain global warming. "Thanks to Faber-Castell, I know that we will get help for the families," says Edgar Tamara, a small Colombian farmer who cooperates with the company, "I believe in the project, which will also help our very damaged environment to recover. It has created a lot of jobs here in the Zapayan community" (Faber-Castell, 2014b, p. 2).

Care for the natural environment is a core company value. Since the 1980s, Faber-Castell has actually been carbon negative, as its factories emit considerably less than the company-owned forests absorb. In Brazil, Faber-Castell owns over 25,000 acres of sustainably managed and certified pine forests, which are supplying the world's largest pencil factory in São Carlos (Faber-Castell, 2014b). Over a million saplings are planted every year, and 20 new cubic meters of wood grow every hour (Gasser, 2009).

Faber-Castell also uses its own renewable energy (e.g., compressing the sawdust produced in the factories into pellets which are used as heating fuel) and waste water treatment plants, engages itself in strengthening biodiversity, produces PVC-free erasers, and has developed its own special environmentally friendly coating for pencils.

Risk-consciousness

Like other family-owned German companies of long standing, Faber-Castell generally shies away from too much risk. Risk – the potential of losing essential resources – can bring a company down. And equally devastating for a family business, it could also lead to a loss of independence. Long-term oriented family business managers are very aware of the importance of risk for the survival of their organizations, and consciously try to contain and manage it. It does not mean that they avoid uncertainty altogether – that would actually mean giving up their entrepreneurial spirit. They do, however, try to give a wide berth to unpredictable risks. There is a world of difference between a responsible risk and a gamble.

Faber-Castell, for example, actively tries to minimize risks from currency contracts (boss-magazin.de, 2009). The company also aims to maintain a high equity ratio to be able to cope with any unexpected events. And it follows the old German proverb, "Cobbler, stick to your trade." Having resisted the advice of consultants to enter new business segments such as computer-aided design-related products or e-business endeavors, Count Anton continued to focus on traditional writing implements. This is a domain that his company and its employees understand, have co-created, and continue to shape. He knew on which core skills he could capitalize but did not overestimate the abilities of his company. Instead of embarking on risk-filled adventures, Count Anton preferred to follow traditional principles:

> For me, corporate ethics means "behaving decently" not only around people who are especially dependent on the company (for example, workers who need to retain their jobs) but also around partners such as clients and suppliers. This decency, which is based on values such as social responsibility, trust, honesty, and fair mutual dealings, can be compatible with a healthy striving toward sustainable profitability, as only profitable companies can assume their social responsibilities on a continuing basis.[9]

Faber-Castell as a company follows four core values: providing outstanding quality, building the business on competence and tradition, fostering innovation and creativity, and acting in a socially and ecologically responsible way (Braun, 2013). These core values or "brand essentials" are communicated throughout the company with training sessions and area-specific definitions of dos and don'ts related to each value to guide the daily actions of all employees. The brand essentials also form the basis for Faber-Castell's integrated management system, which helps to contain risks through setting global quality and social and environmental standards, and providing a set of tools to translate them into controllable managerial targets. Standardized processes and reporting systems help to ensure compliance. Faber-Castell's managers' bonus agreements are also clearly tied to targets that are strongly oriented toward the company's overall value-based goals. In line with the general long-term orientation, some, albeit not all, managerial target agreements are also determined on a multi-year basis.

In addition to using traditional risk-management tools, avoiding unknown territory, carrying low debt, and implementing management and control systems to limit risks, we can also regard the emphasis that Faber-Castell puts on caring for its employees, benefitting society, and protecting the environment as a risk-reduction strategy. It helps to increase the "moral capital" of the company, protecting it in an insurance-like way against the risks of losing valuable resources that are dependent on good stakeholder relationships (Godfrey, 2005).

Rejuvenation

Continuity, both in terms of top management tenure and in staying committed to a specific market (in Faber-Castell's case, writing implements), is characteristic of long-term oriented family firms (Sternad, 2013). Continuity, however, is not the same as stubbornly holding on to past recipes for success, which can lead to failure if external circumstances change. "Complacency and hubris constitute a significant threat to the long-term survival of a company," said Count Anton.[10] He was convinced that if brand manufacturers fail, they do so from inside, not because of a changing environment.[11] To never let this happen at Faber-Castell, he strongly focused on ongoing product improvement, which, for him, is "the lifeblood of long-term success and sustainability" (Chalmers, 2012).

Companies that want to survive in the long term need to adjust themselves to the market realities of their times. In other words, they need to constantly rejuvenate themselves. Rejuvenation does not mean breaking with one's tradition – just the opposite: it means making the organization young and vital again, giving it new vigor and energy. "Tradition means keeping the glow, not the ashes, alive," said Count Anton:

> The success of Faber-Castell throughout the centuries is a result of appreciating and respecting years of experience, striving to make the ordinary extraordinarily good, being open to new ideas and acting responsibly with entrepreneurial spirit. These values apply not only to the brand but to the entire company as well and form the basis of both our identity and our long term success. (Faber-Castell Cosmetics, 2015)

Faber-Castell does not attempt to make revolutionary changes. Instead, the company has constantly tried to make continuous improvements and find optimal solutions for its customers. Pencils – "products which may cause a yawn," as Count Anton wryly said on a *CNN* TV report (cnn.com, 2012) – are basically the same as they were a few hundred years ago. Yet, Faber-Castell has repeatedly found innovative interpretations of the basic product. A prime example is the "Perfect Pencil," a simple yet elegant solution that includes a sharpener and an eraser. It became an instant success, just like the triangular pencil for children that has ergonomic dots for a better grip.

Count Anton was not afraid that the cultural techniques of handwriting and drawing would disappear in this age of digitalization. Indeed, he also recognized a trend back to a culture of writing: "If they want to say thank you in a personal way, people increasingly turn to paper and pen again. The cause is probably all these impersonal e-mails that we receive every day" (Gasser, 2009). *The Economist* (2014a) has illustrated several examples of this seeming paradox. Many traditional businesses, based on fountain pens and Swiss watches, for example, are thriving in the internet age of disruptive innovation. People do not just buy something because it is more efficient, but also because it provides deeper value in the form of aesthetic satisfaction. The real value of these products goes far beyond their pure function, and knowledgeable consumers are willing to pay a premium for the meaning that these cultural artifacts convey to them. Tapping into these market opportunities, as Faber-Castell clearly demonstrates, demands a careful balance between tradition and change.

Even in the internet age, Count Anton still saw a lot of growth potential especially for colored pencils in countries such as India or China where many children could not afford laptops. He was convinced that the development of educational systems in these countries would also trigger a higher demand for pencils (faz.net, 2006b). He also never got tired of pointing out that pencils are more than just writing tools, referring to the fact that neuroscientists observed that children can strengthen their mental abilities and fine motor skills through using hand-held products (Dohner, 2014). Therefore, he was always convinced that "the pencil will not just simply vanish" (Dohner, 2014).

Count Anton and his team were trying to promote the use of writing and drawing tools wherever they could, whether it was through training and sponsoring young artists with the Faber-Castell Academy and the Faber-Castell International Drawing Award or through supporting non-profit organizations that are improving school education in developing countries. Although these actions are clearly aligned with Faber-Castell's business interests, they also serve a deeper purpose. Together with the high-quality writing implements that Faber-Castell produces, they contribute to keeping handwriting and drawing, these essential human cultural techniques, alive and capable of stimulating the creativity of both children and adults. Maybe one of them will be the next Vincent van Gogh, who was an avid user of A.W. Faber pencils and found that they "produce a marvellous black and are very agreeable to work with" (Van Gogh, 1883).

Thinking in generations rather than quarters

With its emphasis on the long term, Faber-Castell is a typical representative of the *Mittelstand*, the backbone of the German economy. These family businesses – often world market leaders in their fields – are mainly competing on the quality of their products and services rather than on any cost advantage. These companies' managers, often family members themselves, are not responsible to transient investors who want to see quarterly results. They have a totally different time horizon that spans decades rather than months.

"The family business has the advantage that it is not a matter of profit; it's like your home," says Mario Preve, the Chairman of the more than 170-year-old Italian rice producer Riso Gallo in an *Ernst & Young* publication on family businesses:

> I always say that it's like the relay race: someone passes you the baton and then you pass it on to someone else. We say that we didn't get the company from my parents, we are borrowing it from our children. And this is important. We are thinking of how it affects our offspring. We don't think in quarters, we think in generations. (EY, 2013)

Count Anton Wolfgang von Faber-Castell fully agreed:

> We family entrepreneurs naturally find it easier to think in terms of generations and to see through projects whose fruits will not be reaped for perhaps decades, only after setbacks. In a listed company, this attitude would have got me fired at least three times by now, especially in the days when shareholder value was the be-all and end-all, and the goal of short-term profit eclipsed any long-term considerations. (EY, 2014, p. 56)

The EY Family Business Center of Excellence asked 280 family business managers about the most important reasons for the sustainable success of their businesses. One factor by far outweighed all the others: a long-term management perspective (EY, 2013, p. 8). Long-term oriented family businesses often show an amazing degree of durability and longevity, even in times of economic tur-moil. "One reason family businesses are so able to withstand shocks is that they are specifically built to do so," says Philip Aminoff, the owner of a Finnish family business and former president of the European Family Businesses Group: "a long-term family business has usually seen a number of catastrophic events, either internal or driven by technological innovation or geopolitical forces" (EY, 2013, p. 9). The secrets of how to survive in times of crisis and how to thrive over decades and centuries will never be found in monthly or quarterly financial figures. They lie in the deep values and long-term oriented business principles that are carefully passed down from generation to generation. The owner-managers of the German luxury jewelry producer Wellendorff, for example, write generation reports – one by the grandfather, one by the father, and one by the son – instead of quarterly reports (Hofer, 2014, p. 19).

Eternity as the business horizon in a Benedictine monastery

In our search for long-term oriented companies that create real value, it was not easy to outclass the over-250-year-old family firm of Faber-Castell. However, a few hundred miles south of the German pencil empire's headquarters, smack in the middle of the Austrian Alps, we came across a much older organization, a community rather than a family firm, which has been in business for almost one thousand years.

In 1074, the Benedictine monastery of Admont was founded in a secluded location surrounded by the dramatic rock summits of the Ennstal Alps. From its earliest days, the monks have followed the traditional motto of their order's founder Saint Benedict of Nursia, "ora et labora et lege" (pray and work and read). In addition to having established a spiritual center, they created the world's largest monastery library – a highlight of Baroque art – and have also taken on the responsibility for setting up economic structures in the region. Today, the Admont Monastery is, among other things, an enterprise that employs almost 600 people in a diversified range of businesses – from agriculture and one of Austria's largest forestry operations to timber-processing, electric power supply, real estate, and tourism services.

Why does a Catholic monastery develop and own a successful group of businesses? "Business has a serving function for us," says Admont's Abbott Bruno Hubl (Höfler, 2009). It enables the monastery to run the only high school in the region for more than 570 students, a high-quality nursing home, a meeting house and student dorm, a combined museum for fine art, contemporary art, and natural history, and offer pastoral care for 26 local parishes. "Not least, it is also about creating jobs," adds Abbott Bruno, "Earned profits are also serving the common good" (Kump, 2012, p. 17). For Admont, a village with less than 3,000 inhabitants, and its surroundings, the monastery's businesses are the main driver of regional development.

The monastery – like other enterprises that create real value – sees its business activities as instrumental for reaching higher aims. "I do not serve shareholder value with my work here, but purposes for which the monastery and I take responsibility," says Helmuth Neuner (Höfler, 2009), Admont's Business Director, whose office, appropriately, directly faces Abbott Bruno's:

> The nice thing about Admont is that on the one hand, we are doing business within the context of the usual laws of the market economy and do our best to work with our employees in a profit-oriented way; on the other hand, however, we use the income for the region, for operating the business, for the people in the region, and for the monastery itself. (Unterberger, 2008, pp. 20-21)

To make sure that its deeper purposes can continue to be fulfilled in the long run, the monastery's businesses need to be managed with a long-term perspective. "The thinking always needs to be sustainability-oriented," says Abbott Bruno. "Only short-term profits – that is not the right way" (Höfler, 2009).

The Admont wine revival

Between 1139 and the dark years of the expropriation of the monastery by the Nazis in the late 1930s, Admont owned a vast vineyard estate in the Štajerska region in what is today Austria's neighboring country of Slovenia. For almost 800 years, wine had been one of the main sources of income for the monastery, which in turn strongly contributed to regional development in Štajerska, building streets and schools, and providing people with sufficient means to earn their living and support their families. The monastery's wine was renowned all over Europe, sold well in England and was avidly consumed at the Austrian royal court in Vienna.

After World War II, under Communist rule, the estate was first nationalized and then more or less completely run down. In the course of privatization efforts in Slovenia in the 1990s, the Admont Monastery decided to reacquire the estate despite its degraded condition. It has since invested €12 million into re-cultivating the vineyards, refurbishing the existing buildings, and opening a new production site. "Currently, we produce 300,000 liters of wine – a relatively large quantity, but we do not earn any money with it," explains Helmuth Neuner. "It is also not our intention to make profits right away. That is our most important advantage compared to other investors who need to earn their money back in a very short time."

If it is not about earning money, then why does the monastery invest in the business? "If you contribute to the development of a region – even if it is only a small region – for a long time, you have a responsibility," says Neuner (Sternad, 2016, p. 4):

> We want to assume this responsibility again. In the long run, we, of course, also want to earn something again, but at the moment, we focus on building the substance, improving the substance, and creating value in the substance. If we would sell it again today, we would not get anything for it. But how does it look like in 200 years? I am convinced that food staples – and I consider wine a food staple – are something that people will always need. In the long term, when we will be able to improve our name and make the wine more known again, we will also get returns. We just need to establish our new brand – Dveri Pax. It takes time, but we will take our time. (Sternad, 2016, p. 4)

Neuner believes that a good reputation built on trust and credibility can only be developed with quality and consistency:

> Only high quality lasts. It will become apparent. People will taste the wine and will buy it if it is good. We will provide high quality every year, or we won't offer the wine to the market at all. Thus, we will reach at least a balanced business result within the next five to ten years. (Sternad, 2016, p. 4)

Forests, houses, industry

For centuries, the Admont Monastery lived from wine-growing in Štajerska and forestry in the mountainous regions of Austria, until it nearly went bankrupt in the 1930s. The monastery was unable to pay wages, needed to ask for credit at the local grocer, and had to sell some of its precious art collection to survive. What happened?

The price for timber had collapsed, and since timber from its forestry operations was Admont's main source of income, the monastery almost collapsed (along with its business).

> We learned that we could not rest on one pillar alone, it did not work in this way. We needed more pillars," says Helmuth Neuner. "It is important, however, also to understand the other pillars. Many others who thought that they needed to diversify failed. Their new pillars were breaking away because they did not have the necessary skills to manage them. (Sternad, 2016, p. 3)

In the 1970s, the monastery focused its diversification efforts on the timber-processing industry. It founded STIA, a producer of wooden floors and panels. Another subsidiary, DANA, was developed into a successful door manufacturer with over 500 employees and a market share of more than 60% in Austria. These businesses, however, were quite cyclical, and in general, volatility is the enemy of the long-term economic stability to which the monastery aspires. DANA had also outgrown its domestic market. As the monastery had neither the inclination nor the necessary skills to internationalize the brand, it decided to sell the business to a global player with the resources and abilities to further develop DANA. However, the monastery decided to keep STIA, even though it presented similar management challenges. Its location right next door resulted in a tightly integrated connection with the monastery itself, for example through providing its heating, and led to the monastery having a strong perceived responsibility for providing employment for the local population.

Helmuth Neuner, backed by his supervisory board (which consisted of all the monastery's monks), decided to invest all the proceeds from the sale of the DANA door factory into real estate. "Why real estate, why not a forest?" asks Neuner. He answers:

> In forestry, the yield is well below 1 per cent. In real estate, I had a yield of 5-6 percent from the beginning: returns that I cannot guarantee in industry. A 0.5 per cent difference in yield will double your assets in a century. Thus, if I invest in real estate, I have the same substance as in a forest, but a much higher chance to accumulate property. (Sternad, 2016, p. 3)

During the last two decades of Neuner's tenure as Admont's Business Director, he has built up real estate assets equal in value to the over 60,000 acres of forests that the monastery has owned for centuries.

In addition to acquiring new real estate assets, Neuner has also focused on developing the necessary skills for successfully managing them. Initially, Admont started as a junior partner in a joint venture with an insurance company that was already highly experienced in this business. After completing three joint projects, while at the same time ensuring that his own staff was developing essential real estate management skills, Neuner decided that it was time for the monastery to proceed on its own. Meanwhile, Admont has also been offering its real estate management services to external clients: "We help other church-related institutions in developing their real estate," explains Neuner:

> We never pull them over the barrel. We are transparent, open, honest and very correct. That's our highest credo. Thus, others can participate as well. Now that we have built a reputation, more and more potential partners are asking us to cooperate with them. (Sternad, 2016, p. 3)

Following an ancient rule

Despite the differences between Faber-Castell and the Admont Monastery in terms of industry sector and ownership, we observed several striking similarities in their long-term oriented management approaches. In both cases, *reputation-building* through consistency and a relentless quality-orientation plays a key role, whether through establishing a premium brand for writing implements at Faber-Castell or through investments in high-quality winemaking and mutually beneficial real estate development at Admont.

Regardless of their long traditions, both organizations constantly strive for *rejuvenation*; Faber-Castell through innovative reinterpretations of its core products such as the "Perfect Pencil," and the Admont Monastery through entering new business segments. But rejuvenation is different from total change, because it also means maintaining continuity and an affinity with one's roots.

Both organizations' top managements care for their *resource bases* at least as much as they care for profits. Admont's Helmuth Neuner prefers to call the resource base "substance" in line with the founding father of the Benedictine order. The monastic community at Admont still follows the almost 1,500-year-old *Rule of Benedict*. The *Rule* contains precepts for all the members of the community, among them the cellarer, the person in charge of the material things in the monastery:

Let him regard all the utensils of the monastery
and its whole property
as if they were the sacred vessels of the altar.
Let him not think that he may neglect anything.
He should be neither a miser
nor a prodigal and squanderer of the monastery's
  substance.
Rule of Saint Benedict, Chapter 31 (OSB, 2015)

Admont's Business Director, who we can regard as a 21st-century equivalent of the cellarer, sees substance not only in forests and real estate, but also in people. In fact, anyone in a leadership function in the monastery's business will usually remain there until retirement. "This makes selection more difficult," says Neuner, "but considerably improves cohesion and the working atmosphere" (Henrich, 2009). Just like Count Anton Wolfgang von Faber-Castell, Neuner

emphasizes values in leading both the organization and its
employees:

> In conversations with employees, attitudes, dignity, and humil-
> ity are important – things that also Saint Benedict put into the
> foreground. To my mind, humility is one of the most impor-
> tant elements of leadership – it's about letting the other per-
> son live, giving him or her the chance to develop, and taking
> delight in how the other one is able to do something. (Sternad,
> 2016, p. 5)

Reputation-building, rejuvenation, resource-orientation – all
three focal areas of long-term oriented management can be found
in Faber-Castell and the Admont Monastery. But what about the
fourth principle, *risk-consciousness*? "We do not enter any sphere
of risks," says Abbott Bruno. "We cannot afford that for moral reasons" (Höfler, 2009). As with Faber-Castell, the monastery therefore tries to keep the equity ratio of its businesses high and shuns
currency transactions and derivatives. It prefers reaping the fruit of
honest, sustainable work to taking easy pickings and follows the
time horizon that Saint Benedict envisioned:

[W]hile there is still time,
while we are still in the body
and are able to fulfill all these things
by the light of this life,
we must hasten to do now
what will profit us in eternity.
>   Rule of Saint Benedict, Prologue (OSB, 2015)

Beyond monks and aristocrats

Is long-term orientation a luxury that only companies run by German aristocrats and Benedictine monks can afford? Aren't these very special cases far from the realities of business in other realms such as fast-moving start-ups or public corporations that are subject to the short-termism of Wall Street? Our answer is an emphatic no!

Although quarterly thinking is widespread in Corporate America, there are exceptions. Take Seventh Generation, a U.S. company that devotes itself to creating healthy and environmentally friendly natural household cleaning and personal care products. The name of the company derives from an old maxim of the Iroquois Confederacy: "In every deliberation we must consider the impact of our decisions on the next seven generations" (Ecoheart, 2013).

Since it was founded in 1988 by Jeffrey Hollender, the company has been at the forefront of the sustainability movement in the U.S. "All too often, businesses are asking the wrong question," says Hollender in an interview with *Lifestyles Magazine*:

> That's important because the question shapes the answer. For instance, if you ask, "What can we do to build market share?" you'll get a different answer – and create a different future – then if you ask "What can we do to build a more sustainable economy?" Here's the question that should be asked: "What does the world need most that our business is uniquely able to provide?" (Ruhling, 2011, p. 129).

We would rephrase this question as "How does our business create *real value*?" Hollender is convinced that a company's purpose and values count more than the actual products or services it offers (Ruhling, 2011, p. 128). He aimed to create a consumer-goods company with a mission of providing safe and healthy products with the least negative environmental impact. His successors still follow him in this long-term endeavor.

The current CEO of Seventh Generation, John Replongle, has given his team clear, measurable, long-term goals such as producing zero waste, sourcing all natural materials from sustainable farms that are devoted to improving soil fertility, water quality, and biodiversity, or creating the best workplace in North America (Seventh Generation, 2014). Although their aim is to achieve these goals within seven years rather than seven generations, their actions still have (positive) long-term impacts. The long-term goals are not just lip service, but are directly linked to financial incentives for Seventh Generation's employees and managers. "Our goal is not a billion dollars," says Replongle. "We do not measure success in sales; we would rather be a company that focuses on meaningful work" (*Burlington Free Press*, 2012). Despite this attitude of putting purpose and long-term impact before just making money, Seventh Generation has shown impressive business results since it was founded. It was the second-fastest-growing company in Vermont over a decade and has become the leading natural home products brand in the United States (*Brattleboro Reformer*, 2008; Ecoheart, 2013). Its products can now be found in almost every natural grocery store in North America (Ecoheart, 2013).

There is another outstanding example of a person who sees an alternative to the narrow-minded quarterly results-focused pressure of the capital market. Clearly understanding the damage that can be done when companies underinvest and neglect both their customers and their brands just for the sake of hitting short-term earnings targets, this person argues that CEOs who "always promise to 'make the numbers' will at some point be tempted to *make up* the numbers" (Berkshire Hathaway, 2003, p. 21). As an investor, his "favorite holding period is forever" (Berkshire Hathaway, 1989). He also calls it a "til-death-do-us-part attitude" (Berkshire Hathaway, 1990). Despite going against conventional Wall Street wisdom, this person became the most successful investor of the 21st century and the richest man in the world (Forbes, 2008). No prize for guessing: this long-term thinker is the famed Warren Buffett.

Buffett tells all executives in the companies owned by his NYSE-listed holding Berkshire Hathaway to manage their businesses as if they were the only asset that they and their families would ever own and as if they could neither sell nor merge them with another business for at least a century (Cunningham, 2014, p. 55). Thus, he demands of his executives the same time perspective as his own – an extreme long-term orientation. He is fully focused on maximizing long-term value, not on achieving quarterly profits (Cunningham, 2014, p. 55). This does not mean that Buffett completely neglects all current results. He does, however, refuse to give them precedence when there is a trade-off between reaching short-term goals and ensuring positive long-term outcomes for the company (Cunningham, 2014, p. 55).

Although he is the head of a publicly listed company, Buffett's long-term oriented investment and management style shows surprising similarities to Faber-Castell and the businesses of the Benedictine monks of Admont. Like the German count and the Austrian monks, Buffett acknowledges the importance of the four habits of long-term-oriented enterprises, *reputation-building*, *resource-orientation*, *risk-consciousness*, and *rejuvenation* (see also Figure 2.1).

One of his mantras is: "We can afford to lose money – even a lot of money. But we can't afford to lose reputation – even a shred of reputation" (Berkshire Hathaway, 2011, p. 104). For him, reputation primarily means being true to one's word. "We will behave exactly as promised," he says, "both because we have so promised, and because we need to in order to achieve the best business results" (Berkshire Hathaway, 1991). If a company is consistently delivering on what it is promising, it is creating consumer trust – one of the resources that Buffett has always sought when judging investment opportunities.

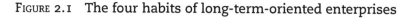

FIGURE 2.1   The four habits of long-term-oriented enterprises

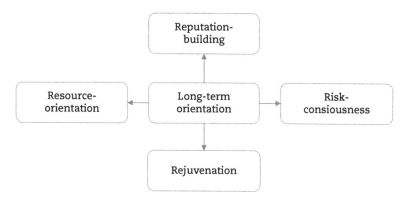

Resource-orientation for Buffett primarily means looking at the intangible part of the value of a business or 'economic goodwill,' as he calls it. In his eyes, economic goodwill is strongly determined by the accumulated trust in a brand (Cunningham, 2014, p. 257). He does, however, also have an eye on other intangible resources such as good relationships with business partners or managerial talent. "We have found splendid business relationships to be so rare and so enjoyable that we want to retain all we develop," he says (Cunningham, 2014, p. 302). And he sees attracting and retaining exceptional managers as one of his most important jobs as a CEO, since he believes that great businesses are built on "unstinting care and exceptional talent" (Berkshire Hathaway, 2001).

In addition to being clearly oriented toward building and extending an intangible resource base, Buffett is also a prime example for risk-consciousness. He is convinced that risk-control is a task that a CEO must never delegate (Cunningham, 2014, p. 82). He is also famous for his high regard for the "margin-of-safety" principle (Cunningham, 2014, p. 114). Buffett prefers to invest in companies that possess competitive strengths that will last for decades in industries in which sea changes are relatively unlikely (Cunningham, 2014, pp. 117-118). Actually, he seeks to avoid business problems rather than solving them when they arise – "avoiding dragons rather than slaying them," as he calls it (Cunningham, 2014, p. 126). Like many family-owned firms, he tries to be conservative in financial matters and cautious, so he does not overleverage his businesses with debt (Cunningham, 2014, p. 128). Buffett says he would never want to be in a position in which there is even a one percent risk that a major shock could lead to serious financial distress for his company (Cunningham, 2014, p. 127). "We try to be alert to any sort of megacatastrophe risk," he wrote in one of his famous letters to Berkshire Hathaway's shareholders (Berkshire Hathaway, 2003, p. 15). For that reason, he also keeps large amounts of cash – usually $20 billion – in his company's coffers to provide for unforeseeable events (Berkshire Hathaway, 2015, p. 35). Buffett knows that he sacrifices some profits with this risk-conscious attitude, but in return he is getting a good night's sleep and the freedom to grab the best new investment opportunities even in times of economic crisis when everyone else is hunkering down (Cunningham, 2014, p. 131).

Last but not least, Buffett also recognizes that businesses need rejuvenation if they are to remain competitive (Cunningham, 2014, p. 130). "The pace of change in terms of what customers are doing, how they pay us, how they come to us – it's breathtaking," he said in a radio interview:

> Any company that interacts with consumers and thinks that last week's technology and approach is going to work five years from now is probably making a mistake. That does not mean that they leave the old totally behind, but they'd better be in touch with what their customers are doing. (PYMNTS.com. 2013)

With his family-business-like focus on the long term, Warren Buffett has clearly departed from the conventions of Wall Street. He is an outlier in his temporal orientation, just as he is an outlier in terms of business success. For the 50 years between 1965 and 2014, Berkshire Hathaway outperformed the market, with a compound annual gain of 19.4% for book value per share and 21.6% for market value per share compared to a mere 9.9% for the S&P 500 index (Berkshire Hathaway, 2015). At the beginning of 2015, Buffett's company had a market capitalization of over $350 billion.

The example of Berkshire Hathaway makes it clear that the principles of long-term orientation can also work exceptionally well for a business in an environment dominated by short-term pressures. But isn't Berkshire Hathaway actually the epitome of a money-making machine as opposed to an enterprise focused on creating *real value*? From an organizational perspective, that's perhaps true, regardless of whether the main goal is reaping short-term profits or creating value in the long term. But if we change our perspective and look at what Warren Buffett actually does with all of his profits, we may come to a different conclusion. In his will, Buffett arranged to bequeath five charitable foundations with the majority of the Berkshire stock that he owns, "thus carrying out part of my lifelong plan to eventually use all of my shares for philanthropic purposes," he says (Cunningham, 2014, p. 321). Creating real value and a long-term orientation go together. And a business with a deeper purpose and a drive to create real value does not necessarily have to bow to the myopic will of Wall Street.

In brief: long-term orientation

- Creating lasting real value usually takes time and leaders who are able to think and act with a long-term perspective.

- Long-term-oriented companies understand the value of building a positive reputation as a provider of quality products and services, as a trustworthy and reliable business partner, and as a good employer that cares for its employees and customers as well as for its community and the natural environment.

- Long-term-oriented leaders think about the impact of their decisions on the next generation. Instead of narrow-mindedly focusing on short-term profits, they give priority to creating potential for the future in the form of extending the tangible and intangible resource and skills base of their organizations.

- In order to preserve the sustainability of their organizations, long-term oriented leaders actively try to identify and contain major risks. They also tend to be conservative in financial matters in order to provide for hard times.

- An organization's long-term viability is closely linked to its ability to constantly rejuvenate itself. Rejuvenation does not mean giving up on the past. Instead, it means being open to creatively adapting oneself to a changing environment while remaining aware of one's roots and skills and staying true to one's values.

3

Lasting relationships: cooperation instead of competition

Competition has been shown to be useful up to a certain point and no further, but cooperation, which is the thing we must strive for today, begins where competition leaves off.

Franklin D. Roosevelt (1912)

I am not a destroyer of companies. I am a liberator of them! The point is, ladies and gentleman, that greed – for lack of a better word – is good. Greed is right. Greed works. Greed clarifies, cuts through, and captures the essence of the evolutionary spirit.

Gordon Gekko in the movie
Wall Street (Weiser and Stone, 1987)

The dominant narrative of business is simple: individual businesses strive to be competitive, to offer the best products and services at the lowest prices to the most consumers, and to achieve the highest possible financial returns for their shareholders. They exist in a world that conventional wisdom tells us is "dog-eat-dog," where the law of the jungle prevails, the survival of the fittest obtains, and "business is business." It is an upside-down world where, to paraphrase Gordon Gekko, "greed is good!" (Weiser and Stone, 1987). Poor Adam Smith is trotted out with regularity to support the notion that no good deed will be done altruistically, but rather only due to the self-interest of the doer:

> It is not from the benevolence of the butcher, the brewer, or the baker that we expect our dinner, but from their regard to their own interest. We address ourselves, not to their humanity but to their self-love . . .(Smith, 1904, Book 1, Chapter 1, p. 2)

Of course, this is a gross simplification of Smith's philosophy. His conveniently and largely ignored first book, after all, was *A Theory of Moral Sentiments*, in which he argued that the virtue of what he called "sympathy" was the highest of mankind's qualities, a natural, deep-seated concern that individuals have for the well-being of others, and of economic behavior that was embedded firmly in a moral context. Nevertheless, it is the mantra of the market's "invisible hand" that is remembered by most and the notion of self-interest that is a foundation of the dominant ideology of business. In such an environment, competition is king. To believe anything else (they would have us believe) is to be soft, fuzzy-headed, and something of a fool.

This mindset colors business activities all along the value chain, surfacing not only in the cut and thrust of the marketplace, but in the prosaic, quotidian activities of most business organizations. Businesses haggle with their employees over pay, benefits, and performance, put pressure on their suppliers over price, delivery, and quality of raw materials, and constantly try to squeeze higher margins out of their distributors. In fact, hardnosed bargaining dominates the value chain, until an agreement is sealed and a *transaction* effected. Indeed, some firms see themselves as no more than a means, or an instrument, for bundling transactions – which are no more than exchanges, representing the buying and selling of goods, services, labor, or any other resource. Transactions are about giving and taking – presumably at arm's length, and with the help of information supplied by "the market" that values these transactions. And they are always valued monetarily; money is the ultimate arbiter, and there is only one bottom line. At its base, a condition of nature as sure as tomorrow's rising sun, is unbridled individualism and the pursuit of self-interest – the magnetic pull that makes the world, and its liberalized and competitive economy, go round. Today's corporations, collections of self-interest-seeking individuals who have transacted with shareholders to pursue *their* self-interest, are perfectly adapted to such a world. Or so we are told. But increasingly, this "stylized fact" of economics is being questioned, for instance by American futurist and radical critic Jacque Fresco:

> Competition is dangerous, socially offensive, considered right and normal, because you are brought up to that value system. What kind of competition did Jesus have? What kind of competition is there in your body? Suppose your brain said, "I'm the most important organ!" And the liver said, "I am. And I want a Free Enterprise system!" You'd rot away in a month if every organ of your body went out for itself. (Fresco, 1974)

His view itself may be extreme, but we think that Fresco may be on to something. Are we really creating value if we just engage in squeezing out the most from others? We might create surface value in pure monetary terms, but we will never reach the deeper, emotional layers of *real value* in this way – value that comes in the form of meaning, identity, and a higher quality of life. As we discussed in the first chapter of this book, meaning comes from "self-transcendence," connecting to others in a way that positively affects them. Identity, in turn, is derived from our social relations and identification with others. And numerous studies tell us that our perception of well-being, happiness, and quality of life is closely linked to the quality of our relationships (Argyle, 2001; Dolan *et al.*, 2008; Linley *et al.*, 2009). Can we even imagine a good life without good, mutually beneficial relations with others? If we agree that doing business is an integral part of our lives, why do we then still assert that it is all about self-interest? Are we really all schizophrenics, longing for good relationships throughout our lives with the exception of our business endeavors, wherein we turn into radical egoists?

Cooperative firms

> The only thing that will redeem mankind is co-operation.
>
> Bertrand Russell (2009, p. 204)[12]

There is another, deeper, and happier, reality. It is that humans are at least as naturally collaborative and cooperative as they are competitive and aggressive! They are distinguished by their mindfulness and consciousness, and cooperate as much as they compete, and (sometimes) even do for others as they would do for themselves. They *relate* to each other as much as *transact* with each other. The two genes in their makeup – their thirst for (and even joy in) competition and a bent for cooperation and teamwork – may live in a sometimes uneasy stasis, but the human impulse for cooperation is undisputed. As Irish economist David McWilliams wrote:

> we know that humans like to share and collaborate. The ability to share, inform, exchange ideas and therefore organise through language is what propelled humans into poll [*sic*] position in the animal kingdom. We like to involve others in our world, to talk and exchange ideas. A sense of humour is nothing more than sharing your own funny ideas and hoping to get a laugh. Humans have always shared ideas and we have always collaborated for the greater good. (McWilliams, 2015)

The future appears to belong more to organizations that practice *co-opetition*, a mindset that combines competition and cooperation. The duality between competition and cooperation is also mirrored in the range of business organizations. There is a wide span between hypercompetitive multinational firms that are owned largely by institutional investors and non-profits of every size and description supporting every cause and need imaginable. But there *are* also business firms that attempt to bridge this gap and merge these dualities – a full range of alternative business enterprises that have been garnering considerable attention.

Alternatively structured business firms, often called "social enterprises," may include community-owned corporations, "B" or Benefit Corporations (Honeyman, 2014) that have an explicit social mission and operate to a "triple-bottom-line" standard, commercial arms of charitable organizations, mutual enterprises and credit unions, cooperative enterprises, and many sorts of hybrid business organizations that do not fit neatly into any category. Some of them, such as cooperatives, are not nearly as rare (or as new) as many seasoned business professionals might believe. Indeed, interest in these "alternative" forms of business organization is at last beginning to attract serious attention from practitioners, academics, and social entrepreneurs alike; a refreshing change from the days in which they were dismissed out of hand. Gone, hopefully, are the days when they were viewed as having weak business structures rather than, as we believe, possessing all the attributes required for success. These are organizations that focus on lasting *relationships* rather than fleeting transactions and where the goal of making money is but one objective among many, and even then, only as a means to an end.

Cooperative enterprises, which include producer-owned, consumer-owned, and worker-owned cooperatives, as well as credit unions and utilities, are not trivial economic actors. Worldwide, the 300 largest cooperative enterprises represent more than $2 trillion in sales, employ over 100 million people, and have more than 800 million members (Logue and Yates, 2005; International Cooperative Alliance, 2012). This is ironic in that their employment exceeds the estimated 69 million people employed by the foreign affiliates of transnational corporations (UNCTAD, 2012). In particular, cooperatives have experienced significant growth in the developing world, at the so-called "base of the pyramid," and are often found at the forefront of fair-trade campaigns (Prahalad and Hammond, 2002; Hart and London, 2005).

Perhaps in reaction to some of the more egregious by-products of globalization, advocates of sustainable development have often posited the value of business enterprises that are of smaller scale, rooted in local communities, and possessed of democratic, participatory governance structures (Gladwin *et al.*, 1995). Worker cooperatives in particular, defined as "enterprises that are owned and controlled by employees," appear to meet these requirements (Lawless and Reynolds, 2004). To such advocates, worker cooperatives represent an important component of an emerging "fourth sector" in the global economy, or a "third way," a local, entrepreneurial response to the excesses of a neoliberal global economic system, its multinational enterprises, and big government. Indeed, the International Labor Organization (ILO), a constituent arm of the United Nations, promotes cooperative enterprises as a key element in its drive for fair and inclusive globalization.

In Italy, worker-owned companies comprise 4% of all workers in the country (Pencavel *et al.*, 2006). The Emilia-Romagna region, in particular, is rich in worker cooperatives, which number in the tens of thousands (Williams, 2007). Canada is one of the most cooperative-minded countries in the world, with a total of 9,000 cooperatives that employ over 150,000 workers (Saskatchewan Co-operative Association, 2015). Worker cooperatives in the United Kingdom and France range in the thousands and have been growing at a steady rate since 1980 as well (Williams, 2007). In the developing countries, India has the largest cooperative movement; it has about half a million cooperatives and approximately 210 million members (Zamagni and Zamagni, 2010), although many of these are agricultural rather than worker cooperatives. On the other hand, in the United States, the world's largest economy, worker cooperatives are found only at the margins of economic life; they are few (approximately 300) and small, a minute portion of all firms in the nation.

The point is that cooperative enterprises, founded upon principles of mutuality and economic democracy, are viable organizational forms that have the capability to model a new, and different, way of doing business, where firms are no less globally competitive for delivering a range of social benefits and public goods – monetary and non-monetary – to their members and their communities. Cooperative enterprises show how *real value* can be created through lasting relationships, where people agree to work together on an equal basis and share equally the fruits of their labor.

In the following sections we tell the stories of two such cooperative organizations, both of them owned by their workers. Mondragón, probably the most famous example of a successful worker cooperative in the world, offers a primer on how the principles of cooperation can be extended to large, complicated industrial enterprises that are deeply engaged in global competition. Their story is both exemplary and salutary. We will also study Equal Exchange (USA), which organized itself on a cooperative basis and has developed ongoing, mutually beneficial relationships with small, indigenous coffee producers in developing countries in order to further its overarching mission of creating real value through furthering fair trade.

"Humanity at work" – the Mondragón Corporation[13]

> We . . . have to tackle an unpredictable future where trust and hope will be necessary, together with co-operation on the basis of our diversity and the development of new sustainable profitable businesses which help transform our society.
> Javier Sotil, former Chairman of the General Council of Mondragón Corporation (Mondragón Corporation, 2015a)

Beginnings

There are few multinational enterprises that can claim roots in Catholic social teaching and a founder who was a humble parish priest in a backward region in a country devastated by civil war. This is curious enough, but the Mondragón Cooperative Corporation (MCC) can claim another and perhaps even more significant distinction: it is the world's largest federation of worker cooperatives. Founded, and still deeply rooted, in Mondragón, a town of approximately 23,000 people in the hilly Basque region of northern Spain, it has become an exemplar and indeed a "poster child" for the inherent possibilities of cooperative enterprise. It is a Horatio Alger, "rags-to-riches" story set in a European context.

Founded in 1956, the endeavor was inspired and driven by Father José María Arizmendiarrieta, an energetic and idealistic young priest with a practical bent and a bias for action. As a priest, Arizmendiarrieta was concerned with the spiritual and moral development of his flock, but he also saw how the lack of employment and even more, the lack of hope, was having catastrophic consequences for his community. He believed in the important role of work in the formation of character, and saw that jobs were necessary to effect real human development and provide the essentials for living a good and fulfilling life. But in right-wing, conservative (even neo-fascist) Franco's Spain, and particularly in the impoverished Basque country that had fought and lost to Franco in the Spanish Civil War, creating jobs represented a formidable task.

Arizmendiarrieta's task was even more difficult, because he did not want *only* to create jobs. He also wanted to recognize and celebrate the dignity of work in firms where workers shared responsibility and rewards and where solidarity and cooperation in support of a common purpose were the norm. In the post-civil war Basque country, no such firms existed; the people would have to create them themselves.

Mondragón's official history relates the priest's beginning efforts:

> Before setting up the first cooperative, José María Arizmendiarrieta devoted several years of his life to training young people in caring and participatory humanism based on Christian values, and to acquiring the necessary technical knowhow. Equipped with an extraordinary mixture of idealism and pragmatic talent, recently arrived in Arrasate/Mondragón he

> set about to revitalise the community. Based on his motto ideas
> keep us apart, needs bring us together, he first set up a football
> team in order to rebuild personal relationships. (Fernández,
> 2015, p. 12)

It was a wise decision to begin with sports activities and education, and the school he founded in 1943 not only taught technical skills, but incorporated a liberal dose of cooperative principles and Father Arizmendiarrieta's own (somewhat radical) social vision. It was the beginning of what was to be Mondragón's continuing emphasis on education. And, it began to develop a cadre of educated, competent, and pragmatic idealists who were ready to put their ideas into action. In today's parlance, they were budding entrepreneurs with one important difference – they would travel their road, and build their businesses, together. There was no room for only one founder, or one "great man." It would be a cooperative effort.

After several false starts, the first cooperative enterprise, Ulgor,[14] was founded in 1956 by five idealistic technical school graduates who – urged on by Father Arizmendiarrieta – left their jobs at the largest local employer (Unión Cerrajera) and literally went door-to-door in the Basque country to raise sufficient start-up capital to invest in a paraffin stove manufacturing business. This business succeeded, and quickly evolved into a multi-product industrial enterprise, becoming the flagship enterprise of the entire Mondragón cooperative federation.

Then the floodgates opened and other cooperative enterprises rapidly followed. The first consumer cooperative, Eroski (now one of the largest retailers in Spain) was founded a year later. In 1959, the Caja Laboral Popular, the cooperative financial institution that became the central locus of financing cooperative growth, was founded. Cooperatives not only did their banking with Caja Laboral, but invested in the bank which, in turn, provided financing to existing cooperatives and new enterprises. This was a critically important addition to the system, and attacked one of the major problems common to many cooperative enterprises – insufficient capital availability.

Expansion continued rapidly, but it was not helter-skelter. The structure of the Mondragón cooperatives had been carefully thought out. Fundamentally, it was envisioned as a federation of cooperatives, each independent and autonomous but related to the others, with a stake in the success of each other, and all committed to Mondragón's founding principles and to the basic notion that the federation is a nexus of relationships among many cooperative enterprises. The notion of solidarity undergirded the entire enterprise.

It has been a successful formula financially – the envy even of the investor-owned multinational corporations who have a very different driving vision and values. In 2014, the Mondragón Corporation (the federation of independent, autonomous Mondragón Cooperatives) had sales of €11.9 billion from 260 cooperatives and associated businesses. It had facilities in 41 countries and sales in more than 150, with more than 74,000 employees, 83% of whom are worker-owners. Mondragón had 15 R&D and technology centers, as well as its own university, a renowned culinary school, and a number of management and training centers.[15] The range and scope of its activities is impressive, ranging from banking and consulting services to supermarkets, to automobile parts and components for household appliances. By any definition, Mondragón is a big business, but it is surely in a category all its own.

A values-based business

Mondragón was a "social enterprise" long before the term became fashionable. Its business model is rooted in ten basic principles which incorporate and expand upon the original cooperative principles articulated by the Rochdale Pioneers – the founders of the "prototype" of the modern cooperative – in 1844, and the current cooperative values institutionalized by the International Co-operative Alliance (ICA), the global umbrella group for cooperative enterprises.[16] They are intended to inform the structures, governance, strategies, and decisions of all of the Mondragón units (Mondragón Corporation, 2015c):

- *"Open admission"* (No discrimination. Membership is open to all.)

- *"Democratic organization"* (Worker-members own and control the company.)

- *"Sovereignty of labor"* (Labor is the most important factor of production. Created wealth is distributed on the basis of labor.)

- *"Instrumental and subordinate nature of capital"* (Money is not the most important thing; capital is hired by labor, not vice versa.)

- *"Participatory management"* (Participation, transparency, consultation, negotiation.)

- *"Payment solidarity"* (Sufficient and fair pay for work.)

- *"Inter-cooperation"* (Between Mondragón cooperatives, and Mondragón and other cooperatives around the world.)

- *"Social transformation"* (Aiming for an "economic and social reconstruction" and "the construction of a freer, fairer and more caring Basque society.")

- *"Universality"* (Fostering universal values such as peace, justice, and development, and showing solidarity with others who strive for "economic democracy.")
- *"Education"* (To promote all of the above-noted principles, Mondragón must use part of its resources to promote education.)

Fundamental to most of these principles and providing a base to their enactment is the idea of long-term relationships. There is also a very distinct approach toward the relationship between human beings and money. Clearly and explicitly, in word and in deed, Mondragón operates as if money is *not* the most important thing, let alone the *only* thing. Money is of course an important part of the equation, the essential lubricant of any economic entity, but it is a necessary but insufficient component of a successful values-based business. There must be more. The subsidiarity of capital to labor has been an article of faith since the very first days of the Mondragón venture, demonstrating a relationship that is utterly fundamental to the Mondragón experiment. It is of course also profoundly at variance with most businesses, where capital is king, and hires (transacts with) individuals, businesses, and resource holders of all sorts to achieve its aims. But Mondragón turns this transactional approach upside down, replacing capital dominance and a transactional approach with economic democracy, worker "sovereignty" and a cooperative, relationship-based approach to business.

Similarly, the advancement of workers (people) over capital (profits) changes the internal dynamic of the firm, as expressed in Mondragón's comprehensive, complex, and multi-dimensional governance systems. It colors decisions on strategies, patronage dividends, loans to member enterprises, and much else. Naturally, there have been critical accounts of Mondragón cooperatives such as the study by U.S. anthropologist Sharryn Kasmir, who argues that they are falsely idealized, portrayed as apolitical institutions while the negative experiences of many shop-floor workers are ignored (Kasmir, 1996). Yet, without doubt, it is an achievement, even a triumph, to maintain a functioning system of economic democracy within the extensive network of businesses and operations that is Mondragón. It also, of necessity, demands real and substantive worker owners' participation, consultation, negotiation, and transparency throughout the governance process of the firms. Workers govern not only their own firms, but must help to govern the entire federation and multiple inter-cooperative relationships.

Mondragón is also a network of reciprocal and enduring relationships among the individual cooperatives, tied together by bonds of fraternal connection and solidarity. The individual cooperatives have pooled their R&D, educational, training, banking and insurance services, created benefit plans for their employees, and jointly focused on maintaining an employment "safety net" for the job security of their worker-owners. If worker-owners in a Mondragón cooperative are no longer required due to business conditions, the federation makes every effort to place those worker-owners in other cooperatives in the network.

This does not happen automatically; rather, it is a result of continuing "give and take" among legally (and often operationally) autonomous enterprises, using the elaborate governance structures that Mondragón has evolved over time. There is a General Assembly (of all worker-owners) and a Governing Council (a Board of Directors elected by worker-owners) in each independent cooperative. They make all strategic decisions. The next level is the Division, with a Governing Council elected by the Governing Councils of the individual cooperatives. The Division, however, only facilitates, negotiates, and generally tries to coordinate the activities of the individual cooperatives in particular business sectors. It dictates nothing; the individual cooperatives always have the final say. (If they are unhappy, an independent cooperative can leave the federation; and sometimes they do.) But importantly, at divisional level, there is also a "profit pooling" whereby all cooperatives contribute a percentage of their annual profits (15 – 40% – depending on how integrated they are) to a divisional common fund; this has the effect of assisting those enterprises that are doing less well. This is real solidarity! They also contribute to a revolving capital fund at corporate level, used to fund new cooperative enterprises, purchases, joint ventures, etc. At corporate level there is a Cooperative Congress, made up of representatives of all members' cooperatives, and a Standing Committee that acts as a Board of Directors of the federation, but they hardly function like the Board of Directors of a shareholder-owned firm. The relationships between the individual cooperative enterprises and the institutions on the divisional and federal level clearly differ from the typical "command and control" approach of large corporations. Instead, Mondragón's internal relationships are based on "ongoing communication, persuasion and negotiation" (Lafuente and Freundlich, 2012).

There are many more governance and coordinating bodies throughout the Mondragón federation; it is complex and extensive, and theory would probably suggest that it shouldn't work – it flies in the face of orthodox notions of decisive, "the buck stops here" theories of "great man" leadership and management. It may be messy and complicated, and take time and effort, but it works – in the same way that people who want real relationships to work, must work at them themselves, day in and day out. Relationships are not transactions; they are alive, and dynamic, and enduring. Transactions, on the other hand, are the moral equivalent of a "one-night stand." There is an exchange, and then it is over! The Mondragón cooperatives, relationally based and cooperatively inclined, have demonstrated that they are in it for the long term.

Solidarity in the face of a crisis

Sometimes, of course, we learn more from our failures than our successes, and Mondragón, like other organizations composed of human beings, has yet to achieve perfection. But we can learn something about the heart of the enterprise from the way that it has handled its failures, and probably none of these failures has been more dramatic, even traumatic, than the bankruptcy of the original Mondragón cooperative – Fagor (formerly Ulgor). The way Mondragón handled this crisis is instructive.

First, we must appreciate the importance of Fagor, both materially and symbolically. Fagor was Mondragón's most important associated cooperative, producing a wide range of consumer appliances including refrigerators, washing machines, and dishwashers on a large scale. It was reportedly the fifth-largest such concern in Europe, employing around 5,500 at its facilities throughout Europe, including 2,000 in Spain (Alperovitz and Hanna, 2013). It had realized steady growth over its nearly 57 years, although as a manufacturer of durable consumer products, it was always susceptible to the vagaries of the business cycle and particularly the housing market. Even more so, and despite its size, it was increasingly finding the going very tough as it tried to compete with low-cost Asian competitors and with technologically sophisticated German rivals. A Spanish housing boom helped for a while, and to achieve further scale Fagor management orchestrated the acquisition of a French competitor, which saddled the firm with a significant debt load. It proved to be an ill-fated and ill-timed decision.

When the Spanish housing boom went bust in 2008, and economic recession struck the EU, Fagor found itself in a vulnerable position. As demand tumbled, the debt that Fagor had accumulated by the acquisition began to weigh it down even further. As one affected worker said at the time:

> The housing bubble popped, and that combined with a finan-
> cial crisis, so credit was cut back, consumption dropped, prod-
> ucts came in from low-cost countries, and raw material prices
> rose . . . We're a cooperative, but we don't live outside the mar-
> ket. (Mount, 2013)

It was a time to test the cooperative federation's mettle, and the other cooperatives in the Mondragón system came through. Over the course of several years, Mondragón supplied some €300 million in crisis funding to help stabilize Fagor. Some observers found it quite surprising that workers in other Mondragón cooperatives would be willing to cut their own salaries to assist a brother coop-erative that was failing, but that is effectively what was done – until such time as the hemorrhaging threatened to swamp the entire Mondragón federation; at that point, they had little choice but to remove Fagor from life support (Buck, 2015).

Fagor, with accumulated debt of €850 million, was allowed to go bankrupt in November 2013. This had a devastating effect, and the symbolism was unmistakable. After all, Fagor was the first, and the largest, of the Mondragón cooperatives – a central part of the "cre-ation story" of Mondragón and once considered the flagship of the enterprise. Over the decades, too, it had contributed much of its own surplus to fund other cooperatives' expansion and meet the ongoing funding needs of other Mondragón cooperatives. Now it was being let go. In the wake of this failure, some claimed that the cooperative "experiment" was over – that Mondragón was now "just like any other corporation."

But this hardly seems true. Fagor was a business that failed due to competitive conditions and management's (and by extension, the worker-owners') bad decisions, and not the cooperative system. Mondragón's response to Fagor's difficulties was nothing less than heroic. That other cooperatives in the system were willing to go to the wall and, at no small pain to themselves, fund several iterations of rescue plans, is not insignificant. It is solidarity in action, even to the extent of literally "throwing good money after bad" when it became clear that Fagor could not be saved. After Fagor collapsed, parts of its operations were taken over by other white goods producers. Mondragón then relocated the majority of those Fagor employees who lost their jobs, approximately 600 (worker-owners got preference), to other jobs within the Mondragón system. This was the "Mondragón way" that they had always lived by. Employees who were not placed elsewhere were given generous benefits to help cushion the blow.

It was the first and only bankruptcy of a Mondragón cooperative in its nearly sixty-year history, and it hurt. The cooperative structure itself is no replacement for good business sense! Each member cooperative must itself be a viable business. But the Mondragón family of companies tried first to save the enterprise (at no small cost to the other cooperatives) and then tried to salvage a livelihood for Fagor's worker-owners. This is not the norm for a multinational enterprise but is fully consistent with the Mondragón way. The ties among the Mondragón cooperatives are dense and enduring, and the ties between individual cooperatives and worker-owners exemplify common cause and solidarity. What other multi-billion-euro enterprise has a maximum pay ratio of less than 8 to 1 (from highest paid chief executive to lowest paid full-time employee)? We are fairly sure of the answer: none.

Mondragón may be a commonly cited example of solidarity, cooperation, and dense and long-lasting relationships, but it is not the only one. Nor is it the only one that wants to change the world, or the only one that aims to create *real value* instead of just making profits.

Equal Exchange: small farmers, big change

Fairness to farmers. A closer connection between
people and the farmers we all rely on.

(Equal Exchange, 2015)

In 1986 three young men with a passion for social justice and a
belief in the virtues of fair trade found themselves working together
at a food cooperative in the Boston area. Rink Dickinson, Michael
Rozyne, and Jonathan Rosenthal were not only true believers in the
nascent movement to transform the relationship between food producers and consumers, but they were also motivated to act on that
belief. Further, they did not think small; they wanted to change the
world. They met weekly over the course of several years to study
and plan how they could effect changes in the food system that
would improve the lives of both producers and consumers. After
much discussion, the founders created both a vision and an idealistic and ambitious mission to guide the development of their
planned company. The firm would be:

- A social change organization that would help farmers
  and their families gain more control over their economic
  futures.

- A group that would educate consumers about trade issues
  affecting farmers.

- A provider of high-quality foods that would nourish the
  body and the soul.

- A company that would be controlled by the people who did
  the actual work.

- A community of dedicated individuals who believed that honesty, respect, and mutual benefit are integral to any worthwhile endeavor. (Equal Exchange, 2015)

To do this, they chose to enter the global coffee business, which was notorious for its exploitation of small farmers (though there are exceptions such as the Italian company illycaffè, as we detail in Chapter 6 in this book). It was characterized by middlemen who made huge profits, small growers, generally from developing countries, who made little or none, markets dominated by huge multinational corporations who relentlessly drove down prices, and not least, rampant human rights abuses of both growers and migrant laborers. Some 25 million small farmers produced 80% of the world's coffee, but they reportedly received only 7 to 10% of the retail price of coffee (Fairtrade Foundation, 2012). This was an area where the founders believed Equal Exchange could make a real difference, and create value in its real, meaningful sense.

Wading into the organic, fair trade coffee business, Equal Exchange began with very limited capital of $100,000, contributed by the founders and their friends and family, who were explicitly warned that they might never see their money again. As expected, Equal Exchange lost money during its first two years, but broke even in the third and hasn't fallen back, even during those times when the larger economy has faltered. In fact, Equal Exchange had an average annual sales growth rate of 23.6% from 1987 to 2014, and in 2014 had sales of $61.1 million and before tax income of $2.2 million. Structured as a worker cooperative, it has 145 employees, 117 of whom are worker-owners. This is a remarkable accomplishment and one of which many shareholder-owned firms would be envious.

In the beginning, the founders went through a rather steep learning curve: for example, they didn't actually know how to find the small-scale farmers that they endeavored to trade with under the enlightened terms that they had envisioned. They spent a great deal of time trying to identify democratically run farmer groups, and to determine product quality, dependability of supply, and sustainability. This was all compounded by their lack of proficiency in Spanish, the language of the majority of their growers.

It took time, but gradually Equal Exchange developed relationships with grass-roots farmer groups in Latin America and Africa and, early on, joined the European Fair Trade network, which was far more sophisticated and extensive than anything then happening in U.S. markets. With the knowledge, connections, and momentum gained from this network, Equal Exchange expanded its reach to farmer cooperatives worldwide.

At its core, both Equal Exchange's cooperative structure and its business model were based on long-lasting relationships of trust, reciprocity, and solidarity between the worker-owners of the firm, between the firm and the coffee growers with whom it traded, and between the firm and its varied customers (including many faith-based organizations). The firm has retained its idealistic drive, its commitment to worker democracy, and its desire to change the world. Former Equal Exchange spokesperson Rodney North shared this insight:

> A lot of us take pride in creating more coop jobs, constantly showing the viability and the vitality of our coop – and by growing we are extending fair trade benefits to more farmers, so that is the real impetus. When I arrived there were only 13 people, now we are at 150, and I was sure that whatever democracy we had was going to be diluted with size. But in fact, our democracy has been stronger in recent years than it was when I arrived.[17]

Like Mondragón, Equal Exchange limits the pay ratio between the highest paid (the management) and lowest (blue collar) worker, which is currently 4 to 1. Its focus on transparency in compensation, and moderate differences in pay, reflects its continuing commitment to solidarity among worker-owners united in pursuit of a common objective.

In 1997, Equal Exchange joined with Lutheran World Relief to launch their Interfaith Program. This important and long-running relationship has allowed Equal Exchange to connect with communities of faith (currently more than 8,000) throughout the United States who want to live their values by promoting the principles of fair trade and ethical business. As a minister involved in it said:

> We live our lives unjustly in so many avenues, but fair trade is one way to ensure justice, and there is no reason to buy cheap coffee on the backs of poor farmers. (Gogoi, 2008)

Partnering with these faith-based organizations who actively promote and sell an expanded line of fair trade products (now including tea, chocolate, nuts, and bananas) through fundraisers and other outlets has allowed Equal Exchange to significantly extend the reach of its sales activities well beyond what it would have through simply selling through cooperative or organic food stores, its mail order business and its own cafés. In a business based on values, cooperation with like-minded organizations is essential and can be highly effective. In this case, the relationship with faith-based organizations has been a critical and enduring component in Equal Exchange's ability to continue to grow its sales of fair trade products.

But perhaps the most important relationship that Equal Exchange has is with the 40 or so small grower organizations, many of them associations of cooperatives themselves, with whom it partners around the world (including Central and Latin America, Africa, and Asia); after all, small coffee growers are the reason that Equal Exchange exists. It is a unique partnership; as a coffee buyer, Equal

Exchange tries to pay its growers *the most* they can for their coffee beans, while still maintaining competitiveness in the market and making a profit. For their part, its coffee growers try to supply Equal Exchange with the highest quality, most sustainably grown coffee possible. Together, Equal Exchange and its partners create *real value* in the form of providing quality organic coffee to consumers, ensuring a decent livelihood for the growers, and creating meaning for all people who are investing themselves in this long-lasting "exchange between equals."

Equal Exchange does not buy coffee beans grown on large coffee plantations; rather, it focuses on small, typically family-run farms. Its interests in coffee growers (and growers of other products it now sells) extend well beyond paying them a "fair" price; it encompasses helping growers with different methods of growing and crop diversification, quality improvement and achievement of the stringent criteria for organic growing, continuing education and training, improvements in living conditions, women's empowerment, and many other aspects of the growers' lives. Additionally, Equal Exchange helps farmers to escape the wild swings of the global commodity markets in coffee by purchasing coffee from them under guaranteed, long-term supply contracts, providing credit facilities, and making a portion of the payment in advance of actual delivery of the crop – all helping coffee growers to smooth out the income cycle.

The basic imperative of Equal Exchange continues to be to create *real value* through improving the quality of life of these small producers and their families, and to enter into business relationships with them that are more than mere commercial transactions. They are long-term, cooperative, symbiotic relationships that are characterized by trust and that lend dignity to the growers and their families and quality to the buyers and consumers. Equal Exchange demonstrates that it is possible to develop productive, beneficial relationships that lead to outcomes that are good for their customers, for their small farmer suppliers and for the planet. They are also, not coincidentally, modestly profitable for the worker-owners of the Equal Exchange cooperative itself.

Conclusion

It is not only organizations formally structured as cooperatives that demonstrate long-lasting, cooperative, relationship-based behavior; although it may be more complicated, publicly-owned corporations can do so as well. In fact, it is often a characteristic of the very best global firms. As researchers at Booz & Company noted:

> Although some companies will dub any concluded business deal a relationship, top-performing companies focus extraordinary, enterprise-wide energy on moving beyond a transactional mind-set as they develop trust-based, mutually beneficial, and long-term associations, specifically with four key constituencies: customers, suppliers, alliance partners, and their own employees. (Gulati *et al.*, 2002)

Some multinational behemoths such as Starbucks have adopted an explicit social mission and strive to be attentive and responsive to their stakeholders. Such firms demonstrate that public companies *can* care, while earning a respectable profit. Starbucks has long been a leader in treating its employees, even part-timers, significantly better than the industry standard. It provides employees with a range of benefits including low-cost medical insurance, paid time off, profit sharing, and, most recently, access to free university-level education. Good treatment of employees, in turn, spills over into Starbucks' relationships with its customers, who can expect a certain standard in both the products that Starbucks sells and the services that it provides (e.g., a pleasant and clean café ambiance, diverse product offerings, and other performance elements). It also has an array of programs targeted at its coffee growers and intended to assist them in improving product quality, mitigating risk, and improving their communities. Starbucks is definitely far from perfect, and indeed it has suffered some setbacks in pursuing its social mission, but it clearly understands the importance of building enduring relationships. "The culture is very relationship-oriented," said a Starbucks vice-president. "It's built on trust. We talk about partnerships and mean it in every sense of the word" (Gulati *et al.*, 2002).

A firm that treats all of its stakeholders, whether employees, suppliers, customers, the community, or the natural environment, as ends in themselves rather than instrumental stepping stones to financial profits is a firm that understands that the creation of real value and a better quality of life for more people is a fundamental responsibility of business – not an add-on. Such firms are committed to long-term, collaborative relationships, not throw-away, transient transactions of convenience.

In this chapter, Mondragón demonstrated to us that promises can be kept not only in good times, but in bad. Equal Exchange showed us how a small firm that wants to change the world can grow in size and profitability without losing its idealism and cooperative zeal. These firms, and many others, that are able to create real, enduring value are invariably those firms that understand that the basis for all good relationships is trust, and that for trust to be established, promises must be kept. Healthy, long-lasting relationships, not cold-blooded, short-term transactions, pave the road to real value creation.

In brief: lasting relationships

- Cooperation and competition are both basic human impulses – twin approaches that must be deployed in a well-balanced combination if an enterprise aims to remain successful in the long term.

- Companies that foster lasting relationships with their employees, customers, suppliers, and communities, rather than focusing on short-term transactions, are better positioned than other firms to create real enduring value for both their stakeholders and themselves.

- Long-lasting relationships as a basis of joint real value creation are grounded in common values and mutual respect between equals.

- A cooperative enterprise, an organizational form that is founded on the principles of cooperation, solidarity, and participation, can combine exceptionally high levels of both value creation and reciprocal fairness.

- Companies create enduring relationships through nurturing an environment of trust. Such companies keep their promises to all of their stakeholders.

4

Local roots: the place-based enterprise

> *Not knowing where you are,*
> *you can lose your soul or your soil,*
> *your life or your way home.*
>
> Wendell Berry (2011)[18]

To create real value, you must know *who* you are and *what* your mission is. But it is difficult if not impossible to have a sense of self, and a sense of purpose, without also knowing *where* you are. In other words, you need a sense of place. So it is with enterprises that try to create real value; they have a firm foundation at home, are grounded in real physical and cultural places that are populated by living human beings, and are possessed of a profound sense of stewardship and responsibility. In other words, they *care* about the places in which they are rooted. But they may also, under the right circumstances, reap very special competitive advantages from their embeddedness in a place. Of course, to 21st-century business managers who have been trained to look abroad for their opportunities, such an assertion may seem counterintuitive or even naïve. Perhaps the poet John Keats (1919) captured this peculiar myopia long ago with his famous couplet: "I cannot see what flowers are at my feet/ nor what soft incense hangs upon the boughs."

After all, the dominant institutions of this age are the powerful multinational corporations that employ vast repositories of financial, intellectual, and human capital to locate and exploit opportunities around the world. These firms are engaged in a game of multiple-point competition and relentless exploitation of marginal advantages wherever they can be found. They are consummately cosmopolitan and sophisticated players who are essentially stateless (except in the most formal and superficial sense) and whose mobility and flexibility provide them with the ability to leverage opportunities and outflank purely domestic firms. Their very rootlessness allows them to arbitrage options that pit countries, states, and cities against each other as they compete for multinational investment. Such firms utilize sophisticated tax minimization strategies to realize income in the most tax-advantaged locations, often to the detriment of their home countries. They lack a special sense of responsibility to any particular place, but instead call themselves "citizens of the world" and claim to have responsibilities everywhere that they are located. But how deep can such "responsibilities" go? In a sense, such multinational enterprises have no home. They are everywhere, indeed, but in a more real sense, are they actually *nowhere*?

At best, such leviathans have only a primitive understanding of what after all is really a very dense notion – that of "place." They equate place with the mere location of resources of various sorts that they require, such as labor. The places where they produce and market their products and services are instrumental means to an end – profit. Indeed, in the pursuit of profit, they are often accused of leading a "race to the bottom" in labor standards as they inexorably attempt to reap marginal cost advantages. Their ties to place, and to community, are tentative, uncertain, and transient. Robert Reich, an economist and former American Secretary of Labor, lamented the sundering of the ties between corporations and their home countries:

> The bonds between company and country . . . are rapidly eroding. Instead, managers are more distant, more economically driven, more coldly rational in their decisions . . . having shed the old affiliations with people and place. Gone is the tight connection between the company, its community, even its country. Vanishing too are the paternalistic corporate heads who used to feel a sense of responsibility for their local community. (Reich, 1991, p. 78)

Indeed, by implication, those firms that are *not* multinational have been presumed to be backward, hidebound, disadvantaged, and doomed to failure in the brave new global economy. They are perceived as quaint anachronisms, at best; relics of a different time, short of both competency and ambition. Anchored in one place, they lack the global reach of the multinationals and their ability to arbitrage opportunities in a variety of competitive spaces. This compromises their ability to relentlessly drive down costs and reap market advantages. In many ways, such anchored firms have been defined more by what they are *not* than by what they *are*. And since they are *not* multinationals, and *not* mobile or footloose, or *not* possessed of facilities in dozens of countries, they are assumed to be disadvantaged and peripheral players in the global economy, fighting a battle with one hand tied behind their backs, scarcely the equal of the global corporations.

But this is simply untrue! In a world that is said to be dominated by cosmopolitan behemoths, firms anchored at home – local firms rooted in and deeply attached to a specific place, often through dense ties of relationship and care, can derive very real advantages and capabilities from that place. These advantages are exceptionally powerful in the ways in which they harness the power of difference. Through capitalizing on the distinctiveness of a place firms can generate an "edge" that is unique and often inimitable, and generate feelings of affiliation and identity that help them to create real value. There is power in place! Even in this age of globalization, the "local" is actually more important than ever.

Place itself is a rich, dense concept – and a powerful one. It conjures up images of home, safety, love, affection, rootedness, and any number of other attributes. It represents a physical location with latitude and longitude, a landscape and ecology, and a built environment – that much is clear. But place is more than that; it is also socially constructed. Human beings (and their organizations) create places through living in them and creating meaning; a place is "a territory of significance" distinguished from others "by its name, by its particular environmental qualities, by the stories and shared memories connected to it, and by the intensity of meanings people give to or derive from it" (Relph, 2009). People affect (and create) places, and places affect (and create) people – and their organizations. In a larger sense, place helps to fashion both community and culture. As poet Gary Snyder puts it, "People who work together in a place become a community, and a community in time, grows a culture" (Snyder, 1995, p. 236). Place is therefore a foundation of human meaning. But to be "placeless" is to be cut off from the wellsprings of meaning that are resident in place.

Being "at home" means being deeply embedded in a place. Place-based enterprises are anchored where they draw their resources, where they are inspired by tradition, history, stories, and the unique natural and built environments of "their" home place. If multinationals have mobility and flexibility advantages, then place-based enterprises have a sense of place that represents a potentially potent competitive advantage in its own right. Place-based enterprises, with their deep "sense of place," derive identity from their home. In turn, they have a strong sense of stewardship and an ethos of sustainability and responsibility. Who, after all, is going to befoul their own place? They enjoy a symbiotic relationship with their home place, focused on long-term success rather than short-term exploitation. With their deep roots in place, they are less likely to outsource, less likely to misbehave, and more likely to be a positive social, economic, and environmental force in their communities. In short, they are more likely to create *real value*.

In this chapter, we will visit several business enterprises that are deeply rooted in place, drawing their inspiration and identity from the rich fabric of their local surroundings. We will travel to a remote island off the west coast of Ireland to study several enterprises on Inis Meáin, and to England to learn about an "alternative" form of organization that is crusading to stem the loss of that most venerable of British institutions (besides the monarchy) – the local public house. Along the way we'll also make note of other dynamic, entrepreneurial, locally based enterprises that demonstrate some of the many ways that an organizational "home" can foster the creation of meaning, identity, and value. We believe that you *can* indeed go home again!

Inis Meáin and the power of place

> We don't just sell knitwear, we sell design and place. In the fashion world, the talk nowadays is about quality, heritage and tradition.
>
> Tarlach de Blacam[19]

The place: Inis Meáin

Inis Meáin is the smallest island in the Aran Island chain located 30 miles off the west coast of Ireland. It is an Irish-speaking community of less than 200 year-round inhabitants, and is easily the quietest and most "traditional" of the Aran Islands, with few facilities for tourism and little development. This small island, little more than 3.5 square miles of limestone in the Atlantic Ocean, is an iconic place – a mecca for Irish (Gaelic) language enthusiasts and for those who want to sample an "authentic" or "traditional" way of life on the western periphery of Europe.

Often described as "barren" and "windswept," Inis Meáin is surprisingly rich in flora and fauna, and relatively untouched by the environmental degradation that has begun to impact on other parts of the once pristine Irish landscape. It has also preserved the use of the Irish (Gaelic) language in everyday life, and is seen as a last redoubt of traditional skills and crafts that have elsewhere been lost. Among these crafts is traditional knitting and the famous "Aran knits" that were to inspire the creation of the Inis Meáin Knitting Company.

The inhabitants of the island practice a sturdy ethos of self-sufficiency. Although there are daily ferry and air services to the island, connections to the outside world are still tenuous at best. When the weather is stormy, as it often is, the island and its people are on their own. People have to look out for each other.

Inis Meáin represents, at the very least, an unusual locale for a globally competitive business. It meets none of the criteria usually considered necessary for siting production and distribution facilities: infrastructure, transportation links, a large pool of skilled labor, and adequate supporting and related businesses. It is a business location consultant's nightmare! Nevertheless, it serves as the home base for entrepreneur Tarlach de Blacam, owner of the highly successful Inis Meáin Knitting Company.

It may seem a fluke, a pure aberration, but we think not. De Blacam, in fact, has tapped into the very heart of a wholly unique place, full of character, tradition, and meaning – and has found a way to create a business every bit as unique, as tough, and as meaningful as the place that inspires and supports it.

The entrepreneur: Tarlach de Blacam

Tarlach de Blacam is a consummate Renaissance man – "a man of many, *many* traits. Irish (Gaelic) scholar, inspired designer, humanitarian, menswear entrepreneur" (*The Block*, 2013). A native of Dublin, he earned a degree in Celtic Languages from Trinity College in 1972 and seemed destined for an academic career. But within a year of graduation, his interests took a more active bent, centering on community development in the Gaeltacht (Irish-speaking area).

> I married Áine Ní Chonghaile from Inis Meáin when she was working as a teacher in Dublin in 1973 and we decided to move to the Aran Islands in the same year to start a new life there. Inis Meáin was where I had been sent for regular trips to learn Irish (Gaelic) in 1968 and while a student at Trinity. This was the island where most of the scholars and writers of the great Anglo Irish and Gaelic literary revival of the early 20th century went to learn Irish/Gaelic. (*The Block*, 2013)

Initially, de Blacam involved himself in various development projects intended to create permanent employment on the island, but eventually came around to starting his own enterprise, the Inis Meáin Knitting Company [*Cniotáil Inis Meáin*], in 1976:

> to try and stem the tide of emigration and to build a living, sustainable community on the island . . . One of these projects was the knitwear company Inis Meáin Knitting Co. Permanent employment was essential for the sustainability of the island. We started a small factory with 6 domestic knitting machines in 1976, hand-finishing all sweaters. We employed mostly young islanders who had learned knitting skills from their parents. These were young people who were not prepared to work from home for the cottage/tourist industry. They were people who would have emigrated if our company was not there. (*The Block*, 2013)

At first, Inis Meáin produced primarily for stores that sold standard, traditional Aran sweaters to the tourist trade. This in itself was not unusual; there were many such knitwear companies on the West Coast of Ireland. But over the next few decades the company evolved very differently, into a competitive space far removed from that of providing simple knit souvenirs for tourists, ambitiously entering the sophisticated, cosmopolitan, and high-end fashion knitwear sector.

The products

Inis Meáin's contemporary designs are deeply rooted in the island community's long tradition of hand knitting. Tarlach and Áine noted that there was another tradition of island knitwear designed for home use and not for sale in tourist shops and Irish import stores abroad. These were simpler and more distinctive knits, with different stitches and more colors, used for everyday wear. In other words, they were authentic and grounded in the life of the island.

The de Blacams were very taken with these traditional designs, and adapted them to meet contemporary needs and fashion sensibilities; these prosaic fishermen's garments, knitted on the islands for hundreds of years, thus became the inspiration for Inis Meáin's unique line of high-end knitwear.

Their designs draw on traditional styles, colors, and skills literally developed over centuries, which the couple refines and reinterprets for each year's new collections. They introduced luxurious (imported) yarns and vibrant colors that reflected the islanders' love of color; the company's designs mimic the changing colors of the sea and sky that surround the island, and use many of the distinctive knitting patterns commonly used by individual island families. These were not the typical Aran sweaters sold to the tourist trade. As de Blacam explains:

> I think people can have a stereotypical view of sweaters. I saw beyond the Aran jumper, and looked at the complexity of the design in both the traditional work wear [fishermen's clothes] and dresswear [confirmation/communion knitwear, for example] and thought I could bring elements of it into contemporary living. (*Sunday Business Post*, 2012)

For example, Inis Meáin's 2011 line included a sweater named the 'Máirtín Beag' after a local fisherman who used to favor it; it was a product grounded in a place, reflecting a powerful heritage, and graced with the name of a person who used to wear it. This blending of traditional craft and contemporary design produced a sweater that was both new and functional, yet with an air of tradition and comfortable familiarity.

Every collection, and every product, is connected to and rooted in place. Today, the firm's range of products is wide, encompassing sweaters, cardigans, dresses, coats, and shawls. They are knit from the highest quality (Irish and imported) yarns including cashmere, silk, linen, alpaca, and merino wool. The garments are designed by

Tarlach and Áine, inspired by tradition, and produced on the island. They are classic and modern, functional and fashionable. Says de Blacam:

> This is our inspiration and heritage, but we also meet the market, producing collections twice each year. This is possibly our greatest strength: staying attuned to what is happening in the market but never abandoning the inspiration of where we come from and why we are doing this. (*The Block*, 2013)

The business

Despite the remoteness of its location, and the often inhospitable nature of its weather, Inis Meáin has managed to maintain and even expand its links with the outside world. It has even been called a "chic knitwear outpost in the Aran Islands" (McQuillan, 2011). Even with its small size and unprepossessing location, it has become a serious global player in upscale fashion, offering collections of jackets, shirts, sweaters, and other knitwear. It focuses exclusively on the high end of the market with garments selling in price from €250 to €1,500. Its annual sales total about 11,000 sweaters (average retail price €300) and 3,500 accessories (average retail price €140) with the retail mark-up on these at about 50%. The logo on the products is also quite telling – an upturned *currach*, the lightweight, canvas boat used by the islanders and typically identified with them. The garments are exported to high-end stores the world over, including Barneys, Bergdorf Goodman, and Paul Stuart in New York, Grey Flannel in London, and other exclusive stores in Japan and in Europe. Ironically, Inis Meáin's products may be far easier to find in the States or in Germany than in Ireland!

In addition to its list of exclusive retailers, Inis Meáin also runs a lively mail order trade, prominently displaying on its website the Irish (Gaelic) phrase *Go maire tú is go gcaithe tú é* ["May you live long to wear it"]. It also generates in-house sales in the whitewashed showroom above its workshop, distinguished by floor-to-ceiling windows that open on inspiring Atlantic Ocean views.

But island life has its challenges too, as de Blacam explains:

> Island life of course has added complexity, meeting boats and planes, shipping and traveling when weather is bad. Should I travel today in case the boats and planes can't sail or fly tomorrow? How quickly can I get a spare part for a faulty machine from Italy or Japan? How do I fix that steam press/forklift/boiler or whatever – there are no main dealers or tool shops on Inis Meáin except for what we carry in stock. But everyone is good at something and we all lend a hand to help each other out. (*The Block*, 2013)

The vast majority of Inis Meáin's competitors are Italian knitting brands like Brunello Cucinelli, Cruciani, and Cividini that make high-end, distinctive, quality, artisan products. These companies concentrate on design, produce a small number of niche products, and avoid direct competition with major brands like Gucci. The products are sold by small independent retailers to discerning customers who themselves are independent in spirit and well understand intangible concepts such as "authenticity" and "provenance."

Authenticity and place

If there is one quality that de Blacam insists on being at the core of every product that Inis Meáin produces, it is authenticity. Increasingly, consumers want to know the provenance of a product; they want to know who made it, and where, using what sort of techniques and with what materials. In short, they want to know the story of a product. For a world-class, indigenous, place-based firm like Inis Meáin, the story, backed up by product quality, is everything. Just as a wine is imbued with subtle characteristics by its own unique *terroir*, so Inis Meáin's products embody a sense of place that derives from its unique and complex physical and human environment. What is created is simply inimitable. Place-based firms like Inis Meáin succeed in providing sophisticated global consumers with products characterized by authenticity and a unique and even ineffable character.

Perhaps this is also the secret of how Inis Meáin, selling high-end products into a sophisticated and dynamic market, survives when practically all Irish clothing companies have gone either to the wall or overseas. De Blacam describes the advice he received from a state industrial development organization:

> Like all the other garment manufacturers in Ireland, we were told by Enterprise Ireland about 10 years ago "hey guys, you shouldn't be doing this [manufacturing in Ireland] anymore, you should be doing this in Eastern Europe or in China. Just have a design facility in Inis Meáin." We said "no" but a lot of the people didn't, they all went.[20]

Inis Meáin has survived and prospered by staying true to the traditions of its home place even while adapting to the demands of a dynamic and challenging international fashion sector. This is reflected in its retailing strategy, which seeks to nurture an emotional connection between the customer and the island. Customers understand that the real value that Inis Meáin creates is more than just the tangible, physical product, and are willing to pay handsomely for it. They sense the dramatic landscape of the island with its ever-changing sea and sky, and the heritage and craft of its people, captured in the intricate knits and vivid colors of the garments. Inis Meáin emphasizes this connection in its marketing materials, for example, which feature stark black and white photographs of the harshness and beauty of the island and the resiliency of the islanders. Inis Meáin is selling more than sweaters. The garments carry with them more than a reputation for quality and utility, they carry the images, impressions, and echoes of a people, a place, and a way of life. In turn, they create a deep sense of independence, durability, and place.

But Inis Meáin is not imprisoned by the past; it is very much a 21st-century company. It takes a practical, modern approach to its business operations, using highly efficient, cutting-edge looms and sourcing its yarns from suppliers throughout the world, including local and other Irish providers. The operation is almost totally run by the staff; the de Blacams confine themselves largely to design and marketing activities. Tarlach himself spends endless time on the road, traveling around the globe to attend the world's most exclusive fashion tradeshows and often making calls on the great fashion houses of Europe as he sells his collections and picks up on the latest fashion trends. It may be located on the periphery of Europe, but Inis Meáin is intimately connected to its industry. In fact, the firm collaborated with French luxury icon Chanel to introduce a line of garments to be sold in Chanel's exclusive shops. The Inis Meáin collections have also been showcased at top-drawer events such as the Pitti Immagine Uomo fashion fair in Florence, Italy and the Bread & Butter tradeshow in Berlin, Germany.

Traditional chíc: Inis Meáin Restaurant & Suites

But there is another de Blacam enterprise on the island. Tarlach and Áine's son Ruairí and his wife, Marie-Thérèse, have chosen not to go into the family business, and have instead built their own – Inis Meáin Restaurant & Suites – that is no less embedded in place. Clearly, their connection to the island has done them no harm: they were described as the 'hottest, hippest couple in Irish food' in the 2009 *Bridgestone Irish Food Guide* (McKenna and McKenna, 2008).

Their five-star restaurant and five-suite hotel is rated among the very best in the country, and probably the most difficult to get into. Customers must reserve months in advance. This seasonal business is distinctive and unique in almost every way. It provides guests with books and bicycles rather than televisions and minibuses. It has built a customized facility constructed with local stone that blends into the very rock that is so characteristic of the island. All of the rooms have windows overlooking a sometimes tumultuous and always changing Atlantic Ocean. *The Irish Times* has called it "Ireland's ultimate destination restaurant' and 'the very best of new Ireland in a part of the country that still feels pleasantly unspoiled" (*Irish Times*, 2008, 2010). Clearly, the younger generation of de Blacams have followed in their parents' footsteps by building something extraordinarily unique and special.

The distinctive identity and integrity of place

The restaurant's home page proudly proclaims: "Elemental Eating – Inspired by prime ingredients from our pure location" and Ruairí and Marie-Thérèse work tirelessly to keep that promise.[21] Most of the restaurant's ingredients are locally sourced, whenever possible from the island itself or from the Atlantic Ocean. For example, while much of Ireland now sources its potatoes from Poland (yes, it is true!), Inis Meáin's potatoes are grown on the island in the small fields, ringed by grey stone walls, that have been literally created by generations of islanders who built up the soil with the seaweed they carried there. Local fishermen, still plying the traditional trade of the island, supply the restaurant with fresh lobster and crab, and scallops found on a bank less than a mile from the island. And they are always striving to learn more, and more deeply, about their special place:

> We grow our own vegetables, salads and herbs on the site of the restaurant. Our shellfish is caught around the coast of the island. We only serve wild Atlantic fish and homestead-reared meat . . . [but] . . . availability of quality produce, both wild and cultivated on the island is entirely dependent on weather, seasonality and practicality, however each year we aim to develop our knowledge and skills to cultivate, harvest and pre-serve more island food. (inismeain.com, n.d.)

Ruairí and Marie-Thérèse have striven to combine these unique local food resources with the dramatic landscape of the island and world-class hospitality and service. Not only have they done so, but they have created an experience that possesses the deepest integrity – a unique dining and recreation experience that is true to the tradition, culture, and history of the island, its environment, and its people.

This same level of integrity is seen in the respect that is shown to the natural world and the emphasis that is placed on environmental sustainability; the restaurant has a sophisticated water-harvesting system that allows the use of waste and grey water for their vegetable gardens. Similar respect is shown to the cultural history of the island and its native language; all the menus are bilingual, printed in both Irish (Gaelic) and English.

Of course, the "magic" that Ruairí and Marie-Thérèse conjure up doesn't just happen. It is created deliberately, and creatively, in a way that balances economic, cultural, human, and environmental goals, and pays due respect to the past, present, and future. As Ruairí de Blacam notes:

> What we do looks easy because we make it look easy. But simple is very difficult since everything has to be thought through long and hard. The easier it looks the better we are doing it.[22]

They have done it well enough that the rest of the world has taken notice. The well-known Irish chef Darina Allen, founder of the famous Ballymaloe Cooking School, has called Inis Meáin Restaurant & Suites "one of my favorite places to stay anywhere in the world" (Allen, 2012). The *Financial Times* classified it as one of the dozen best restaurants of 2011, with its food writer noting that "None of this had really prepared me for the sense of place that I felt throughout dinner" (Lander, 2011).

Inis Meáin's offerings have achieved a standard that is comparable to the best in the world, but they remain deeply anchored in and dependent upon their local place. This enterprise and its offerings are authentic, distinctive, inimitable, and quite simply full of character. Indeed, it is an enterprise that is enabling its owners to live out their own values by creating sustainable, real value for themselves, their customers, and the place and community that sustain them.

The future

> I believe that the future is bright for us. There is a great revival of interest in authentic products like ours and the provenance of those products and long may it last.
>
> Tarlach de Blacam (*Irish Examiner*, 2014)

The de Blacam enterprises, anchored on a small island that is itself off the coast of an island, draw their competitive advantage, and even their identity, from the place they call home. And what they draw from the island they have tried to reciprocate, honoring their shared traditions and heritage, providing jobs and economic stability, and deepening their roots in the community. They have managed to remain distinctively Irish even while competing and winning in one of the world's most daunting and cut-throat market sectors – the fashion industry.

For years, the EU classified Inis Meáin (the island) as a "peripheral," disadvantaged area within the community, but the de Blacams have turned disadvantage into advantage, drawing on the ethos of self-reliance, skilled craft tradition, and the folklore and heritage of a very special place to provide unique products (and experiences) that are like no other. No less than the "stones of Aran" themselves[23] the Inis Meáin businesses are deeply rooted in a unique place that provides their enterprises a character, distinctiveness, and authenticity that cannot be duplicated. The de Blacams, in turn, are committed to the survival of their enterprises on Inis Meáin as much as to the preservation and flourishing of the island and its people, traditions, and culture.

The power of place in a globalizing age

The example of Inis Meáin is a salutary one. As a firm that trades on the heritage, history, and craft tradition of its own unique island culture, Inis Meáin is at the same time a progressive, forward-looking, and globally competitive firm, determined to meet the needs of its demanding global customers and unafraid to compete toe-to-toe with the most prestigious and successful fashion houses in the world. Although its base of operations on a rock in the North Atlantic presents its own peculiar challenges and operational difficulties, it also provides this enterprise with resources and capabilities that are distinct and meaningful, creating real value that is almost impossible for competitors to duplicate. Drawing on the island tradition for its core competence, its story, and its identity, Inis Meáin has found a way to tap into the *genius loci* or the "spirit of place" in a way that colors all aspects of the business. It is difficult to know where the island ends and the business begins. For their part, the knitting company and restaurant behave as stewards, creating value for the community as the biggest employers on the island and a continuing draw for visitors who come to experience a place they've perhaps only experienced at some remove through a cardigan or sweater.

Place-based enterprises, however, come in many shapes and sizes and not all of them explicitly and directly serve a global market; many serve local markets, becoming part of the fabric of their communities. These locally rooted businesses cater to the communities in which they are embedded, adding a distinctly local touch to their offerings and reinforcing their communities' own sense of identity and distinctiveness. Indeed, they are often central to the lives of people in small communities, engaged rightly enough in profit-making endeavors but serving at the same time a distinctly social purpose.

Of course, in becoming a part of the dense fabric and commercial and social ecosystem of a locality, these businesses help to create and sustain just the sorts of unique and distinctive places to which tourists who crave "authenticity" flock! In our global experience economy, we search for products and services that are valuable, unique, distinctive, and possess a basic, intrinsic integrity. Locally based businesses, thoroughly at home in their own place, help to provide just such an experience.

These place-based enterprises exist at the coal face of the conflict between "the local" and "the global." As multinational enterprises enter more and more industry sectors, very few places are off limits and little is sacrosanct. Chain-store retailers and super-sized shopping malls devastate downtown areas and city centers once vibrant with shoppers and small, local retailers; the local hardware store is replaced by the mega-DIY stores, the local restaurants displaced by the big restaurant franchises, the independent cinemas replaced by corporate entertainment giants. Even that local gathering place and informal social center – the local post office – seems everywhere to be under threat, as the large shipping companies and couriers like UPS, DHL and Federal Express squeeze out the national postal services. In the United Kingdom, even local public houses that have survived for hundreds of years have been driven to the wall. But there are grounds for hope. In our next section we look at one organization that has mobilized the power of local communities to fight against the homogenizing power of globalization under the battle cry of "save the pub!"

Saving the "local" – the cooperative public houses of Britain

> This royal throne of kings, this sceptred isle,
> This earth of majesty, this seat of Mars,
> This other Eden, demi-paradise,
> This fortress built by Nature for herself
> Against infection and the hand of war,
> This happy breed of men, this little world,
> This precious stone set in the silver sea,
> Which serves it in the office of a wall
> Or as a moat defensive to a house,
> Against the envy of less happier lands,
> This blessed plot, this earth, this realm, this
>   England.
>   Shakespeare, King Richard II, act 2 scene 1

Of all the institutions that characterize "this sceptred isle" of England and, more broadly, the United Kingdom, surely one of the most revered is the "local." From time immemorial, the local public house has been where local folk have gathered to socialize and gossip, talk and listen, celebrate and commiserate, and most importantly, be among their fellows. Every neighborhood, town, and village had one or many of them. As the great writer George Orwell put it, Britain without its pubs is simply "unthinkable."[24]

Yet not even the local pub, where time supposedly stands still, is exempt from the vagaries and challenges of our global economy. Quite simply, like Britain's small village shops, the traditional British pub is under siege. For example, between April and December 2013, some 28 pub closures per week were reported throughout the UK (Plunkett Foundation, 2014). Why is this happening? Is global capitalism eating away at the nation's soul?

There are a host of possible reasons. There is the availability of cheap alcohol at the large retail multiples such as Tesco and Sainsbury's, where proportionally more people are making their purchases, even in the face of a 30% drop in per capita consumption of beer in the UK between 2003 and 2011 (Heath, 2014). There is the fact that around 40% of Britain's 48,000 pubs are actually owned by large, publicly owned "pubcos," the corporate pub chains (Heath, 2014), who lease the premises to operators who then are "tied-in" to purchasing all products from the pubco, at such high prices that the operators cannot make a profit and subsequently go out of business. There are the developers who sense an opportunity to take advantage of rather lax planning laws that allow them to buy pubs and convert the sites into more lucrative convenience stores or other businesses. There is the ban on smoking, the endless choices for home entertainment, strict enforcement of drink-driving regulations, and high taxes and red tape. But whatever the reasons, the results are clear. The British pub is dying out, particularly in rural communities.

Parliament, it seems, is not insensitive to the threat; in fact, it even created the post of Minister for Community Pubs. In this role

Brandon Lewis, who later became the Minister of State for Housing and Planning, noted that "[t]he local pub is often at the very heart of the community and an important aspect of life for many people. When it closes, many communities feel powerless to save it" (Plunkett Foundation, n.d. a). The Oxford Rural Community Council, in 2013, painted a bleaker picture:

> The role of the village "local" as a vibrant social centre at the heart of the community is as important as ever, but the future of the pub in our rural communities is coming increasingly under threat. Changing economic and social factors are making it more and more difficult for the number of rural pubs to be maintained as sustainable businesses.
>
> Each pub closure represents a loss of a local service, a social hub and an employment opportunity; in some cases the closure of the pub signifies the end of locally based services within a community and can threaten the vibrancy of the village itself. Little surprise then, that many residents are up in arms when the future of their local is threatened, and want to do all they can to keep the pub going, even if it means dipping into their own pockets and buying the pub themselves.

The groundswell of local concern over disappearing public houses, and the willingness of local citizens to not only dig deep into their own pockets but to organize themselves to take over the ownership and active operation of these threatened local pubs, lays the groundwork for the next part of our story – the development of a nationwide movement to save the pubs. Local citizens could only save the public houses by combining their resources, their talent, their passion, and their energy – but they needed an organizational form by which they could accomplish this. This is where the Plunkett Foundation enters the picture. The pubs would be saved through fostering locally owned cooperative public houses. Indeed, the movement to save the pubs has been accelerating over the last few years, based upon this almost forgotten form of business organization – the cooperative enterprise. The Plunkett Foundation has led this charge to "cooperatize" the locals, and in the process fostered a variety of positive community side effects by creating a critical mass of locally owned, place-based enterprises.

The Plunkett Foundation and the gospel of cooperation

The Plunkett Foundation was founded by Sir Horace Curzon Plunkett in 1919 to foster the development of cooperative enterprises around the world, particularly in rural areas. A self-described "Anglo-American Irishman," Plunkett's life work centered on spreading the gospel of cooperative organization, which he did with Messianic zeal. Plunkett believed cooperatives to be a revolutionary movement that would improve the lives of people through self-help, member-ownership of their own enterprises, and democratic control, leavened with the application of business principles of fair dealing, quality, and efficiency. Cooperatives, as Plunkett envisioned them, were locally rooted businesses that were intended to be competitive and profitable. They were not philanthropic organizations, but businesses that also performed a very useful social service and had the power to literally transform rural life for the better.

Plunkett espoused the view that people had to take control of their own economic and social destiny, and that this would foster "better business and better living" for all.[25] The modern cooperative movement itself began in England in 1844 with the Rochdale Pioneers, a group of unemployed weavers who combined to form a consumer cooperative. Their Rochdale Principles have endured to form the core of the cooperative philosophy and ethos today. In summary, cooperative enterprises should be structured to have:

- democratic control (one member one vote)

- membership open to all

- fixed return (only) on capital

- dividend on activity

- no credit

- pure goods

- provision for education of members

- a non-political, non-sectarian orientation

The primary principle of cooperation is nicely captured in an old Irish proverb: *Ní neart go cur le chéile* or "There is no strength without unity." It is only logical that, as local citizens began to mobilize to save their local pubs and searched for an appropriate organizational form to employ, they latched on to the idea of turning the pubs into locally owned cooperative enterprises.

> A cooperative pub is where a significant part of a community comes together to form a cooperative to try and save and run their local. Cooperative pubs are set up on a "one member one vote" basis rather than a "one share one vote" basis. This creates a democratic way of running a community business and ensures that everyone has a say in how they want their local pub to be run. (Plunkett Foundation, n.d. b)

The Plunkett Foundation had been involved with community efforts to save local village stores for years, running conferences and distributing informational publications including stories about pubs that had successfully been converted to cooperative ownership. Their success can be gauged by the fact that in 1994 there were just 27 community-owned shops in the UK, and 20 years later there were 316 (Birch, 2014). But while they had enjoyed considerable success in organizing the conversion of local shops to community-owned cooperative shops, they had not had equivalent success with the pubs. Pubs were expensive to purchase, financing was difficult to arrange, and there was no government assistance. Additionally, the entire process took a lot of time, during which many landmark pubs were lost to developers.

But the closure of the pubs became a political issue, with Labour and Conservative parties both demanding that steps be taken to stop the loss of village pubs. This led to the passage of the Localism Act, which through a "community right to bid" provision gave communities the right to register "assets of community value" and delay the sale of such assets to developers for six months so that they could try to arrange for their preservation as community-owned cooperatives. This kicked the drive to save the pubs into high gear, and preservation efforts were further fueled by the creation of the Power to Change Trust, a £150-million fund (funded by a national lottery) for supporting community-led enterprises throughout Britain. More recently, Community Pubs Minister Marcus Jones announced a new government program worth £3.62 million over two years to help support community efforts to "cooperatize" local pubs that will "bring significant social, economic and environmental benefits to their communities" (Department for Communities and Local Government and Marcus Jones MP, 2016).

Saving the "local"

By early 2015 there were 34 cooperative pubs in the United Kingdom, with more in the pipeline. The Plunkett Foundation runs a cooperative Pubs Advice Line, supported by the Department for Communities and Local Government, to assist with the planning and organization of cooperative pubs, as well as a dedicated website.[26] Their successful efforts are proof positive that residents of largely rural communities, when moved to action in protection of their place and the institutions (such as the local pub) that make their local communities unique, can combine their energies and resources effectively and powerfully. The place-based cooperative enterprise is proving to be an alternative form of organization that fits like a glove. To date, not one cooperative pub in Britain has failed. Of course, they are a relatively new phenomenon, and such a record may not endure, but the point is that their success so far proves that it can be done.

Perhaps the best example is The Old Crown, in the small village of Hesket Newmarket in Cumbria, the first cooperative pub in the UK. It dates back to the 18th century and is the only public house in the village. It was run by private owners as a combination pub and micro-brewery until 1999, when the owner of the brewery decided to retire. Fearing that it would be gobbled up by a larger corporation or even shut down, 58 local people combined to buy the brewery and run it as a cooperative enterprise. A few years later, the pub itself was placed on the market and 125 local citizens were again moved to action, fearing that a large chain would buy the pub and change it into something they didn't want. The pub was duly purchased, and a second cooperative was formed which would maintain the connection between the pub and the brewery. Another sally against the homogenizing forces of globalization! But more was preserved than just a connection between a pub and its beer. As The Old Crown put it on its website:

> The aim is that The Old Crown should continue to be a warm, cosy, friendly pub selling good food and tremendous beer brewed at Hesket Newmarket Brewery behind the pub. No pretensions, no standing on ceremony, just a great British institution doing what it does best – making customers old and new feel relaxed, comfortable and happy. . . .
>
> The cooperative ownership of this important resource demonstrates the strong sense of community spirit in this small Cumbrian village. The cooperative is based on democratic and

voluntary principles, with members contributing on an equal basis to the capital of the enterprise and actively participating in policy formulation. The members of the cooperative strongly believe that ventures of this nature contribute to the economy and social fabric of Cumbria, securing local employment and fostering pride in the community. (Old Crown Pub, 2015)

No less a personage than His Royal Highness the Prince of Wales, a regular visitor to Cumbria, has declared himself a supporter of The Old Crown, having twice sampled the beer on tap there during very public visits. But why would the royal family take an interest in such a campaign? Why indeed would the two major political parties in the UK, adamantly opposed to each other on most issues, be tripping over themselves to be perceived as "protectors" of the local pub? Why would common folk who have never invested a pound sterling in a business or a stock or bond take a chance on becoming part-owner of a cooperative pub?

It is because this campaign has tapped a deep nerve in the collective psyche. Community members responded to the threatened loss of local businesses that have, for literally hundreds of years, created value and meaning. The alacrity with which communities have reacted, and the emotion and passion that are at the core of this movement, make it clear that – whatever cynics may mutter about the unseemliness of supporting "gin mills" and "booze joints" – the local pubs have been engaged in much more than "mere" commerce for centuries. These are enterprises that have created value – for themselves surely as businesses, but in many less tangible but no less important ways for the communities in which they are embedded. As gathering places, socializing spaces, and that place "where everyone knows your name," public houses have served well their purposes and their communities.

The British public house represents a particular kind of place-based enterprise – one that happens to be more inward-looking than outward-looking, more focused on building community than making a profit for shareholders, and rather content to create its magic in particular places and for its own community. The charm, unique identity, and very spirit of these pubs are products of the communities in which they are embedded. Their four walls contain literally hundreds of years of collective community histories. Pubs are meaningful places as well as businesses, nested within other meaningful places. Their roots are deep, and their memories long. Is it any wonder that local people were driven to action, forming cooperative enterprises to ensure that the social and emotional value that these pubs create is continued? What we are now seeing is actually quite remarkable – communities themselves flexing their collective muscle to purchase and operate these small village enterprises.

It makes for a great story – a David and Goliath tale of small rural communities using their slingshot against the tyrannical "pub-cos" that are determined to replace every last village pub with a plastic replica "faux" English pub where the drinks are cheaper (and more nondescript) and the operation is modern and efficient. But this is more than a story. The campaign to save The Old Crown and similar public houses provides lessons for businesses further afield and well outside of this local context.

For one thing, this campaign shows that there is power in the "local." That rather than representing marginal activities at the periphery of the global playing field of the multinationals, real physical and cultural places are sources of distinct and inimitable resources, providing competitive advantages in ways that are deep, intrinsic, and often well hidden from the global behemoths who see only the surface and have only a one-dimensional, superficial view of the richness and dense-with-meaning resources of place.

The place-based enterprise

Place-based enterprises, such as Inis Meáin or the British cooperative pubs, are embedded in and interdependent with unique places.
They are as much a part of a physical and cultural place as the
landscape, the built environment, and the people who live there.
Place-based enterprises pursue goals that encompass both economic self-interest and the interests of the communities (or places)
in which they are embedded. They are place builders rather than
place destroyers. They have an ethos of ecological sustainability, a
distinctive sense of place, and a deep sense of social responsibility.
The overall health of their home place is important to them, both
morally and instrumentally; indeed, their financial success is utterly
enmeshed with the success of their place. They are inextricably
connected. It therefore makes sense that their organizational goals
tend to be balanced, addressing financial, community, and ecological outcomes. Such firms are usually also under local ownership and
control, with their assets being firmly anchored in place. They can
be for-profit, not-for-profit, or even hybrid forms of enterprise (like
the above-noted cooperative public houses).

Place-based enterprises are businesses that are both rooted and
"at home" in the places where they are embedded; they possess a
"sense of place" – a deep understanding of, and appreciation for,
the place they call home. This deep and nuanced understanding of
the rich context in which they engage in their work in turn precipi-
tates actions that are socially and ecologically good, as well as economically profitable. They also represent businesses that are far less
likely to pull up stakes and move operations halfway around the
world in pursuit of a marginal financial advantage.

In this, local ownership is not irrelevant. As with Inis Meáin and
the cooperative public houses of Britain, ownership roots businesses in place, linking commercial success with community

wellbeing. When ownership is largely held within a community, rather than by large remote institutions or individuals who constantly deploy and redeploy their capital across the globe, there is a more intimate understanding of the reciprocal responsibilities that enterprise and community have for each other – and far less chance that "rooted" capital will fly away, like hot money does, at the first opportunity.

Take, for example, the story of the Green Bay Packers, arguably the most legendary franchise in the U.S.-based National Football League (NFL). The Green Bay Packers have been a publicly owned, non-profit corporation since 1923. Although the rules of the NFL prohibit corporate ownership and mandate that clubs be owned by individuals or partnerships, the Packers were "grandfathered" since they became a public corporation before the current rules of the NFL were promulgated. "The Pack" has over 360,000 small owners, with a majority coming from the state of Wisconsin. There are limits to the number of shares that any one person can own, and shares cannot be transferred except to be sold back to the club for a fraction of the original cost, or transferred to relatives or heirs. The stock pays no dividends, and prospective buyers are warned that they should not buy shares if they are looking for a profit (Sanders, 2012).

Green Bay itself is a relatively small city of 104,000 people, and the smallest city in the United States with a major league sports franchise. Without local ownership, there is little doubt that the team long ago would have fled to a larger and far more lucrative market. Big league sports franchises, like multinational corporations, regularly move to greener pastures. Local ownership, however, has rooted the team in Green Bay, with no discernible negative effects on either performance (the team has won more NFL championships than any other) or the community. Indeed, the Green Bay Packers mean everything to the city of Green Bay and its people; it has put the town on the map. Tourists travel to Green Bay, and not just during football season, to see the place that is home to America's favorite team. If Green Bay gave its name to the Packers, the Packers have further defined Green Bay itself as "Title Town, USA." Rooted in Wisconsin, the Packers have a national and even international following – a storied franchise that is surely unique in the annals of American sport.

Such enterprises, rooted in place by local ownership, serve to anchor capital and buffer places from the worst effects of hyper-mobile international capital and other externalities of the global economy (Imbroscio *et al.*, 2003). But place-based enterprises can come in many forms, and thrive in many contexts. Just look at French skincare products company L'Occitane, founded by Olivier Baussan in Provence in 1976. The company produces a variety of skincare products, beauty treatments, and fragrances largely derived from the flora and traditional techniques of Provence. These botan-ically based products use only natural ingredients such as lavender, olives, and almonds, most of them grown in Provence and the source of many local remedies and treatments. L'Occitane's retail outlets, like its other advertising and promotional activities, rely strongly on recreating the experience of being in Provence and focus intensely on linking the company and its products to its home – the source of its inspiration and identity as well as its raw materials. "Provence is crucial for our appearance all over the world, because this region stands for a long tradition in perfumery, know-how and high cred-ibility," says Reinold Geiger, L'Occitane's long-standing CEO (Böhler, 2010, p. D6). "Thus, we made use of the region. A natural approach has been of particular importance to me. Moreover, Provence is an area with a history – also a history of fragrance" (El Mohandes, 2008).

Now a public company after a 2010 initial public offering, L'Occitane is sold in 90 countries around the world and has over

6,000 employees; it recently even opened a store in Grand Central Terminal in New York City. Closer to home, however, it has been leveraging its Provençal roots by branching out into the world of tourism – partnering with a tour operator to design customized L'Occitane tours of Provence. Having developed into a nearly €1-billion company, it still maintains its roots "at home" and continues to focus on creating shared value with its communities, treating people fairly, and respecting the natural environment. "If you are growing up in Provence, amidst gorgeous nature, you automatically think ecologically," says Geiger. "When you are fortunate to have a well-functioning enterprise and see the miserable conditions in this world on a daily basis, you want to give something back. For me, that's a matter of course" (El Mohandes, 2008).

Surely L'Occitane is not immune from the growth imperative that so many businesses face, and the very real pressures that accompany such growth. After all, becoming, and remaining, globally competitive while having local roots in a real place does not do away with struggle and stress. Place is no panacea. But place-based enterprises in particular industries have often proven themselves the equal of the rootless multinationals. They are not limited to small "mom and pop" operations or artisanal enterprises; they can be businesses of scale and scope that have chosen to maintain their links with home, not only out of a sense of obligation, but also as a source of enduring, sustainable competitive advantage. They understand that there is real value in place, and that "who we are" is strongly influenced by "where we are." They do not believe the conventional wisdom that says that mobility and statelessness trump rootedness in and attachment to any particular place. If business enterprises can have a heart, then surely home is where that heart is – a source of identity and inspiration, a place to be cared for and sustained, and in some cases, the key to unique capabilities and resources that give both meaning and competitive muscle to those enterprises that understand the power of place.

In brief: local roots

- Despite a dominant ideology that holds that the scale, scope, and mobility advantages of multinational enterprises will inevitably trump smaller and more "rooted" players, this is at best a limited or even myopic view.

- People increasingly care about where a product comes from, who made it, and how it was made.

- Place-based enterprises, rooted or anchored in unique and special places, may have access to deep sources of competitive advantage – distinct, authentic, and inimitable resources that stem from their affiliation with a place.

- Companies with a sense of place and local roots also have a strong sense of stewardship. They practice an ideology of shared value creation for themselves and for the places of which they are a part.

- In a reciprocal way, place-based enterprises create identity and meaning for the communities in which they are embedded, while, in turn, also gaining real value in the form of identity and meaning from their local surroundings.

- Don't overlook the power and value of place!

5

Limits recognition: self-restraint works wonders

Our freedom fades when it is handed over to the blind forces of the unconscious, of immediate needs, of self-interest, and of violence. In this sense, we stand naked and exposed in the face of our ever-increasing power, lacking the wherewithal to control it. We have certain superficial mechanisms, but we cannot claim to have sound ethics, a culture and spirituality genuinely capable of setting limits and teaching clear-minded self-restraint.

Pope Francis, Encyclical Letter
Laudato Si'. (2015, p. 78)[27]

In his 2015 encyclical on climate change, *Laudato Si'*, Pope Francis criticized the widespread acceptance of a "techno-economic paradigm" that "leads people to believe that they are free as long as they have the supposed freedom to consume" (2015, p. 150). His encyclical made a strong case that the model of relentless growth advocated by economists and the financial community was based on falsehoods: that the world has an unlimited supply of natural resources, that it is possible to renew these quickly, and that any negative effects can be easily corrected by technology. Maintaining that everything in life is connected, the Pope called for an "integral ecology" in which humanity understood its role as an integral part of nature. The tone of the encyclical left no room for misinterpretation: "The earth, our home, is beginning to look more and more like an immense pile of filth" (2015, p. 17). Pope Francis warned that "compulsive consumerism" and a lack of appreciation for limits damage society:

> "When people become self-centred and self-enclosed, their greed increases. The emptier a person's heart, the more he or she needs things to buy, own and consume. It becomes almost impossible to accept the limits imposed by reality. In this horizon, a genuine sense of the common good also disappears." (2015, p. 150)

Since an economy exists to serve the common good, so businesses are ultimately shaped by moral principles. Closely related to the common good is the idea of "the commons," those shared resources necessary to sustain life. The earth's climate, air, and oceans are prime examples of the commons – ecological endowments belonging to all and meant for all. Yet much of the destruction of the commons is powered by the goal of profit maximization. Many businesses, as long as they operate within the limits of the law, see little need to set limits, practice self-restraint, or act responsibly. They see freedom as a *carte blanche* to do whatever they want, as long as it doesn't interfere with the freedom of others to do what they want.

But freedom is not mere license: it is balanced with self-restraint and self-discipline. True freedom matches rights with responsibilities, and growth and development with a recognition of limits. Freedom is also connected with doing meaningful, high-caliber work and becoming what author Robert Pirsig (1974) in *Zen and the Art of Motorcycle Maintenance* called a "person of quality." In the same vein, American writer Matthew Crawford (who oddly enough also sells motorcycle parts) offered the idea of "freedom for excellence" and suggested that individuality evolves through the quality of one's relationships with others. In other words, genuine individualism only occurs within healthy communities (Crawford, 2015). Freedom is about quality and excellence, exercised by both individuals and business enterprises possessed of no little character, in the creation of *real value*.

Companies run by leaders of character invariably possess a spirit of excellence and care. They take to heart the ancient Greek concept of *arête* or personal excellence, the self-imposed duty to be the best one can be. It is this, which Plato called "virtue," and not money that leads to the greatest happiness or contentment:

> I tell you that virtue is not given by money, but that from virtue comes money and every other good of man, public as well as private. (Jowett, 1999, p. 531)

Yet the accepted wisdom is that companies must grow profits and revenues every single year, or even every single quarter, unremittingly and infinitely. But this is a tenet that we cannot allow to pass unchallenged. Indeed, there are companies that strive to be great, rather than big. Bo Burlingham's book *Small Giants* (2005) is full of such examples. One of them, the Union Square Hospitality Group in New York, wants to excel by creating a great place to work, treating customers with exceptional kindness, and contributing to their community rather than by growing into the USA's largest chain of restaurants. "Small giants" like this eschew conventional thinking and focus on satisfying goals of excellence rather than just making money, in the process respecting the limits of both people and the planet. "In effect, they are attempting to build a better way of life in their own corner of the globe," writes Burlingham (2005, p. 117). In other words, they focus on creating *real value*.

Despite these vivid examples of a different model, it is still the norm to assume that relentless growth is imperative for a firm to survive. It remains a central maxim of mainstream economists, financial analysts, and CEOs of Wall Street firms alike. Some even argue that "a no-growth policy makes the firm's prospects highly unattractive in finite time and bankruptcy practically certain in the long run" (Gordon and Rosenthal, 2003, p. 25). The logic of proponents of the growth imperative is that larger firms will achieve economies of scale which allow them to reduce prices, increase market share and profit margins, and generally undercut their smaller competitors. The big fish eat the small fish. In theory, this sounds plausible; but the reality looks quite different. After all, in both the U.S. and the EU, over 99% of all businesses are small and medium-sized enterprises (SMEs) (EU, 2015a; SBE Council, 2015). Between mid-2009 and mid-2013, 60% of net new jobs in the U.S. were created by SMEs (SBE Council, 2015). In the EU, SMEs accounted for 85% of net new job creation in the 8-year period between 2002 and 2010 (EU, 2012). On the official website of the European Commission, we read that "SMEs are the true back-bone of the European economy, being primarily responsible for wealth and economic growth, next to their key role in innovation and R&D" (EU, 2015b). Does that really sound like smaller firms are unable to compete? Is there really no alternative to the choice between growth and death? And are those who set limits for themselves really worse off?

In this chapter we tell the stories of entrepreneurs who recognize limits, and who nevertheless (or maybe because of it) help their companies, employees, communities, and the planet to flourish. We first look at two multinational carpet manufacturers, the U.S.-based Interface and the Dutch firm, Desso. Their leaders understand and respect ecological limits, and have redesigned their business models with the aim of eliminating all waste and achieving 100% environmental sustainability. We will also discuss two unusual business enterprises who recognize that their employees – like the natural world – also have limits. They focus on helping their employees develop and grow rather than subjecting them to excessive levels of stress. Even more surprising is that they are in the financial industry. Middelfart Sparekasse in Denmark and Raiffeisenbank Ichenhausen in Germany upended conventional banking wisdom with their unconventional HR practices, and with remarkable success. Next, we examine a company that limits inequality in the workplace. Suma Wholefoods, a UK natural food cooperative, implemented a radical solution to income inequality by paying all workers exactly the same. Finally, we relay the stories of two small German enterprises, deckchair producer Richard Henkel and the Clemens Härle brewery. Neither wants to grow. Instead, they prefer to focus on their deep values of excellence and an ethic of trust and their strong roots in their communities. All are examples of voluntarily setting limits and of the enlightened self-control that leads to the freedom to do things differently – a freedom through which these companies excel, stand out of the crowd, and create *real value*.

Limits of the environment

It's no coincidence that most companies profiled in this book are European rather than American. As an opinion writer in the *New York Times* pointed out, Americans seem "hardwired to the notion of individual self-reliance" and lack of restraint (Cohen, 2015). But in many parts of Europe social solidarity is still valued as an ideal and "a prudent safeguard and guarantor of human decency" (Cohen, 2015). Robert Paarlberg in his book, *The United States of Excess* (2015), notes that Americans consume food and fuel in amounts that are absolutely unsustainable, which leads to U.S. per capita carbon dioxide emissions at about twice the average of other OECD countries. Paarlberg argues that there are several reasons for this excess, including a general resentment against government regulations, an emphasis on individual rather than social responsibility, and an almost religious belief in science and technology.

We would surely miss the big picture, however, if we merely stereotyped companies in certain parts of the world. After all, companies are created and run by individuals, and each individual, regardless of his or her cultural socialization, can freely choose to recognize limits and act in a responsible way.

Intelligent elimination of waste at Interface

Take Ray Anderson, for example, the man who developed Interface into the world's largest manufacturer of commercial carpet tiles. In 1973, he laid the foundations for the company when he led a joint venture between a British company and a group of American investors (Interface, 2015a). Interface began with just 15 employees but grew quickly, and by 1978, sales had reached $11 million. After going public in 1983, it grew within a few years to become the undisputed world leader in soft-surfaced modular floor coverings. Today it is a billion-dollar corporation, selling in 110 countries and manufacturing in four continents.

In 1994, Anderson read Paul Hawken's book, *The Ecology of Commerce*, which indicted business as the major culprit in the decline of the biosphere. However, Hawken also saw business as the "only institution large enough, wealthy enough, and pervasive and powerful enough to lead humankind out of the mess we were making" (Anderson and White, 2009, p. 14). After his epiphany, Anderson shifted the company strategy and redirected its industrial practices toward an ethos of sustainability. This led to Mission Zero™, the company commitment to become a regenerative enterprise by sourcing 100% recycled material and eliminating "any negative impact Interface has on the environment by 2020" (Interface, 2015a).

A good example of Interface's sustainable innovation is its FLOR® carpet squares that can be freely combined and configured to be used in any kind of floor-covering application. The squares are connected with non-toxic adhesives. There is no need to glue carpet tiles to the floor, and the system also enables the cleaning or replacing of individual squares instead of whole rooms. Interface also invites customers, if they can't find a place to recycle worn or damaged tiles, to send them back and the company will recycle them.

Instead of selling carpets, Interface leases carpet services with an emotional value proposition, the "warmth, beauty, and comfort" of floor covering (Hawken *et al.*, 1999, p. 17). Carpets used to be replaced when they began to look worn out. Old carpets were dispatched to landfills, adding to the growing trash mountains. Anderson recognized that there was a limit to the amount of waste that the planet could absorb. Unlike others, however, he also realized that it was in his power to do something about it. Instead of selling broadloom carpets, which needed to be thrown away as a whole even when only parts of it no longer met the standards of cleanliness, he started to offer easily replaceable carpet tiles and floor-covering "services." Customers no longer "bought" the carpet but rather "rented" it from Interface, which kept the floor-covering clean and "in shape." In regular inspections, worn-out carpet parts, which are usually only a fraction of the total floor covering, are replaced. As a result, Interface customers use around 80% less material and get a better service at a lower overall cost (Hawken *et al.*, 1999, p. 140).

Another venture that supports the Mission Zero™ goal is the company's Net-Works program. In cooperation with non-profit organizations and a yarn producer, Interface set up a project in which abandoned fishing nets were turned into carpet tiles. The initiative not only contributed to cleaning beaches and opening new sources of income for people in poor fishing villages but also enabled the company to source recycled raw material inputs; carpet tile production drew closer to a closed, restorative loop.

Anderson wrote a book, *Mid-Course Correction*, in which he describes how he changed his course toward putting environmental concerns at the center of his business. In a moving TED Talk he gave in 2009, titled "The business logic of sustainability," he explained how he challenged people at Interface (after all, a company with a petroleum-intensive product) "to take from the earth only what can be renewed by the earth, naturally and rapidly – not another fresh drop of oil – and to do no harm to the biosphere. Take nothing: do no harm" (Anderson, 2009).

Contrary to conventional wisdom, Anderson asserted that his mission of totally eliminating waste was incredibly good for business. Costs came down instead of going up, reflecting hundreds of millions of dollars of savings in pursuit of zero waste. At the same time, the sustainability-orientation proved to be an "unexpected wellspring of innovation" (Anderson, 2009) for making better products. To Anderson, a shared purpose was key:

> Our people are galvanized around this shared higher purpose. You cannot beat it for attracting the best people and bringing them together. And the goodwill of the marketplace is astonishing. No amount of advertising, no clever marketing

campaign, at any price, could have produced or created this
much goodwill. (Anderson, 2009)

Ray Anderson realized that real value also stemmed from the
emotional benefits that people – employees, customers, and business partners alike – derive from a business. Sadly, he never reached
the top of the mountain he called "Mount Sustainability"; he
passed away in 2011. But his vision lives on as Interface continues its
journey toward its Mission Zero™ goal. To take one example: by
the beginning of 2014, the company's plant in the Netherlands
reported that it was running exclusively on renewable energy, had
curbed process water usage to almost zero and sent zero waste to
landfills (Interface UK, 2014). This is impressive by any standard.

Abandoning graves at Desso

Staying in the Netherlands, we find an equally inspiring story of a
carpet manufacturer pursuing a radically different business model.
Desso, based in Waalwijk, a small city in the province of North
Brabant, was founded in 1930, and since 2014 has been part of the
French Tarkett group, a global leader in the flooring and sports
surface business. Desso, with two factories and customers in over
100 countries, pursues a mission to "develop unique products
that deliver a much improved indoor environment that maximises
people's health and wellbeing and ultimately their performance"
(Desso, 2015a). Desso plans to transition to a service-based model,
like Interface, in which it leases out its carpets and later takes back
old tiles in order to recycle and reuse the underlying materials (Laurence, 2009).

It is estimated that people spend some 90% of their time indoors,
where they inhale various potentially unhealthy things like fine
dust. Desso seeks to answer these questions: "How can we make
our carpets work better for people? How can we create the 'Great

Indoors'?" (Desso, 2015b). Since 2008, Desso has systematically addressed these questions, scrutinizing the interactions between carpets and people as well as the whole system of carpet production, use, and disposal from a sustainability perspective (Cook, 2014). The company's management concluded that it had to reshape its business model from a linear "take, make, and waste" or "cradle to grave" thinking to a circular approach which is oriented toward the reuse and recycling of all products and materials.

This new approach has been popularized under the term "Cradle to Cradle®" by U.S. architect William McDonough and German process technician and chemist Michael Braungart. Their idea was simple and compelling: every product should be designed to allow for the disassembly and reuse of all its constituent materials at the end of the product life. The result is zero waste. We're not talking about mere eco-efficiency here, trying to decrease waste and at the same time increase productivity, but about "eco-effectiveness" (McDonough and Braungart, 2002) in which, through intelligent design, all materials remain useful for further applications. Materials are fully reused as input at a new "cradle," while nothing is left for the "grave." McDonough and Braungart had a clear role model for their circular thinking: "Nature operates according to a system of nutrients and metabolism in which there is no such thing as waste," they write. "The Earth's major nutrients – carbon, hydrogen, oxygen, nitrogen – are cycled and recycled. Waste equals food" (McDonough and Braungart, 2002, S. 92).

If products are designed in the right way, all output can become input again. Taking wise decisions at the design stage is always better than worrying about how to minimize the negative impact of badly designed products. Following this philosophy, Desso has changed the composition of product materials, focusing on toxin-free and recyclable alternatives. Thus, it tries to achieve several objectives at the same time: decreasing resource use, avoiding waste, and creating a healthier indoor environment for people.

Desso also emphasizes creativity and functionality. Creativity helps in creating the right room atmosphere for each individual customer by offering a wide selection of carpet designs and textures. Functionality is about providing what the company calls "real practical value" by, for example, developing innovative solutions to reduce the amount of dust and noise (Desso, 2015b). At base, Desso cares for environmental sustainability just as much as about beauty and the quality of people's lives. Thus, "real practical value" also translates into *real value* in the sense of our book.

Rudi Daelmans, Manager of Sustainability at Desso, cites the example of AirMaster® as an innovation that not only covers the floor and looks nice but also offers health benefits.[29] A trailblazing product, AirMaster®, through its special construction, captures fine dust particles and in this way reduces the amount of fine dust in the indoor air. This means that people with AirMaster® carpets may encounter fewer lung problems; this is of particular importance to people who are asthmatic. Adding functionality to its carpet tiles can have beneficial health and wellbeing effects on human beings, and is a great illustration of how materials in the built environment can potentially improve people's lives.

Like other companies profiled in this book, Desso recognizes the importance of positive emotions and experiences for creating real value. While Daelmans understands the challenge implicit in translating an emotional feeling about sustainability into action, he says that a positive story is far more powerful than just saying: "O.K., we have to minimize our impacts".[30] Communicating that something is beneficial is far more inspiring than telling your customers that you are just less negative by reducing your carbon footprint.

Offering products that benefit people as well as the environment also positively affects employees. It is energizing and motivating for employees to get positive feedback from customers. Daelmans says that when all of a sudden Desso was in the news, this led to two outcomes. First, people felt they had to live up to expectations, or "walk the talk." Second, it had a positive motivational effect. When newspaper reporters and film crews appeared on the company's premises to report on Desso's sustainable business concept and employees started reading positive stories about Desso in the newspaper or on television, "then that brings a feeling of pride," says Daelmans. "Obviously we are doing something that is interesting and beneficial to people's lives. And that was good!"[31]

Limits of people

An obsession with work and money are harmful to the health and wellbeing of employees. The Japanese even have a word, *karoshi*, to describe somebody who dies from too much work. In contrast, Denmark is well known for employers who aim to create workplaces that are oriented toward the wellbeing of employees. There should be no mystery then that the word, *arbejdsglæde*, which means "happiness at work," exists only in Danish and the other Nordic languages (Kjerulf, 2014). To most Danes, it seems a job isn't just about getting a salary, but also about enjoying themselves (Kjerulf, 2014). Danish society is known for its high level of trust, which is a key factor in the country's wealth and happiness as high levels of trust reduce transaction costs (Jensen, 2014).

Yet even by Danish standards, Middelfart Sparekasse, a regional savings bank with 260 employees and 14 branches, headquartered on the island of Funen, is exceptional in developing a culture of happiness and trust in the workplace. It is one of only a very few companies that has appeared on every *European Best Workplaces*

List since its inception in 2003 (greatplacetowork.dk, 2013). The bank shows great confidence in its employees, and allows them unusual freedom and responsibility. It believes that sowing trust and mutual respect will reap more passionate and committed employees. For example, client advisers have the authority to set interest rates themselves, as the company's management is confident that they know best what's adequate for a specific local market. Thus, Middelfart Sparekasse creates the kind of work culture in which both responsibility and success are shared. Employees at Middelfart Sparekasse are more than just small cogs in a large wheel – they know that they matter and that they make a difference.

Unlike other banks that are tightening supervision and increasing pressure on their employees, the management of the Danish bank assumes that employees naturally want to give their best for the company, so there's no need for constant supervision. What sounds more than unusual for a financial institution works surprisingly well, says the managing director of human resources, Knud Herbert Soerensen: "You'd be amazed what happens once people are empowered to make decisions" (CNN, 2011). Using the concept of self-directed leadership, employees are encouraged to take responsibility, even if that means they make decisions with considerable financial impacts on their own (CNN, 2011). As a consequence, the bank has both satisfied employees and customers who receive a highly individualized service: "There's no one solution and we believe the only way to treat people the same is by treating them differently," says Soerensen. "As a result, 80% of new customers come to us through referrals" (CNN, 2011).

Of course striking a balance between the welfare of employees and a successful business requires special skills. The bank believes this is built "on a balance between leadership and self-management, between team and individuality, between soft and hard values, between the human and technology, and the balance between work life and privacy" (greatplacetowork.dk, 2013). Striking a balance also means setting limits to each of these factors. The creation of a unique culture at Middelfart Sparekasse is fostered by the creation of a special environment where employees work. Its recently built head office is one of the most energy-efficient and worker-friendly workplaces in Denmark, and is now regarded as the best office building in the country (Niko, 2015). Workers choose from more than 20 different mood lighting options according to their own preferences and appropriateness for the activities in which they engage. Not only that, but the new building was designed as a social center for both employees and the local community. It includes open working spaces and a canteen for employees, but also a plaza, cafés, and shops in a staggering architectural structure with exceptionally large window fronts.

Founded as a savings bank designed for the common good in 1853, the commitment of Middelfart Sparekasse to the local community remains strong. After more than 160 years in business, the bank still creates value for its employees and customers through the exercise of old virtues such as trust, honesty, and mutual respect. What we find so impressive is the practical and trusting nature of its workplace. Of course, that should not surprise us since, as *The Economist* put it in February 2013: "The main lesson to learn from the Nordics is not ideological but practical."

Raiffeisenbank Ichenhausen eG in Germany is another bank with a distinctive people-centered philosophy that focuses on limits (Raiffeisenbank Ichenhausen, 2015). A small bank, it has less than 50 employees and 7 offices and a logo that goes *die etwas andere Bank* ("the slightly different bank"), a phrase recently added at the suggestion of the employees themselves. It is unusual in the banking world because it pays its employees a fixed salary with no targets for product sales. The changes in the bank's approach go back to the year 2002 when targets, which accounted for variations in remuneration, commissions, or bonuses, based on the volume of products sold, were abolished. Since then, it exclusively pays fixed salaries. Employees in turn receive generous freedom and additional responsibilities. At the heart of the bank's approach to human resource management are the personal goals and desires of each employee. The bank maintains that the relationships of trust and responsibility it generates lead to high levels of employee satisfaction and therefore very low employee turnover.

This approach ensures a needs-based customer service since employees no longer have any financial incentives to sell products that customers may not need, or that are simply not the right fit. Customers therefore end up with the product that suits them best, not the one with the highest commission. The effect was also quickly noticeable in the market: in the first year after the compensation and responsibility system was changed, sales, margins, and the portfolio of sold products increased significantly – high market shares in all relevant business areas were the outcome (Kronawitter, 2013a).

In his 2013 book *Führen ohne Druck* ('Leading without Pressure'), the bank's Chairman of the Board, Ernst Kronawitter, writes that motivation and a strong team spirit are the keys to the success of banking without targets and sales-related compensation (Kronawitter, 2013b). Instead, he says, individual motivation driven by personal goals and the desires of each employee and a strong team spirit matter most. He is convinced that "excessive supervision definitely does not contribute to the motivation of employees" (bankingclub.de, 2015). Suggesting that the Raiffeisenbank Ichenhausen model is suitable for other business sectors, Kronawitter points out that a human-harmonious working environment and a profitable business are not necessarily incompatible. If you recognize the limits of people, you will get the best out of them.

Limits to inequality

A recent study of people in 40 countries found most believe that CEOs earn way too much money (Kiatpongsan and Norton, 2014). Yet, they fail to realize the magnitude of the gap between CEOs and other employees. On average, people believe CEOs make ten times that of unskilled workers. In reality, however, the income disparity is often on an entirely different scale. In the U.S., for example, CEOs of S&P 500 companies received an average annual salary of $12.3 million in 2012. That is almost 354 times the average worker's pay of $35,000 (and miles away from the 6.7 times the average worker's pay that Americans consider adequate) (Kiatpongsan and Norton, 2014). The disparity has widened in recent years with CEO compensation increasing steadily since the recession while the pay of the average worker has stagnated.

Even in the UK, where the disparity is somewhat less, average CEO pay in 2012 was 84 times that of the average worker (Kiatpongsan and Norton, 2014). Yet astonishingly, amid this excess there is a company where everyone is paid exactly the same wage, about £13 an hour. This is probably the largest organization in Europe with a general equal pay policy (Roberts, 2014). Like the well-known John Lewis Partnership, one of Britain's leading retail businesses, Suma Wholefoods is completely owned by its employees. It is the UK's largest independent natural food wholesaler and distributor with around 150 employees, sales of almost £34 million in 2013 and activities in over 50 countries. Yet it has neither CEO, managing director, or permanent chairperson.

This remarkable story of an organization where worker equality, participation, responsibility, and engagement are central to success started in 1975 when Reg Tayler and his friends set up a wholesale food co-operative in the back kitchen of a house in Leeds (Suma, 2015). From there, they supplied cereals, dried fruits, and brown rice to wholefood shops in the north of England. They soon reached the limits of the back kitchen and rented a garage nearby, followed by the acquisition of a small warehouse and a retail shop, which was soon turned into a separate independent co-operative. In 1977, Reg decided to sell his business to his seven employees. Together, they founded the Triangle Wholefoods Collective, operating under the brand Suma. In the wake of rapidly rising consumer demand in wholefood, Suma steadily increased its business in the following decades, facing the need to relocate to larger premises several times on the way.

Suma's workers receive wages that are well above the typical local rates (Co-operatives UK, 2011). Aside from equal pay, Suma distinguishes itself by giving employees the possibility to work in several different roles and responsibilities. In this way, Suma allows people to engage in both manual and mental work. It is not unusual to meet directors working in the warehouse, marketing people in a delivery truck, or financial managers handling customer orders (Suma, 2010). This is possible because professional jobs are split up. So instead of having one financial director, for example, this role is fulfilled by a team.

"When workers are this engaged with their organization, business performance is hugely more efficient," says Bob Cannell, a long-time Suma employee-owner. "We can spend much less on supervisory management and use people's creativity much better" (Co-operatives UK, 2011). Instead of appointing a CEO, Suma's employees elect a management committee and discuss business strategies together in general members' meetings held several times a year, or electronically via the intranet between the meetings. Decision-making is about finding consensus rather than overruling others. If an idea does not get enough support, members will continue to refine and improve it until everyone agrees (Roberts, 2014).

Most people who start working at Suma also expect to retire there. Having a job at Suma virtually means having a job for life. Such a policy is only possible with a rigorous selection process. To become a member, prospective employees have to pass a three-month trial period in the warehouse, with manual labor and clear performance expectations to "sort the workers from the shirkers" (Suma, 2010). A few months later, the new recruits face another hurdle: a vote of the existing members. The company puts it nicely:

> New recruits are warned that we don't have a boss, we have 120 of them. . . . We take "diamonds in the rough" (able people who have missed out in the education lottery) and propel them into creative and high power positions within months of recruitment. (Suma, 2010)

Worker turnover is negligible, at a rate of around 2% per year for full-time staff. People simply do not leave a place where they feel good and enjoy their work. The company takes pride in the fact that it has never had lay-offs or fired anyone for other than disciplinary reasons (Suma, 2010). This shows that though Suma members are supportive of each other, they also expect certain standards of behavior of their peers. It is not about anarchy, but about collectively creating real value for everyone.

Another Suma member, Julius Nicholson, neatly sums up his feelings in an interview with *The Guardian*: "One of the best things for me is that there are no fat cats, no big car in the car park, and no grafting all hours just for the money to go straight into someone else's back pocket." He adds:

> We all work hard and we share the fruits of our work equally, which is amazing. I once went on a trade union day and there were a lot of people there from traditional industries. We each had to say a bit about our company and one trade union guy went all misty-eyed and said, 'You're talking about utopia.' It made me feel really lucky. (Roberts, 2014)

Limits to growth

We have already seen that companies can do exceptionally well if they recognize limits with respect to the environment, to people, and to inequality. But there is still another type of limit worth discussing, albeit one that Wall Street apostles will hardly accept – the limits to growth.

Earlier, we questioned the received wisdom that businesses must grow infinitely to avoid bankruptcy. We believe that the growth imperative hypothesis is badly flawed, and the assumption that businesses will inevitably lose competitiveness when they fail to "scale up" is not necessarily sound. Granted, the size-cost-price-profitability relationship postulated by the supporters of the growth ideology may well work under the assumption that customers all behave like the fabled *homo economicus*, the rational man who strives purely to maximize his economic self-interest. But as we argue throughout this book, pure economic rationality is a myth; it is not how our brains work. We are driven by emotions at least as much as by our forebrain. We seek meaning, beauty, and good personal relationships, not only purely functional goods at the lowest possible price. We long for the deeper, emotional side of *real value* – and emotional value is not subject to the basic growth law that postulates that higher quantities automatically lead to lower costs, more market share, and higher profits. In fact, deeper emotional value can be destroyed by growth, as things like place-attachment are lost, or mass standardization hollows out the soul of a product, or as CRM databases replace personal relationships.

From a *real value* perspective, infinite growth just does not make sense. It is the *optimal*, not the maximum size that counts. In the optimum, economies of scale and efficiency advantages are used to a certain extent, but not to the detriment of the deeper, emotional value that the organization can still create for its customers, employees, and partners. That's actually how growth works in nature. No doubt, plants and creatures have to grow to survive – but only until they reach the optimal size that their species needs to thrive. Beyond that point, they may grow in complexity, in experience, or in wisdom. They may still embark on a qualitative growth path, but they no longer grow in size. Unchecked growth only occurs when a natural system gets out of control. For instance, in the case of unstoppable cell growth, we have a name for this phenomenon – *cancer*.

On a societal and macroeconomic level, there is a clear trend – accelerated after the financial and economic crisis of the years 2008 – 9 – toward a discussion of alternative models that decouple human progress and quantitative growth. Already in the 1970s, Herman Daly introduced the idea of a "steady state economy" in which the physical size of the economy stays constant at a sustainable scale that does not exceed a certain limit defined by the Earth's carrying capacity (Daly, 1973). In such an economy, progress is not about growth in size, but about increasing efficiency and non-material goods such as knowledge or service quality. At approximately the same time, Ernst F. Schumacher (1973) criticized the negative effects of an unsustainable "gigantism" on people's quality of life, and advocated a new approach that recognized that "small is beautiful."

In a memorable speech, the novelist, farmer, and conservationist, Wendell Berry reminds us that we seem to have forgotten that we are not gods, but merely human:

> [B]eginning in science and engineering, and continuing by imitation into other disciplines, we have progressed to the belief that humans are intelligent enough, or soon will be, to transcend all limits, and to forestall or correct all bad results of the misuse of intelligence. Upon this belief rests the further belief that we can have economic growth without limit. (Berry, 2012)

But times are changing and increasingly the doctrine of limitless economic growth is being questioned. Supporters of the "degrowth" movement, for example, also known as "décroissance" in France or "decrecimiento" in the Spanish-speaking world, believe that the optimal level of economic activity has already been exceeded in many developed countries (Kallis, 2011). Consequently, they go so far as to demand that economies be downsized to a level that is socially and ecologically viable in the long term. A German variant, the "post-growth" approach, refers to empirical findings that human wellbeing more strongly depends on immaterial values rather than economic growth, at least above a certain income level.[28] Supporters of the post-growth concept advocate the sufficiency principle, a decrease in material consumption, a central role for regional supply systems, and, more generally, a "liberation from excess" (Paech, 2012). What all those ideas have in common is that they question the linkage between economic growth and the creation of value – and of *real value* in particular.

This discussion of the limits to growth does not stop at the societal and academic level. More and more business leaders realize that they have a choice; they can decide to leave the rat race for growth. For them, quality comes before size. Fearing that quality and real value could be lost with increasing scale, they deliberately decide *against* further growth. In the following section, we consider two examples from Germany, a country where entrepreneurs with a post-growth attitude have been getting increasing public attention.

Inner growth at Richard Henkel GmbH

Richard Henkel GmbH is a manufacturer of steel tube furniture and a specialist in surface coating technology based in a small town in Southern Germany. At the beginning of the new millennium, the company experienced a sudden and unexpected growth in revenues;

its competence in coating metal parts was in high demand with the rise of the cell phone industry. The growth came at a price, however, as the company soon faced a shortage of skilled workers. Its employees had to work around the clock in three shifts, leading to increased stress levels and pressure on their high standards of quality. At that time, the company just barely managed to meet the expectations of its customers. CEO Susanne Henkel was particularly concerned that there was no more time left for real conversations, leading to a lack of new ideas that usually originate from intense interactions between employees (Stieber, 2013). To make things worse, the coating market experienced a strong downturn in the year following its sudden rise. In Henkel's opinion, the growth path just involved problems and risks, with no returns at all. Consequently, she decided that she never wanted to go through such a growth phase again (Stieber, 2013). Actually, it became an explicit goal for the company *not* to grow any more – at least not in terms of revenues. Henkel was not even bothered by losing a few customers. "A good profitability, weekends off for the staff, and in the end, there's still something left. What more can you wish for?" is how she described her new priorities (Stamp, 2014).

Since then, the company has followed a strategy that Henkel calls "inner growth." It is about getting better, more efficient, more innovative, and more ecologically friendly, and not about becoming bigger in terms of size. Henkel concentrates on constant process improvements, developing new technologies, increasing energy and material efficiency, and reducing waste. Using closed cycles, analyzing energy losses with the help of thermographic cameras, setting strict energy efficiency standards, and introducing a new lighting system that works with mirror reflectors instead of energy-consuming lamps are just some of the measures that the company implemented to decrease both resource use and costs at the same time.

For Susanne Henkel, it is qualitative, not quantitative growth that counts. Instead of producing more, she wants to offer "more valuable" products (swp.de, 2012). As a result, Henkel is able to offer highly durable premium products. The steel frames of the company's deck chairs can be used for decades. The plastic stringing can still wear out over time, but in the case of a Henkel product, that is no reason to throw the whole chair away. The company offers repair services for all its products, combined with a full recycling of the plastic strings. For the customer, the payoff is clear, as repair services are much cheaper than replacement of a whole piece of furniture. The environment benefits too from the reduced steel and related energy consumption.

And the business is flourishing with this strategy. When the global economic crisis hit Richard Henkel GmbH in 2009, it faced a strong decline in demand – in all areas but the repair department, which more than doubled both its work and revenues. As repair services have considerably higher margins than the production operations, the company managed to maintain good profitability levels even during these times of crisis. Meanwhile, Susanne Henkel even actively asks her customers not to replace their old Henkel deck-chairs with new ones, offering them the cheaper repair services instead, "the best customer loyalty activity that you can imagine," she says (Schumann, 2010).

The company has 50 employees, approximately the same number of people that worked for the firm's founder, Susanne Henkel's grandfather. Her intention is to make each of her employees a "knowledgeable efficiency and resource scout" (Henkel, 2012, p. 11). Through focusing on upgrading the qualifications of employees and fully including them in the processes of innovation and continuous improvement, Henkel in essence creates a learning community. In such an atmosphere, new business opportunities arise, including those in international markets. But rather than opening new foreign subsidiaries, Susanne Henkel prefers to grant licenses. "I would rather stay small, compact and capable of reacting to the non-predictable things," she says in summarizing her non-growth strategy (Stamp, 2014).

Clemens Härle: A small brewery with a big impact

Staying small is also a clear strategic goal for Gottfried Härle, the owner-manager of the Clemens Härle brewery, founded in 1897 in Baden-Württemberg, the same German state in which Richard Henkel GmbH is located. The brewery operates in a declining market; average beer consumption has decreased by approximately 25% in Germany over the last 20 years (Neßhöver, 2013). The industry is reacting to this decline predictably – with a price war and calls for further consolidation (Dierig, 2013; Neßhöver, 2013). It's the usual pattern. With increased competition, the big players want to grow by all means in order to cut unit costs, decrease prices, and gain market share. As all the major competitors play this game, they fuel a negative spiral for the industry that in the end fails to increase the consumption of beer (although we couldn't prove it based on some pubs we know, there is after all only a certain quantity of beer that people can drink!) and leads to less income for all and the destruction rather than the creation of value.

Gottfried Härle refuses to act like a lemming. In his opinion, the growth imperative is the completely wrong approach for his company. "Our organizational structure is created in a way that flat hierarchies, flexibility, speed, employee friendliness and customer intimacy are guaranteed. A pronounced growth orientation would be a threat to these values," he says (iöw, 2015). Instead of going with the growth flow, Härle's strategy is to stay small, radically regional, and as eco-friendly as possible. He has followed this strategy for 20 years, and it continues to yield positive results, securing the realization of his overall business goal of "handing the brewery over to the next generation" (taz.de, 2015). Despite the general decline of the industry, the brewery has been able to maintain both the number of employees and beer production at a constant level. Gottfried Härle is convinced that a growth orientation would only bring negative effects: "If we were to grow, we could not cater for the needs of our customers as we do now," he says, giving the example that it would no longer be possible for the brewery to deliver an additional beverage unit to a local restaurant in the evening on short notice. "Moreover, we would compromise the good work climate . . . Today, every employee can come to my office right away. That's not possible in a large corporation" (taz.de, 2015)

The 30 employees are also minority owners under a capital sharing scheme that was introduced by Gottfried Härle's father, who is still actively involved in the company in his nineties. When the employees reach retirement age, they are gradually paid out (Bündnis 90/Die Grünen Baden Württemberg, 2010, p. 7). Thus, they are also directly linked to the economic fate of their employer, to whom they, in turn, are extraordinarily loyal. The average job tenure at the Clemens Härle brewery is more than two decades. "If the drive and creative power of the younger ones are combined with the wealth of experience and the joy of working of the older ones – that's the best foundation for a successful development of the company – and for a good working atmosphere," says Härle (2014).

The brewery's employees are all local, as are the main ingredients such as hops and brewing barley. Also, the majority of other goods and services are sourced from the region. The policy to use mainly organic ingredients sets additional limits to the supply, but ensures the highest quality standards. A considerable portion of earnings is reinvested into the region, as the brewery sponsors local sports clubs, bands, and various associations as well as a theater festival, open-air festivals, and Germany's smallest movie award. As a place-based enterprise, the Clemens Härle brewery lives in a symbiosis with the people and institutions of the small town of Leutkirch and its surroundings. In fact, almost all of the brewery's customers are within a radius of just a few dozen miles. The company does not even want to expand geographically. If a customer from outside wants to buy beer from the company, they have to send their own trucks, because Härle deliberately decided not to offer long-distance delivery in an effort to shorten transportation routes.

That is just one of the many steps that the Clemens Härle brewery has taken to become the most eco-friendly company in its industry. Through replacing an old oil-fired heating system with a wood-chip heating plant that also supplies other buildings in the vicinity, sourcing electricity exclusively from the company-owned photovoltaics system and green energy providers, and running all company cars and trucks with biodiesel, Härle has become the first carbon-neutral brewery in the country. "Instead of Putin and the oil sheikhs, it's the Allgäu farmers who are now profiting from our energy demand," says Härle (haerle.de, 2009), referring to the immediate region in which his brewery is based. The packaging system is designed in a way that allows 100% recyclability. In addition, the company heavily invested in reducing water consumption during the brewing process and in emission control. For more than 20 years, the brewery has analyzed and constantly reduced its resource use and emissions. With such a clear focus on protecting the environment, the Clemens Härle brewery is nationally recognized. In 2009, the company won the German Solar Prize and the following year it was ranked among the three most sustainable companies in the country.

When Gottfried Härle was asked in a newspaper interview how he would cope with cost increases both on the raw material and staff side, he gave a prosaic yet surprising answer: "We increase prices" (taz.de, 2015). In a world in which the large breweries fall prey to each other in a ruthless price competition, Härle, the small local brewer, does the exact opposite, deliberately staying small and making his product more expensive. His regional customers are willing to follow him, as they recognize the value they get from the premium quality, authenticity, local spirit, and eco-friendliness of the brewery – the *real value* that goes far beyond what the multinational beer corporations could ever provide. "Of course, there are alternatives to the growth strategies that large corporations practice" (taz.de, 2015). Härle is very convincing, and his brewery's success over more than a century certainly suggests that he may be on to something.

Being right in the middle

Hidden treasures like Richard Henkel and Clemens Härle have not yet enjoyed much international attention. Yet, they are both examples of a wider phenomenon that we have already come across in this book, in the chapter on *long-term orientation*: the uniquely German *Mittelstand*. These are "mid-tier," small or midsized, often but not always family-run firms, that make specialized products in small towns, far from the usual hubs of economic activity. Staff turnover is usually negligible, about ten times lower than staff turnover at big U.S. firms (*The Economist*, 2014b). With trust a key strength, these companies practice a sort of paternalism with their first loyalty to the workforce, and their second to the community in which they are rooted. Making a profit comes in a distant third. The *Mittelstand* way of thinking is not limited to small firms, though. Take Trumpf, for example, a global market leader in laser machine tools, based outside Stuttgart and employing some 8,000 people. Almost every high-school graduate who works as an apprentice in vocational training at Trumpf later moves on to a full-time position there (Dougherty, 2009). Company principles emanate from the Lutheran faith of the owners, the Leibinger family, and empha-size compassion and discipline in whatever they do, especially when times get tough. Trumpf's CEO Nicola Leibinger-Kammüller expressed this ethos during the recent recession: "What vexes me day and night is the idea that I would have to lay people off," add-ing: "The responsibility I have for our employees is what is dearest to my heart" (Dougherty, 2009).

The Economist (2014) reports that public officials and business-people from around the world are making "pilgrimages" to Germany to learn from the *Mittelstand*, trying to find solutions to problems such as concentration of businesses in a few metropolitan areas, rising youth unemployment, and retaining competitiveness on a global scale. Of course, a business model that works in one society may not necessarily transfer well to another. But there is surely one lesson we can derive from the *Mittelstand* experience: that firms based in developed economies with high wages costs can still be globally competitive – but only if they create workplaces characterized by trust, maintain a strong firm identity that blends both world-class standards and local advantages, and focus on quality in both their products and their processes. Not least, the success of the *Mittelstand* is also based on setting and respecting limits, and on finding the right balance. "We want to satisfy our customers, employees, owners and society in equal measure," states Trumpf in its company principles: "All our dealings are marked by fairness, moderation, and trust" (Trumpf, 2015).

Less is more

A widespread consensus is that by 2050 the global population will reach 9 billion and average temperatures will rise by a catastrophic

3 degrees Celsius (5.4 degrees Fahrenheit) if greenhouse gas emissions continue at the current rate. One thing for certain, these projections imply dire consequences for the future of all living creatures unless human greed, ignorance, and hubris can be reined in. We also see increasing numbers of people suffering from the merciless pressure that the modern work world is putting on them, the growing inequality manifested in societies around the world, and the negative environmental and social side-effects of the inexorable drive for growth.

What gives us hope is that apart from the brief stories detailed here, there are plenty of other inspiring examples of people and companies that practice self-restraint, and respect the needs of the environment, their employees, and the communities in which they make money. An example is Aaron Feuerstein, who owned the textile manufacturer Malden Mills, a company set up by his grandfather in the U.S. town of Lawrence, Massachusetts, in 1906. In December 1995, a fire destroyed his factory. At the age of 70, Feuerstein could have taken the insurance money and retired. He could also have relocated the company to a low-wage country. Instead he continued paying his jobless employees their full salaries during the time in which the factory remained closed, which cost him $1.5 million per week (MoralHeroes, 2015). Together with rebuilding the factory with a focus on making it as employee- and eco-friendly as possible, he invested hundreds of millions of dollars (MoralHeroes, 2015). "I have a responsibility to the worker, both blue-collar and white-collar," said Feuerstein in an interview with the *Parade Magazine*,[32] also referring to Jewish law which emphasizes the need to take care of the "working man" as a brother. "I have an equal responsibility to the community. It would have been unconscionable to put 3,000 people on the streets and deliver a death blow to the cities," Feuerstein continued. "Maybe on paper our company is worth less [now] to Wall Street, but I can tell you it's worth more" (MoreThanMoney, 2002). He realized that *real value* goes far beyond monetary value. Most of his money was lost in Malden Mills' bankruptcy years after these events in the 1990s. Yet, he did not have any regrets. "I did it because it was the right thing to do," he later said (*CBS News*, 2003).

Over two decades ago, Vaclav Havel (1992), the great Czech writer and statesman, said that communism was not defeated by force but by the human spirit. He called this time the "end of the modern era," and with it proclaimed the end of our belief that humans can fully explain and control this world. But with civilization in crisis due to depletion of the biosphere and widening gaps between rich and poor, we should not, Havel argued, simply seek new and better ways of managing society and the economy. What is needed instead is a radical change in our attitude toward the world. We need to abandon "our arrogant belief that the world is merely a puzzle to be solved, a machine with instructions for use waiting to be discovered, a body of information to be fed into a computer in the hope that, sooner or later, it will spit out a universal solution" (Havel, 1992).

In economics, such thinking still holds sway. Yet many assumptions of mainstream economic thinking appear increasingly stale and discredited. For instance, a fundamental tenet, *more is better*, stands in sharp contrast with the spiritual logic, *less is more* or *enough is enough* (Sehgal, 2015). Economic logic suggests that by seeking more money we obtain the resources needed to survive. Paradoxically, spiritual logic holds that by renouncing material wealth we experience greater "inner riches." Pursuit of "external success" is not necessarily accompanied by personal contentment; many are poor in money but rich in spirit. In a world in which we are all connected and dependent on each other, respecting limits is an imperative if we are to survive and thrive. People, and companies, who are oriented toward creating real value understand the need to put moderation before gluttony, and balance before excess.

In brief: limits recognition

- Businesses that recognize that there are limits to the environment and to people are more successful in creating real value and in ensuring its wider distribution.

- Setting self-limits leads not to less but rather to *more* freedom both for individuals and for society.

- Limits recognition is about character and excellence, and can lead to enhanced wellbeing, fulfillment and satisfaction.

- Individuality and individual freedom are fundamentally different from individualism and much richer and more ethically sound.

- People and organizations flourish in an environment where "inner growth" rather than "outer success" through unlimited growth in revenues and assets is the goal.

- A radical overhaul is needed of economists' assumptions about limits such as "more is always better than less", "individual self-interest must be pursued" and "limits reduce overall welfare."

6

Learning community: rooting innovation in meaning

> This I learned . . .
> not of those who taught,
> but of those who talked with me.
> St. Augustine, *Confessions* (1843, pp. 13-14)

Following a deep purpose means trying to achieve a transformation – of attitudes, behaviors, ways of seeing the world, and ways of interacting with others. Such real transformation is only possible through learning. For example, before Mahatma Ghandi fulfilled the great purpose of his life by leading India to political freedom, he had spent over two decades encountering injustice, developing a model of social activism, and achieving political leadership in South Africa's civil rights movement. Just as individuals who – like Ghandi – want to fulfil a purpose must embark on a learning path, so do organizations. Enterprises that want to create *real value* understand that they must first develop into learning communities; only then will they be positioned to achieve their deeper purpose.

A learning community displays a capacity to learn through helping its members continually absorb new ideas, knowledge, and skills while nurturing their personal growth, capabilities, and quality of life. Such a community fosters a culture of creativity and exploration, helping individuals to flourish and live life well through attaining objectives they truly and deeply desire. As individuals learn, so does the organization, developing new resources and capabilities that can be harnessed to create value for customers and the enterprise alike.

After all, deep purpose and learning are powerfully intertwined. On the one hand, fulfilling a purpose requires the ability to learn. On the other hand, purpose together with meaning and identity are keys to developing and sustaining a dynamic learning community. Yet many approaches to organizational learning – for example those primarily focused on analysis or rational decision-making based on sophisticated computer spreadsheet tables – remain dominated by a mechanistic paradigm, based on a crude efficiency-driven philosophy. Founded on an outdated industrial model, these approaches are out of step with the innovative thinking required to serve the needs of modern business and society, since they fail to properly apprehend connections and patterns – a crucial ability in an increasingly complex and interdependent world. In order to survive and thrive in such an environment, the emphasis must be turned toward relationships, integrity, and wholeness and away from reductionist thinking and narrow conceptions of self-interest.

The core mission of a learning community, as we see it, is to foster a network that encourages creativity and innovation in the process of creating value from both tangible and intangible resources. We categorically do *not* mean creating value in a narrow monetary sense. Rather, it's about *real value*, something that people deeply care about, rather than what can be expressed in monetary terms alone. People – customers, employees, and owners alike – strive for meaning and identity, possibilities for self-growth, productive social relationships, and overall wellbeing. Effective learning communities create a rich and complex social fabric that encourages their members to combine many forms of capital – monetary, human, ecological, social, and technological – in surprising and innovative ways in order to create real value.

On this foundation, learning communities accumulate knowledge, rather than merely data. The type of knowledge needed to solve today's global challenges is, as pointed out by Bradley (2011, p. 153), "systemic rather than linear and integrative rather than fragmentary, concerned with process, emphasizing dynamics rather than cause-effect and pattern rather than detail." This implies the need for mindsets that are ecologically rather than hierarchically driven, collaborative rather than just competitive, and holistic rather than functional, in order to tackle the complexity, uncertainty, and change of our 21st century.

A learning community is also a way of thinking, of relentlessly trying to find better ways to use resources to create real value. It cannot be reduced solely to discovering new knowledge *per se*. Of course, knowledge is important. It is the raw material for developing unique capabilities that enable an enterprise to achieve competitive advantages in the marketplace. But new knowledge alone is insufficient to stimulate innovation. While a learning community is essential for nurturing innovation, the latter cannot be developed by relying on scientific research alone. The question of most concern in scientific enquiry is: "*Why are things the way they are?*" For real innovation, however, understanding why is just the beginning. A learning community poses a different and crucial question: "*How can we change the ways things are?*" (Sweeney, 2001).

A recent *Harvard Business Review* article identified "creative abrasion," the ability to use discourse and debate to generate new ideas, "creative agility," the ability to experiment through fast testing, reflection and adaptation processes, and "creative resolution," the ability to make decisions that integrate very different ideas and perspectives, as key capabilities of organizations that want to achieve and sustain a high degree of innovativeness (Hill *et al.*, 2014). It is conceptually similar to the enriching environment of a "skunkworks," an idea introduced by engineers at Lockheed Corporation in the 1940s and today used by some organizations as a way to stimulate innovation in an unconventional manner. A skunkworks project is developed by a small group of highly committed people who escape routine organizational structures in order to roll out an innovative product or service. Relationships of mutual trust, a common purpose, and good communication are critical for such a joint innovation process to succeed, and a common identity and solidarity are critical for the formation of trustful learning relationships.

Transformational learning is founded on active *engagement* rather than on a simple transfer of information. The hallmark of a quality learning experience is knowledge enquiry rather than information receipt. At its best, a learning community also helps individuals develop a personal mission and the confidence to know that they themselves can acquire the knowledge and skills needed for its achievement. This requires a learning environment where people are given time and community support to explore their own selves and recognize meaning through their actions. Through reflection and discussion, both individuals and enterprises can develop a sense of identity and purpose, a great spur for lifelong innovative thinking and practice.

But articulating with any precision the elements of a learning organization is a difficult proposition. It is more effective, perhaps, to offer a few examples that illustrate such organizations in practice. In this chapter we look at two quite distinct enterprises that are in the vanguard of creating learning communities that provide them with a competitive edge and pave the way for the creation of *real value*: illycaffè, S.p.A. (illy) in Italy and Cooperative Home Care Associates (CHCA) in the Bronx, New York.

illycaffè: quality as purpose

Illy is a family-owned, Italian premium coffee company that focuses on quality in all aspects of its business. It was founded in 1933 by Francesco Illy, a Hungarian immigrant who moved to the city of Trieste during World War I. As Central Europe's major port, Trieste had become a center of coffee trade and coffee culture. The city abounded with importers, processors, and roasters of coffee, as well as with elegant cafés which had developed into a focal point of Trieste's rich cultural life.

Illy was only one of many coffee producers in Trieste, but arguably the one with the boldest dream. He aimed for nothing short of offering the best coffee in the world. Recognizing the importance of innovation, he immersed himself in designing a machine that could brew coffee in a way that brought out the very best of its aroma. The result of this experimentation was the Illetta, a revolutionary espresso machine that replaced steam with pressurized water and offered other refinements. It created an espresso like no other. Francesco Illy's other major invention was pressurization, a technology that preserved the freshness of the coffee aromas inside the canisters. Instead of turning rancid when being transported over long distances, pressurization ensured that illy's blend of roasted and ground beans remained perfectly fresh.

Francesco was succeeded by his son Ernesto, a chemist, who ran the company from 1957 and was its president from 1963 to 2005. Ernesto was an avid traveler who successfully internationalized illy's business, first to other European markets, and later to the United States. Following the footsteps of his father, he continued to pursue excellence: "It takes 50 beans to make a one-ounce cup of espresso," he once said. "One bad one, and I guarantee that you'll taste it. It's like one rotten egg in an omelet" (Hevesi, 2008). Consequently, Ernesto invested heavily in research and development aimed at increasing quality in all its facets. He explored the chemistry of coffee with an in-house laboratory that he set up for that purpose, and filed several patents related to improving coffee processing, for example, with a system to automatically detect and pick out bad beans.

The Illy family still leads the company with Ernesto's son Andrea, also a chemist, now President and CEO and brother Riccardo Vice President of illycaffè and President of the holding company Illy Group. When Ernesto handed over the leadership to his children, they together wrote and signed the "Illy pact," a document that succinctly summarizes the values of the company, among them, in the words of Andrea Illy, "that the company is not at the service of the family, but vice versa; our search for excellence in all we do; and our goal to create value for all the stakeholders involved" (Illy, 2015, p. 42). With 2014 revenues of €391 million and more than 1,080 employees, illy is dwarfed by corporations such as Nestlé and Mondelez but has established itself as a prestigious premium brand, based on its "uncompromising quest to provide the perfect cup of coffee" (Chang *et al.*, 2010a).

The company, focusing its business on one single blend of coffee (out of the conviction that there can be only one *best*), tends to avoid mass consumer retailing. "We are a high-end brand," says Andrea Illy, "We are at the top of the pyramid in the coffee industry.

Consequently, our distribution needs to be selective. You cannot be everywhere."[33] Nevertheless, illy coffee is today available in tens of thousands of bars, cafés, and restaurants in over 140 countries around the world, as well as in the more than 200 outlets of the company's stores – *illy Caffè* and *espressamente illy* coffee bar – part of illy's relentless effort to spread Italian coffee culture around the world. "We serve an average of seven million illy coffees per day," says Illy. "Our mission is for them to be simply perfect."

The ongoing search for perfection

Being "perfect" is a grand proposition, especially when equated with notions of being flawless or absolutely unsurpassable. But that's not how they see perfection at illy. Going back to its Latin roots, *perfectus* is the past participle of *perficere* meaning "to bring about" something or "to do thoroughly." It's about the path rather than the destination. "Our route to perfect quality is infinite," says Illy. "There is no limit of how much you should and must improve."

Recognizing that there is always room for improvement is a major precondition for learning and growth, and for getting closer to the ultimate dream of perfection. For illy, learning and innovation have always been at the heart of its business. According to Andrea Illy, innovativeness and a constant striving for perfection lie in both the company's and indeed the family's very DNA:

> My father was an inventor, business man and philosopher. As a child, when friends lend me their bicycles, I tinkered around with them and handed them back in a repaired and refurbished way, because I just enjoy getting things straight in a perfect way. (Lewitan, 2013)

Ingenuity and openness to learning are virtues held in high esteem in the company. "Every time we have an obstacle on our route to perfect quality, we find an innovative solution to circumvent it," says Illy. Whether it was his grandfather Francesco's development of a high pressure espresso maker, his father's introduction of the espresso pod to the U.S. market that allowed consumers to match the quality they could get from baristas, or the new *iperespresso* capsule system that extracts even more coffee aromas, every innovation has been targeted toward improving the quality of the customer experience. The newest innovation, presented at the 2015 EXPO in Milan, is the "personal blender," an electronic system that allows consumers to create their own blend out of the finest ingredients according to their personal taste, all directly from their mobile phone, tablet, or PC. Once the consumers have found their "personal perfect cup," they can keep it on their devices and reorder it from any other illy blending machine.

Innovation is more likely to occur where people of very different perspectives, both inside and outside the company, come together to share ideas. Andrea Illy is an avid "collaborative learner" himself. "I need to understand everything I do, to get to the bottom of it," he says (Illy, 2015, p. 162). He strives to connect with the world's leading experts in varied fields of knowledge, thus fueling his enterprise with new ideas and approaches. When he joined the company in the 1990s, he visited Japan to learn about the TQM (total quality management) philosophy directly from Toyota. He implemented what he learned and dramatically lowered illy's defect rates following the *kaizen* principle of constant improvement. He went to the Massachusetts Institute of Technology to study innovation, then initiated the creation of illy's own innovation system. He collaborated with Porsche to learn about lean management in manufacturing, and explored exponential technologies in Silicon Valley. Still feeling a strong desire to deepen his knowledge (he also describes himself as "a voracious and omnivorous reader" (Illy, 2015, p. 124)), Illy recently also decided to immerse himself in the study of complexity science, which aims to explain the behavior of systems composed of a very high number of interrelated variables.

Indeed, countless variables also need to be considered to create the "perfect" coffee experience, ranging from agricultural issues such as plant genetics and the conditions of the *terroir*, harvesting and post-harvesting processing procedures, transport logistics, roasting, blending, and packaging, to the functionalities of the espresso machine and the way that the cup is served (Illy, 2015, p. 78). All these factors are, again, dependent on various other influences, from the socio-economic conditions under which coffee growers are living to the diligence and passion of the baristas who prepare the final cup. Only if all the factors are calibrated in the right way – in other words, only if an optimal state of equilibrium is reached – will the thousand aromatic substances of coffee unfold their highly stimulating effect. It is a complex system, which, according to complexity theory, is sensitive to even small changes in any of the involved variables. Consequently, as Illy writes in his book *A Coffee Dream*:

> to evolve toward superior problem-solving abilities (and hence collaborate in innovation), we need collective intelligence . . . Each one of us must do our part in constructing a better world, making use of our individual abilities. Because, if we lose sight of responsibility and solidarity, . . . what emerges are an immoral condition and anti-ethical development. (Illy, 2015, p. 179)

Values-driven value creation

From its beginning, illy has been an ethically based company with a mission to create real value by improving the quality of life of people through coffee. Ernesto Illy, for instance, believed that "the ethical dimension should distinguish a company's inner life as well as its business" (Fondazione Ernesto Illy, 2015). He did not accept the status quo of existing imbalances and injustices in the coffee industry, in which a product which improved some people's lives was produced by others who were exploited and compelled to live in poverty.

Ernesto passed away in 2008, but his spirit is still very much alive in the company. His portrait prominently faces his former desk, from which his son Andrea now runs the enterprise. "He still controls me – metaphorically speaking," he says. "I actually like the idea of somebody who controls me." Following his father's all-encompassing stakeholder-oriented philosophy, he is convinced that "companies are basically responsible for the human development." It is a responsibility he takes very seriously.

Illy has been lauded for its performance on measures of both quality and sustainability; it was the first company to receive a Responsible Supply Chain Process Certification from the Norwegian certification body DNV GL. Unlike other protocols which focus on suppliers, this particular certification scrutinizes the transparency, sustainability, and fairness of the company's supply chain management practices. This means the company is obliged to guarantee that all its stakeholders behave properly. Further, it not only requires the company to be fair to its own stakeholders, but also requires it to try to teach these stakeholders to be similarly fair to their *own* stakeholders.

The company's vision is neither to become the market leader nor the most profitable business in its domain. Like other responsible leaders in this book, Andrea Illy sees profits as a means rather than an end. The ultimate end is to build a better world, through coffee, and Illy understands that the ability to offer the highest possible quality coffee to consumers is inextricably tied to the living and working conditions of the coffee growers:

> For a perfect cup of coffee, we need the perfect bean from the grower – and in order to provide us with the perfect bean, the grower must have the necessary knowledge, and must also live under decent socio-economic conditions.

Illy pays considerably more to coffee growers than the average coffee roaster. In turn, the company receives the high-quality coffee beans that it needs to satisfy its customers. It is a virtuous cycle, linking the pleasure that consumers feel when drinking a cup of well-rounded, aromatic coffee with the socio-economic development of the coffee growers and their communities – a cycle that is nurtured by premium coffee companies such as illy. The quality of life of both stakeholder groups is enhanced at the same time – real value creation at its best!

The fruits of real value creation are also reaped in the form of business results. Illy has become one of the fastest-growing private enterprises in the coffee roasting business, with an over tenfold increase in revenues within two decades, based on a business model that has remained solidly cash flow financed (Dawson, 2015).

Unwilling to compromise quality to increase volume, the family's holding company (Illy Group) decided instead to diversify into other luxury food and beverages businesses, including chocolate, tea, and wine. These are "all products of the earth that have a great affinity with coffee and that offer the same combination of sensorial pleasure and inspiration," as Illy (2015, p. 44) remarks. "We want to stick to our unique positioning and excellence, which nobody else can do," he adds. "So our participations amount to a collection of super-premium niches" (Dawson, 2015). Although the new sister companies remain operationally independent, they get full "access to the illy system" and all its research and development, production, and marketing competences (Chang *et al.*, 2010a, S14). Knowledge transfer between the different business areas is explicitly encouraged. As they learn together, they grow together.

A university dedicated to the perfect cup

"Any company is entirely rooted and founded on knowledge," says Illy. "Knowledge is about competences, and competences are about competitiveness. This is the only way for companies to survive." This is especially true for a company that strives to achieve and maintain quality leadership in its industry. Building, sharing, and maintaining knowledge within the company is therefore a major management task at illy. A program called "illy citizen" tries to systematically ensure that the management also listens and learns from the ideas and suggestions of employees. For Illy, taking good care of his "collaborators," as he calls them, is of utmost importance. He is convinced that if they left the company out of anger or demotivation, or did not stay long enough to really learn their jobs, the company would quite simply lose its capacity to be competitive.

The quality of coffee is not only determined by the abilities and motivation of employees and the consistency of the processing and roasting process, but also by the quality of the beans and the preparation and serving process. Thus, in order to fulfill its founder's dream to serve the greatest coffee to the world, illy needs to develop and spread knowledge all along the value chain, far beyond the boundaries of the organization. For this purpose, the company opened its own educational institution, the Università del Caffè, in 1999. Illy's "knowledge hub" is active in more than 20 locations around the world, organized in three departments that target coffee growers, the hospitality sector, and consumers.

A mere 1% of the world's available coffee conforms to illy's demanding standards. But, in accordance with Andrea Illy's conviction that quality can be learned, the university offers support for coffee growers, helping them to elevate their agronomical knowledge and skills in order to grow coffee that will meet illy's high standards. Training is provided on site to growers in the tropical regions, and emphasizes sustainable and environmentally responsible cultivation, harvesting, and processing practices.

On the opposite end of the value chain, the university trains hospitality professionals, illy's front-end to customers. "Our capacity to accomplish our mission and delight consumers, cup after cup, depends entirely on those people," says Illy. How a coffee is prepared is at least as important as the quality of the coffee that is used, or, as an illy executive puts it: "You cannot make a great coffee from bad beans, but you can make a bad coffee from good beans" (Chang *et al.*, 2010b).

After all, the coffee bar owners' success depends on their ability to offer "the perfect cup" to their customers, following illy's value proposition – that they will all have a better business if they serve the best coffee. So the university offers hands-on training in coffee preparation and serving as well as courses about enhancing the overall customer experience and the successful management and marketing of coffee bars. After a three-day course, for example, a participant is certified as a *Maestro dell'Espresso*, which attests that the graduate understands all the factors that contribute to a perfect cup of coffee such as "why espresso cups should maximally be half-full" (Corti, 2013).

Last but not least, the university educates consumers. "We need connoisseurs with the capacity of distinguishing the quality of a generic coffee from ours, just like the sommeliers who are knowledgeable about the different regions, grapes, or ways of processing wine," says Illy. This is what Illy also tries to transfer to coffee, being convinced that "[t]hrough education and training, we can achieve greater discernment and, as a result, a form of sophistication in our appreciation of what is 'good'" (Illy, 2015, p. 58).

Since its opening, the university has trained more than 150,000 people in programs ranging from half-day discovery courses to the world's only master's program in coffee economics and science. It has created a community of people who understand "what matters most" in producing, preparing, and enjoying high-quality coffee. The Università del Caffè has a mission that reaches far beyond the immediate business needs of the company, but at the same time clearly supports it, as Illy explains: "We are seeking to elevate the whole coffee market, because the more sophisticated the coffee market becomes, the more we can thrive in this market."

Another positive effect of the Università del Caffè is that it increases customer loyalty. Illy tries to stay in touch with the university's alumni through newsletters and social media (Chang *et al.*, 2010a). People who understand the qualities of a premium coffee are also more inclined to prefer it over standard coffee. This closer attachment to the product also translates into hard numbers. Illy recognizes a significant increase of revenues at coffee bars or restaurants whose owners or employees have attended a course at the university (Chang *et al.*, 2010a).

Learning together, growing together

The Università del Caffè is an important vehicle for creating a learning community that reaches far beyond the boundaries of the company. It facilitates the creation of a network of mutually beneficial learning relationships among the company, its suppliers, customers, and other partners. It thereby extends illy's long tradition of building trustful partnerships, a major precondition for developing innovative learning communities.

Andrea Illy's sister Anna has long been engaged in creating fellowship with coffee growers in developing and emerging countries (Illy, 2015, p. 41). She spends roughly a third of her time in South America, maintaining direct contact with illy's coffee producers. As a result of her efforts, illy sources all beans directly from the

growers, unlike many in the industry who buy their beans from bro-
kers in the international coffee market. Andrea Illy is convinced
that the highest quality can only be achieved through close cooperation and a joint learning process:

> We meet the producers, make our choice and motivate the
> producers to cooperate with us in various ways. Our quality
> standard is above the market's – and we show the coffee farm-
> ers how to reach our quality level. . . . [We] teach [them] how
> to best grow coffee and what are the working processes that
> need to be performed. Only if the results of this knowledge
> transfer fulfills our quality expectations, we buy the coffee.
> (cremamagazin.de, n.d.).

The success of strong collaborative relationships based on trust is
illustrated by illy's dealings with its Brazilian suppliers. When it
began its search for partners in Brazil in the early 1990s, the country
posed a real challenge. After all, Brazil had a reputation for low-
quality coffee, while premium quality was central to illy's business
model. With Anna Illy's support, the company organized a competition called the *Prêmio Ernesto illy de Qualidade do Café para
Espresso* (Brazil Quality Award for Espresso Coffee), which was
later complemented by an additional prize for the most sustainable
coffee grower. The competition aimed to promote a quality attitude
among growers, and encourage them to improve their coffee growing, harvesting, and processing standards. Year after year, more
growers participated in the illy award, resulting in a significant
increase in overall quality standards, even in regions which had been
considered totally unsuitable for coffee cultivation before (Perrini
and Russo, 2008).

Some of the most active participants in this competition were
invited to join the *Clube illy do Café*, founded in 2000 to further
intensify the relationship between the growers and illy. The club

offers a range of training and knowledge exchange possibilities for its members, thus fostering a new, local learning community.

With these initiatives, a select number of Brazilian coffee producers were given the opportunity, through partnerships based on mutual trust, to gain knowledge and develop competences that would enable them to become producers of high-quality coffee. As a result, they receive higher prices as illy suppliers, and are able to raise their own living standards. A Brazilian Secretary of Agriculture called the Illys "pioneers," adding that as a result of their influence, "[t]hey helped us learn to produce high-quality coffee, first for them and then for everybody else. Today we don't think anymore in terms of quantity of production. We think in terms of quality of production" (Stein, 2002). *Fortune Magazine* concurs, suggesting that indirect, reputational benefits of illy's engagement in Brazil may be even more valuable than the huge amount of money the company contributed to the coffee growers themselves through paying above-market prices:

> the Illy family may have had more impact than anyone on the creation of a high-quality coffee sector in Brazil . . . Illy taught Brazilian growers how to produce high-quality coffee, in the process helping Brazil shake its bad reputation among the gourmet coffee crowd. (Stein, 2002)

The trustful learning relationships between illy and the coffee growers not only benefitted the principal parties, but had very positive spillover effects for the whole industry. When people trust one another they can better cooperate, learn faster from others' skills, knowledge, and attitudes, and are more able to reach a common goal. "Trust grows when people perceive that they are part of a collective effort to deliver value to stakeholders in a way that contributes to the betterment of their world," wrote Harvard Business School Professor Robert G. Eccles and his colleagues (2012, p. 50).

"Work becomes more meaningful, and people become more engaged and productive" (Eccles *et al.*, 2012, p. 50). In short: when people create real value together in a trustful way, they achieve better results for both themselves and others. "Civilization can only improve if we see all the stakeholders," says Illy. "But it's not only about solidarity. It is also about a sustainable value chain, about enabling the growers to deliver us the coffee that allows us to delight our consumers. That's why we must care."

A blend of goodness and beauty

Creating real value means doing something good, for others as well as for oneself. For Andrea Illy, the goodness of coffee means "pleasure in savoring it, awareness of its quality, and recognition of the ethical commitment behind its cultivation, processing and production" (Illy, 2015, p. 102). He also believes that goodness can be enhanced by beauty. He likes to refer to the ancient Greek term *kalokagathía*, which is goodness and beauty combined in one word. "Basically, if something is good, it must be beautiful," says Illy. "And if something is beautiful, it must be good. It is circular – two sides of the same coin."

Recognizing the nature of coffee as a multisensory experience, including the taste, the touch in the mouth, and the aromatic scent, Illy wanted to further "broaden the pleasure" by adding an extra sense – sight. That's why the company not only strives for a quality product, but also for beauty in all it does – from the color of the espresso's *crema* and the design of the cup (which Illy calls the coffee's "dress"), to the packaging and the coffee machines, to the way it uses images and literature in expressing the company's values and philosophy.

It was Andrea Illy's creative and talented brother Francesco who initiated a far-ranging collaboration of the company with some of the best-known artists from all over the world, including Italian architects Matteo Thun (the creator of the iconic illy coffee cup) and Luca Trazzi (the designer of the legendary "round and curvy" espresso machine "X1"), American pop-art painter James Rosenquist (the creator of illy's company logo), Serbian performance artist Marina Abramović and Japanese-American multimedia artist Yoko Ono. As did many of their colleagues, these artists also accepted the call to use illy's ceramic coffee cups as their blank canvas, transforming them into works of art as part of the illy Art Collection, thus adding visual joy for coffee lovers.

In the field of photography, illy has a long-standing partnership with Brazilian social photographer Sebastião Salgado, who shares the company's concern for sustainable development. He carefully documents the life of farmers in the countries from which illy sources its blend, making us aware that coffee is produced by people, not by anonymous commodity markets. For Andrea Illy,

> Sebastião's photographs always remind me to look at the land and at the families who process the coffee. The wise and attentive hands and eyes of the farmers are our allies in the extraordinary challenge of producing the world's best coffee, with reciprocal effects for the happiness of all. (Illy, 2015, p. 208)

With its sustainArt program, illy also supports young artists, focusing on talents from the coffee-producing countries, helping local cultural communities in a manner similar to what it did with the agricultural communities. In addition to its wide-ranging collaborations with visual artists, illy is also active in promoting literature with its own literary journal *illywords* and its sponsorship of a local literature festival.

Illy's remarkable contributions to the arts community are not pure philanthropy. The search for beauty is also a learning activity that drives relentless innovation. "True beauty cannot only be imitation," says Illy. "It must also be the expression of a new, subversive reality" (Illy, 2015, p. 124). Moreover, he sees the role of arts and beauty also as a kind of "universal language" that can help his company to better differentiate and position itself on the market:

> The more beautiful you are, the more sophisticated you are, the higher people perceive the quality that you offer, and the more they recognize and are ready to pay for this intangible value.

This aesthetic experience is an important part of the real value of the product, as is the meaning that such a beautiful and sustainable product conveys to both consumers and producers. Illy's gourmet coffee, sustainably produced and marketed, provides a holistic customer experience of pleasure and beauty that, thanks to its long pursuit of a deeper purpose, may in fact be improving the world.

Trust and meaning – what really counts

The example of illy shows that creating real value must be a collaborative effort, in which the enterprise, its employees, suppliers, distributors, and consumers learn and work together as a learning community to achieve a better life for all. A company must create value that is, according to Andrea Illy "both tangible – economic – but also intangible, in the form of knowledge and reputation. In a word: trust" (Illy, 2015, p. 107).

In the case of illy, value is created through mutually beneficial trustful relationships. Through educating coffee growers, illy receives better quality coffee, while raising the living standards of the growers through the premium prices that they can get for their produce. By educating hospitality professionals, illy ensures that consumers will get the "perfect cup." The coffee bar owners, in turn, get the chance to increase their margins through selling a premium product. Educating the consumer not only enhances their pleasure when drinking coffee, but also increases demand for illy's high-quality offerings. Providing consumers, baristas, and growers with a common knowledge base, in turn, creates a sense of inter-connectedness and community, and therefore meaning and real value. "Because what counts isn't the thing in itself," says Illy, "but the meaning we give it" (Illy, 2015, p. 46).

CHCA: cooperating in care

British writer George Monbiot (2015) argues that in the UK economy there is "an inverse relationship between utility and reward." Those in the highest paid jobs tend to cause the greatest harm, he says, while the ones who work hardest to improve the lives of others end up with the lowest incomes. What he terms the "uselessness" ratio is ever increasing: UK chief executives received pay 60 times more than the average worker's salary in the 1990s. Today, it is at least 80 (some estimates even say 180) times more. Referring to this increasing imbalance as "klepto-remuneration," he cites home care workers as an example. "Is there a more difficult or worthwhile employment?" he asks. Home care workers' already demanding work in assisting people in all their activities of daily living – from dressing and bathing to cleaning and going to the toilet, are combined with an ever-increasing pressure from the side of the employers and impatient and hypercritical family members. As they commute from one home to another, care workers take on the role of a kind of "human loom," says Monbiot:

> stitching the social fabric together while many of their employers and shareholders, and government ministers, slash blindly at the cloth, downsizing, outsourcing and deregulating in the cause of profit. (Monbiot, 2015)

The U.S. home care industry seems little different. About 2.5 million strong, it is one of the nation's fastest growing (thinkprogress. org, 2015). But it also faces a looming labor shortage as the demand for home health services skyrockets with the aging of the baby boom generation (those born between 1946 and 1964) (Ludden, 2012). Despite the need to attract legions of home care workers, it remains a low-status, low-wage industry. Home care aides earn on average less than $10 an hour and are often trapped in unprotected, precarious employment situations. Nearly half of them live in households that are dependent on public assistance such as food stamps, and a third have no health insurance (Rieder *et al.*, 2012). Turnover rates are extremely high, many aides are untrained, and there is little potential for career advancement.

Cooperative Home Care Associates (CHCA), a worker-owned home care agency in the Bronx, New York, is doing its bit to change that. The company goal is to provide good jobs for a class of workers who are often treated quite shabbily, while also providing a critical social service. CHCA is dedicated to providing "reliable, high quality home health care services for those who are elderly, chronically ill, or living with disabilities," while offering reasonable compensation and building a successful, worker-owned business. Importantly, it also focuses on giving its workers "opportunities to learn and grow as members of a health care team" (chcany.org. 2015). Indeed, the impetus to provide learning and development opportunities within a vibrant learning community lies at the very heart of this organization.

Of course, even though CHCA is a worker-owned cooperative, it is also a business that operates in a challenging industry. It has revenues of around $45 million, 2,300 employees and pays a minimum starting wage of $10 (with additional benefits of about $4). While not a requirement, about 70% of its staff have chosen to take up ownership in the cooperative, buying one share for $1,000, paid over several years. This has enabled them not only to participate in the management of their firm, but also to realize an average annual dividend of about $200.

CHCA has, since its inception in 1985, operated with a simple dictate: 80% of its revenue goes toward employee compensation, while the other 20% goes to overhead and other expenses. At CHCA, the slogan "'a quality job and quality care' encompasses everything the company believes,"[34] according to its President, Michael Elsas. We can gauge CHCA's value system by noting that all senior staff, including Elsas himself, make far less money than those in comparable positions elsewhere, earning no more than ten times the average salary at the company, nowhere near the obscene ratios often found in similarly sized companies.

CHCA treats home care workers with great respect and dignity, but at the same time maintains strenuous standards of discipline. Home care work is by nature independent; there is little support available to a worker while actually on the job, since the work involves going into someone else's home, dealing with the family, and caring for the patient independently with little contact with others. Hence, CHCA provides as much personal support as it can. For instance, CHCA is probably the only home care company that doesn't mail people's pay checks out, insisting that a key part of being a community-based company is that employees come in to pick up their pay stubs (even if they have direct deposit), in the process connecting with colleagues and staff. Meetings, workshops, and information sessions are routinely scheduled for those days when employees come into the office to pick up their checks.

As Elsas emphasizes, it is very challenging to run a company where people don't come together every day. He compares his role to that of a local factory manager:

> If they want to have a meeting up there, they shut the factory down, they ring a bell, and everybody goes into a cafeteria or somewhere, and they get to talk to all their workers for half an hour, an hour, whatever it is. I can never do that.[35]

He sees this as both frustrating and challenging but luckily – although he cannot have a community meeting of 2,300 people – somehow the message is getting through that CHCA is a good place to work. Indeed, some 70% of the workers who come to CHCA are referred by somebody who already works there, since it is regarded as a company that cares about its workers. Elsas points out that he is working with people "who spend ten or twenty hours with our mother and father, keeping them entertained, keeping their diapers clean, making sure they don't fall when they get up . . . How do we say that we [as a society] value that?"[36]

Perhaps this special care for employees has something to do with the cooperative form of enterprise in which workers have a real sense of ownership? After all, in line with the ethnic background of CHCA's workers, over 90% of the company is owned by minority women (Flanders, 2014).

While Elsas agrees that being a cooperative is important, he emphasizes that the emotional attachment has more to do with company practices than the structure itself. For example, he says it would be hard to see much of a difference in outcome between CHCA and other non-cooperatives who use the same practices or who treat their workers equally well. To him the cooperative form is merely a vehicle, albeit an effective one, to deliver on their mission. The crucial thing is that while the cooperative establishes principles of ownership, respect, dignity, and participation, it is only by putting these into practice that CHCA is able to achieve its mission. Elsas stresses that to CHCA workers, the sense of ownership is driven more by how the company treats them rather than by whether or not they actually sit on the board of directors or make decisions on company operations and strategy. He also sees a sense of family or belonging as emotionally very close to this sense of ownership.

As a worker-owned cooperative, everything revolves around what's best for the worker, rather than what will make the most money. It is democratically run, but more importantly, it is also a well-run business. While it has to make a profit, Elsas stresses it is not a "profit maximizing" company.[37] Yet interestingly, while an investment in CHCA isn't primarily about achieving a high return, he proudly points out that CHCA's return on the workers' investment has beaten the U.S. stock market by a factor of four over the past 30 years.

Learning with care

In contrast to the central role that culture, quality, and sustainability play in illy's learning milieu, CHCA's education programs have far different goals. They are targeted at low-income, largely Latina, women. About 600 people receive free home care training at CHCA's state-of-the-art facility every year. This produces individuals who know what they are doing and are able to provide excellent care to their patients. Indeed, CHCA trains its entry-level workers for 150 hours, twice the level that is required as a minimum by law (Rieder *et al.*, 2012). The training program results in a dual certification as a Certified Home Health Aide and Personal Care Assistant, and CHCA offers guaranteed full-time employment for all graduates. If they accept this offer, they are employed in an organization that clearly recognizes the importance and value of their work to the community. In addition to competitive wages, they also receive a guarantee of 35 hours of work every week, overtime premiums, career opportunities, and ongoing training and support, not to mention the benefits of worker-ownership such as dividends and participatory decision-making.

CHCA estimates that over 80% of the people who graduate from their training courses start jobs, most with CHCA. In hiring, and it only hires people it trains in-house, CHCA pays special attention to whether or not a prospective employee is a caring person. As Elsas puts it:

> Somebody [who] comes here with a PhD in psychotherapy is not going to impress us as much as a woman who is 27 years old who has spent the last four years taking care of her grandmother. That's going to impress us more – if she can talk about that and describe what that was like, what she liked about it, what she didn't like about it. That's probably who we are going to hire.[38]

One result of this kind of attention to the quality of the person is that CHCA's annual staff turnover rate, around 20 to 25%, is about one-third the industry average of over 60% (phinational.org, 2015). CHCA has a remarkably successful model in taking a workforce, most of whom have little formal education, and turning them into what Elsas calls "mini-entrepreneurs."[39] But it has also enabled individuals to provide much better care to their patients. In Elsas' view, no other group has stronger values than the primarily immigrant women who work for, and own, CHCA. He foresees that in the near future, home care workers will be required to take over more responsibilities, such as patient evaluation, which are now conducted by personnel with medical qualifications. This presents both a challenge – especially regarding training needs – and an opportunity. It means that the scope of practice can be expanded so home care workers can become more truly a part of a medical team, which is not the norm at present. It should also lead to further development opportunities for home care workers.

As a learning community, CHCA has not only committed itself to educating its workforce, it has also striven to be an innovator in its industry. The CHCA community is keen to embrace new technology. One example is smartphones that can monitor and record various elements of a patient's condition, such as skin pallor. Indicators like this could then go immediately to a nurse who might be monitoring a hundred patients from a station. It could decrease the amount of doctor's visits or even hospitalizations which, in turn, could, as Elsas points out, "have a dramatic effect on the cost of health care" (Ludden, 2012). It could also fundamentally change the perception and role of care workers in our society for the better.

Of course, the entrance of younger people into the workforce, particularly if pay for home care workers improves, may have major implications for CHCA. It will present new challenges, both in terms of training and supervision. The CHCA goal must be to create an environment where young people are energized and infused with a cooperative mind-set, where they know they will be given a chance to grow both professionally and personally. Job security is often not a significant concern since younger workers now expect to work with multiple organizations throughout their careers. However, they increasingly seek more meaningful and interesting work, and work environments where relationships, conversations, team-working, and social networking matter. Organizations which focus on the creation of real value and see themselves as learning communities will become increasingly attractive employers in the frequently invoked "war for talent."

Learning in a living network

Learning in CHCA is tightly bound to the organization's informal networks, thereby offering great sources of novelty and creativity. As Fritjof Capra suggested, the life of an organization and its ability to learn, create, and innovate, is tied to what he called "communities of practice" (Capra, 2002). The CHCA leadership is constantly trying to support and strengthen such informal networks. For instance, CHCA developed a "peer mentoring" system and trains its supervisors in coaching to discourage bossing and bullying. Managers in more traditional organizations who believe in controlling an organization through hierarchical structures often ignore the living network of their employees. But organizations are living systems rather than machines. You can control machines but not living systems, explains Capra (2002), as the latter can only be "disturbed." Thus, it is not strict rules and detailed instructions that will move them to a higher development level, but guiding principles and indicative directions, or "meaningful impulses," as Capra calls them. He puts it:

> There is no need to push, pull, or bully it to make it change. Force and energy are not the issue; the issue is meaning. Meaningful disturbance will get the organization's attention and will trigger structural changes. (Capra, 2002, p. 98)

As is clear from CHCA's evolution, a learning community, unlike a traditional bureaucratic organization, will harness the power of meaning through incorporating both a deeper overall purpose and an honest aspiration to help its members reach their personal growth goals. In learning communities, true leadership does not depend on some extraordinary individual to effect change; it is mainly bottom-up rather than top-down. A learning community can foster innovation through eliminating barriers, encouraging its members to interrogate assumptions, and generally acting to help its members achieve their full potential. It functions best on the assumption that people in general, and especially if they are given the chance, are motivated to work to make things better – and not just to make more money. People who have the feeling of contributing to the creation of real value for others while coming closer to reaching their own potential as part of a vivid learning community will not need any "motivation" from the outside. As they themselves find meaning in their work, they will naturally tend to advance the interests of the enterprise for which they work.

Learning to innovate

The world is undergoing a paradigm shift from an industrial age of tangible goods to an innovation age of intangible services and experiences. While the industrial enterprise has been wedded to rationality and control, the innovation enterprise puts far more emphasis on emotions, feelings, empathy, and cooperation. Fostering meaning, delivering experiences, and nurturing identity replace the dominant role that selling physical goods played in the industrial economy. As we discussed earlier in this book, meaning and identity can primarily be found in knowing and using one's own strengths and potential in a way that transcends the self, entering into relationships that are mutually beneficial. In the innovation age, successful enterprises will concentrate on their core competence while networking with others who possess different competences, depending on the needs of any particular project. So, the emphasis is placed on collaborative processes, shared resources, teamwork, relationships, knowledge-sharing, and establishing and nurturing communities of practice and value networks.

In their book *Innovation – The Missing Dimension*, Richard Lester and Michael Piore identify two fundamental processes that lie at the heart of innovation. One process, called *analysis*, which currently dominates decision-making, treats innovations as the equivalent of problems that need to be solved. The other process, called *interpretation*, is more about orchestrated conversations that best emerge from a community that conceives and discusses (Lester and Piore, 2004). Relying on analysis alone based on rational thinking risks choking off vital interpretative spaces required for real innovation. This does not mean that a thorough analysis is unnecessary in learning communities. Far from it! Investigative minds are of utmost importance for understanding the different ramifications of complex problems. But analysis alone is not sufficient for innovation; rather, a balance between the analytical and interpretive processes, together with the courage to embark on new, unbeaten tracks, is required. This is a task a learning community is ideally suited to do and which our examples, illy and CHCA, exemplify so well.

Illy uses a unique blend of science and the arts to create high-quality experiences for coffee lovers, while at the same time improving the living conditions of the coffee growers. CHCA combines professional training and development methods with the determination to create an encouraging and respectful working environment, thus enhancing the lives of both the home care workers and their clients. In both cases, cooperation and real value creation for multiple stakeholders are at the core of the mission. The leaders of these enterprises understand that real value is created together in a joint effort rather than at the expense of others.

Barry Sugarman of the Society for Organizational Learning makes a clear distinction between the "old" bureaucratic model of an organization and a new innovation and learning-oriented model (Sugarman, 2000). He sees the bureaucratic model as working on a basic formula that defines how to run everything in the organization; its role is to transform inputs into outputs. Strategy is formulaic, hierarchy is highly structured, and there is a clear chain of command. Most learning communities are different. Of course, as in all forms of human cooperation, they do have leaders, but these leaders know that their task is to work for the organization, not the other way around. A learning community tends to have flat structures and its members communicate laterally through networks inside and outside of the organization. Change is a constant, and no assumptions, practices, or ideas are sacrosanct; anything can be questioned. The impetus for improvement is a central driver of all activities. In such an environment, networking and cooperation are crucial, as a common purpose is the glue that binds the enterprise together.

According to Sugarman, the differences don't stop there.[40] The bureaucratic model privileges the specialist, whose knowledge is narrowly disciplinary and deep; a learning community, on the other hand, cultivates members who are versatile and possess interdisciplinary and even idiosyncratic skills, sometimes in fields that are not obviously related. The boundaries inherent in the bureaucratic model disappear in a learning community, while the objectivity and dispassion of the bureaucratic model give way to the exuberance and passion found in learning communities, where roles are flexible, and in a sense, work becomes play. Systems are more formalized in the bureaucratic model, while a learning community deliberately encourages more informal communication and coordination channels. And finally, the two types of organizations are driven by very different goals. While maximizing profits and shareholder value play an overarching role in the old-style bureaucratic model, following a common purpose of creating real value lies at the center of what innovative, learning communities are about.

A new type of organization also needs a new breed of manager. As Henry Mintzberg (2004) shows, three elements must feature centrally in management education, namely *science* (or analysis), *craft* (or experience), and *art* (or imagination). To enable learning communities to thrive, it is not enough to teach science. Giving management students the chance to experience and use their imagination is at least of equal importance. They must be capable of integrating different perspectives in cross-cultural and multidisciplinary teams, and learn to think and act holistically to be able to build and lead sustainable organizations that are oriented toward the creation of real value.

Learning is best accomplished in informal networks where people literally learn from each other in a collaborative manner. In the illy and CHCA stories, for example, peer-to-peer learning is especially important, as these companies realize learning is essentially a team effort rather than an individual experience. It's a philosophy that mirrors the description of the best possible adult education by the American education pioneer Eduard C. Lindeman:

> A cooperative venture in non-authoritarian, informal learning, the chief purpose of which is to discover the meaning of experience; a quest of the mind which digs down to the roots of the preconceptions which formulate our conduct; a technique of learning for adults which makes education coterminous with life and hence elevates living itself to the level of the adventurous experiment. (Lindeman, 1926, p. 546)

Dynamic, interdisciplinary work teams, holistic mindsets, and an ability to deal with ambiguity and rapid change are necessary skills for the innovation age. Such skills help learning communities to develop appropriate and productive responses to a global environment which promises only more instability and change. A learning community helps both individual members and their organizations answer questions such as: "how do I know I am doing the right thing?" or "how do I improve my work practice to achieve a desired result?" (Boyle and Bradley, 2005, p. 15). To be effective, the common learning experience must be characterized by a sense of purpose and excitement, and develop in people a strong mission or vocation that they find to be motivating. It is only when people and their organizations firmly believe they can change the world for the better, and that they can create real value for themselves and others, that they will be willing and able to do so.

Learning from stories

Everything in the world is connected to everything else, and this is especially true of the globalized economy. If executives of the future want to develop sustainable innovative enterprises, they will need to understand and recognize patterns and relationships between phenomena while thinking in multidimensional terms. They will need to adapt to the complex social, economic, and ecological systems of our times, and collaborate with others to bring about positive change within them (Gladwin and Berdish, 2010). Learning for innovation should therefore combine traditional efficiency principles – helping people identify how to create value through harnessing in the most productive manner financial, human, social, cultural, technological, and natural resources – and an ethic of relationship-orientation, cooperation, and joint real value creation.

Since both illy and CHCA exemplify cooperation and real value creation themselves, it's no surprise that both Andrea Illy and Michael Elsas often make use of an ancient tool of leaders and teachers alike, storytelling, to help promote learning within their organizations. For Illy, it means following in his father Ernesto's footsteps, who, according to his son always "used beautiful metaphors that gave concreteness to his concepts" (Illy, 2015, pp. 38-39). Like other leaders who understand how the experience economy works, Andrea Illy fully understands the real value that stories can create, recognizing that "storytelling, or the 'narration' of what a dish or particular food contain, can enhance our gustatory perception up to 50 percent, compared to our reaction when this information isn't provided" (Illy, 2015, p. 76).

"Great stories create a rich visual imagery in people's minds," writes Douglas Ready in *MIT Sloan Management Review* (2002), "and great storytellers invite us to walk the landscape created by this imagery." He points out the role of storytelling not only for positioning the company in the customers' minds, but also for strengthening the character of the organization. Above all, stories create identity and convey meaning, and are therefore invaluable for generating the deeper, more emotional side of real value.

Learning communities are highly dependent on leaders who themselves are open to learn and develop. It therefore seems appropriate to conclude by letting Andrea Illy describe the story about his own learning experiences during the recent global financial crisis.

It was already a very difficult time for the whole family, as Ernesto Illy passed away at the beginning of 2008 while macro-environmental conditions were growing steadily worse for the firm. "We had at least three crises in one," recalls Andrea Illy. "The economic crisis that considerably affected the home market Italy, the highest coffee prices on the commodity market in history, and big corporations that attacked the coffee sector like crazy." The situation was aggravated by internal problems as several senior managers were unexpectedly forced to retire following the introduction of a new Italian retirement law. Navigating stormy waters with an inexperienced management team, the company began to lose a lot of money. Illy describes that he felt "like an old, wet cat" at the time:

> You know, cats hate it to be wet! I was very disappointed and also felt guilty, as I did not manage to live up to my own perceptions of responsibility. I felt incompetent and thought that I had failed. After seventeen flourishing years without greater mistakes it was a shock! (Lewitan, 2013)

He even thought about withdrawing from the firm, but eventually managed to see the situation from a new angle, as a learning and growth opportunity for both himself and the organization. He decided to basically rebuild the company, investing in the development of new products, changing organizational structures and management systems, creating new advertising campaigns, and upgrading the whole IT infrastructure, to name just a few of the initiatives started during this watershed period.

The company emerged from the crisis stronger than ever, as its leader understood that real, transformational learning is often not the outcome of our achievements, but our failures:

> Yes, you cannot do anything, neither work nor speak nor love, without making mistakes. You cannot learn to walk without falling. I thank God that I made this mistake, because I will not make it a second time. I can face even bigger challenges in the future, because I understand them and I can analyze them. (Lewitan, 2013)

In brief: learning community

- Real value is created by enterprises that are learning communities. In a learning community, people explore and reflect together, and care for the personal growth of the individual as much as for enhancing the knowledge base and innovativeness of the organization.

- There is a strong link between a deeper purpose and learning. On the one hand, enterprises must never stop learning and developing to be able to fulfill their purpose. On the other hand, a deeper purpose ignites the wish to find better ways of using and combining resources to reach a common goal.

- Innovation occurs when people share ideas. Trustful partnerships within and across the boundaries of an organization, a cooperative attitude, and openness to conversation and discourse are therefore key cornerstones for developing innovative learning communities.

- Thriving learning communities can only be created by leaders who understand that, first of all, they need to be avid learners themselves. These leaders must recognize the complexity that is inherent in our world, and deal with it in a holistic way that includes analysis as well as interpretation, and imagination as well as collaboration with others.

- Nurturing a learning milieu composed of a potent combination of a distinct values-led pioneering spirit and dynamic open culture helps to re-connect people to "who they are" and "what they are here for."

7

Leadership responsibility: individuals who make a difference

"In dreams begin responsibilities."
William Butler Yeats (1916)[41]

It is time that we should wake from slumber and face our responsibilities!
Albert Schweitzer (1998, p. 127)

It all began with one man who decided to dig deeper – literally. In the late 1970s, Ibrahim Abouleish recruited a team of experts to dig a well on a plot of wasteland that he had bought in the Egyptian desert 40 miles north-east of Cairo. The well, dug only with hands and spades, was the first of five wells, all over 300 feet deep, that now irrigate that barren stretch of land. It was the beginning of an astonishing transformation of almost 1,700 acres of desert land into a fertile farm and garden. Alone on his tractor, Abouleish started building roads. He arranged the digging of canals, organized the energy supply, and planted tens of thousands of shade-giving trees, "which can inspire people to inner uprightness," as he once remarked (2005, p. 80).[42]

Today, this once inhospitable land is the heart of the SEKEM initiative for sustainable development. SEKEM includes an internationally successful group of companies in the organic food, textile, and medicine industries with around 1,200 employees and hundreds of associated partner farmers. But SEKEM is much more than just an agro-industrial group of companies. Through the widespread social activities of the SEKEM Development Foundation, it has grown into a thriving community that encompasses its own medical center, kindergarten, schools, vocational training center, research center, university, and a variety of cultural and arts initiatives, which create real value for both SEKEM employees and thousands of people who live in the nearby villages.

SEKEM, named after the ancient Egyptian word for the "vitality of the sun," was established by a man who believed that human beings have the responsibility to "help each other develop" (Abouleish, 2009a, p. 13). He did not see this as an abstract imperative, but as a concrete responsibility set squarely on his own shoulders. He has since worked steadily on fulfilling the purpose that he envisioned for his unique initiative – fostering the development of individuals, society, and the environment through a holistic concept that includes interconnected economic, ecological, cultural, and societal initiatives. In 2003, Abouleish and SEKEM won the highly prestigious Right Livelihood Award, better known as the Alternative Nobel Prize, "for a 21st century business model which combines commercial success with social and cultural development"

(The Right Livelihood Award, 2013). It was just one of the many international awards that Abouleish has received for his singular work of simultaneously creating economic value (jobs, sources of income for the local population, and sustainably profitable enterprises), social value (healthy food, healthcare, education, and meaning), cultural value (artistic expression and beauty) and environmental value (sustainable agriculture and the reclamation of fertile land from the desert).

It takes leaders such as Ibrahim Abouleish to build organizations that create real value. It takes people who deliberately decide that it is *their* job to make a difference and improve the quality of life of others; people who see it as their personal responsibility to change things for the better. Such leaders assume responsibility in its original sense. The roots of the English word "responsible" and its French equivalent *responsable* lie in the Latin verb *respondere*, meaning "to answer." Responsible leaders find answers – answers to questions that they pose to themselves, such as "Why am I here in this world?", "What is my role on this planet?", or "How do I find meaning in my life?", but also to a broader, universal question that human society asks each of its members: "How do *you*, as a human being, contribute to our common good?"

Of course, we must not forget that this is not a book about philanthropy, but about businesses, and about people who want to run businesses in a profitable way. Yet it is about business *people* who recognize that they are first and foremost *people,* and that being human – even in the business world – means much more than just narrow-mindedly focusing on accumulating money. Responsible leaders focus on real value creation instead – on the development of a higher quality of life for customers, employees, and partners as well as for themselves, working to advance their societies and renew the health of the environment. They achieve financial gains through their value creation efforts, but are rewarded even more with a feeling of having contributed to an important cause, with living a meaningful life. Meaning is also what these leaders have to offer to their followers, whether in their role as employees, customers, or supporters. What their followers get is deeper value in the form of emotional benefits that they reap from the feeling of contributing to a cause that improves the lives of others. Responsible leaders instill meaning through giving people a higher purpose.

In this chapter, we will take a closer look at how Ibrahim Abouleish has contributed to a better life for thousands of people working in and around the green oasis that he has created in the Egyptian desert, and at two other examples of responsible leaders, Johannes Gutmann and Helianti Hilman, who were courageous enough to make a big decision in their lives – the decision to leave the well-trodden path of conventional business wisdom and devote all their energy to creating real value.

The man who turned the desert into a garden

Ibrahim Abouleish left his native Egypt at the age of 19. In a farewell letter to his father, he promised that when he returned to his home village, he would build factories and workshops, a theater, a hospital, a kindergarten, and schools (Abouleish, 2005, p. 33) – a fantastic and seemingly unrealistic plan for an Egyptian teenager. After finishing his studies in technical chemistry, medicine, and pharmacology in Graz, he embarked on a promising career as a pharmaceutical research manager in Austria. At the age of 38, Abouleish – by then also an Austrian citizen – returned to Egypt for a visit. He was as fascinated by the brilliance of ancient Egyptian art as he was shocked by the desperate social, economic, and environmental state of the country. He was especially bothered by the poverty and widespread illiteracy, as well as the excessive use of artificial fertilizers and pesticides in agriculture. Unlike others, who lamented the situation but did nothing, Abouleish decided to take responsibility and act.

In a bold move, he quit his highly regarded and well-paid job as the Head of Research in a European pharmaceutical company and convinced his family to return with him to Egypt to farm the desert. "I told our children the story of a man who decided to move to the desert with his children and who created a big garden there," he recalled (Abouleish, 2005, p. 64). He promised his 16-year-old son that he would be allowed to ride a motorbike in the desert and his 14-year-old daughter that she could spend as much time as she wanted with the horses that she loved so much. Thus, like every good leader, he gave each of them a good personal reason why they should leave the beaten track and discover a new territory.

In his unusual endeavor, Abouleish was guided by a vision: he saw himself standing beside a well in the desert, planting and watering flowers, herbs, and trees, with the land turning green and fertile, attracting animals and people alike as "a reflection of paradise on earth," as he calls it (SEKEM, 2015a). Shortly before returning to Egypt he wrote in a letter to a friend that he hoped "that the souls of Egyptian people can be revitalized by a garden in the desert" (Abouleish, 2005, p. 65). Since his early childhood, he had been fascinated by gardens, especially his aunt Aziza's. Her garden was full of blossoming flowers and fruit-bearing trees, and there was also a well. One day, however, young Ibrahim was a bit too curious, and tumbled into the well. Fortunately, he was rescued. This episode taught the young boy a lesson: There were also dangers in this world (Abouleish, 2005, p. 20).

And there were dangers and obstacles aplenty on the rocky road to realizing his vision. First, he could not find local partners for his project as everyone feared the project would be snuffed out by a suffocating Egyptian bureaucracy. When he bought the desert land from the Egyptian state, a Bedouin tribe moved there and claimed it as its own possession. They even threatened to kill Abouleish. He courageously answered their threat by staying alone in the desert the following night – showing them his will to persist – and subsequently found a way to include the Bedouins in his endeavor. But more complications followed. The Egyptian Ministry for Agriculture wanted to close the farm when they heard that biodynamic farming, the organic farming method that was used at SEKEM, involved the breeding of bacteria in compost. They feared that these bacteria could cause health problems across the country. Another time, Abouleish was even confronted with bulldozers and soldiers with machine guns. A general of the Egyptian army had decided to turn the SEKEM land into a military zone because of its good water-supply facilities. As in the other cases, Abouleish did not give way under the pressure and was finally able to solve the issue by gaining access to the highest levels of the Egyptian government.

The greatest threats to SEKEM were still to come, however, and Abouleish had to pay his personal dues. Owing to his relentless efforts, he suffered two heart attacks before the age of 50. And he continued to struggle with outside enemies. Exactly at the time when the chemical industry heavily opposed SEKEM's countrywide initiative to replace synthetic pesticides with organic pest control, a local newspaper ran a story about "the sun-worshippers." It included a photograph showing SEKEM employees standing in a big circle – their weekly assembly ritual that was meant to be a sign of social equality, a way of making people feel part of the community, and an impetus to taking more responsibility for each other (Abouleish, 2005, p. 206). The newspaper article, however, accused SEKEM of worshipping the sun, one of the worst accusations that Muslims could face. Prayer leaders in mosques denounced SEKEM, and there was a realistic fear that public opinion would massively turn against the project. As in prior instances, Abouleish had the courage to directly face the challenge. He invited influential officials and religious leaders to the SEKEM farm and explained everything that was done there with verses from the Koran, thus convincing his visitors that his initiative was fully grounded in an Islamic spirit.

Despite the multiple challenges that he was facing, Abouleish tenaciously followed his vision. He set up the biodynamic farm in the new oasis with the help of European experts and local farmers. He managed to close a contract with an American customer who wanted to buy lace-flower extract. The medicinal flower was planted on the farm and processed in a laboratory that he also set up on the premises. Finally, his efforts began to pay off commercially. Abouleish started to produce medicinal herb teas on the farm, followed by other tea varieties and organic agricultural produce. With the help of partners from all over the world, SEKEM set up distribution structures in Europe, the USA, and Japan, selling medicinal herbs, organic food, and cotton clothes, mainly through wholesalers and retailers that specialized in ecological products. Total quality management and certification initiatives allowed the company to compete in international markets. Today, SEKEM organizes its business operations within a holding structure with several business units: The iSiS Organic subsidiary produces a wide assortment of organic food, Lotus organic herbs and spices; Atos Pharma and SEKEM Healthcare produce natural pharmaceutical and health care products; and NatureTex specializes in organic textiles. As a clear leader in the Egyptian organic market and a successful exporter to Europe and North America, SEKEM has become a star in the organic food world – a star that built its foundations on a very deep well that was once dug in the desert.

Cultivating a larger garden

"All that is very well, but let us cultivate our garden," are the famous last words in Voltaire's novella *Candide, ou l'optimisme* (1918). Responsible leaders distinguish themselves by how they define the boundaries of their gardens. For Abouleish, his own garden does not end at the rows of trees that surround the SEKEM farm. His efforts to create real value reach far beyond.

The growth and profitability of the SEKEM businesses enabled Abouleish to unfold other plans for creating real value and improving the quality of life of people in the region. He set up a medical center, which is used by more than 40,000 people per year. Every morning, a school class is brought to the medical center in an effort to regularly examine and treat the children living in the villages around the farm. Comprehensive education was another pillar of the SEKEM concept. A kindergarten, schools (including a special school for handicapped children), a center for adult education, a vocational training center, and an academy that was later upgraded into a private university were established.

Abouleish strived to create a holistic initiative for the advancement of human development, in which educational, cultural, and spiritual impulses were at least as important as business. Therefore, the arts also play an important role at SEKEM. It offers painting courses for its employees and has its own drama group, orchestra, and choir. Musical, eurythmy (an expressive movement art in the anthroposophical tradition), and theater performances are regularly scheduled in the amphitheater that was built on the premises. "Through our artistic deeds a beautiful garden is created," says Abouleish (2005, p. 194).

Business, societal engagement, the arts – none of these pillars of SEKEM works without the others. Education is the cornerstone of business success, which again enables cultural and social advancement in the community. The creative and scientific activities, in turn, are a main source of vitality for the whole SEKEM ecosystem.

"I developed a vision of a holistic project able to bring about cultural renewal," said Abouleish. "But I would need to create concrete institutions for all this so that the project did not remain solely an ideal" (2005, p. 63). Thus he set up several institutions to provide services to the community. The Cooperative of SEKEM Employees, amongst other tasks, tries to improve the living conditions of employees and their families, for example, regarding hygiene, sanitary standards, and water supply. A social fund supports employees financially at special times in their lives, such as marriage, birth, or death. The SEKEM Development Foundation focuses on education, health care, social development, the arts, and science. Through its work, the 13 villages around SEKEM profit from the development of infrastructure, medical services, and various cultural and educational offerings. The foundation also grants microcredits to small enterprises in the region (SEKEM, 2014).

But the impact of Abouleish's work reaches far beyond the immediate surroundings of the SEKEM farm. SEKEM also devised an efficient organic method of protecting cotton plants and convinced the Egyptian ministry of agriculture to apply the method on a wider scale. Eventually, based on SEKEM's initiative and supported with training and support activities by the Egyptian Biodynamic Association (another institutional offspring of SEKEM), hundreds of farmers across the country have started to use the organic method for controlling plant pests. With the help of the new method, they increased crop yields by nearly 30%, and helped to curb the use of synthetic pesticides in Egypt by more than 90% from over 35,000 to around 3,000 tons per year (ebdaegypt.com, 2015).

Keeping the balance

In the biodynamic method practiced at SEKEM and its associated farms, plants get their nutrients and energy from the local
ecosystem – especially through the use of compost – rather than from
the addition of synthetic fertilizers from outside. Every functioning
ecosystem needs to maintain a dynamic balance. That means that
no single type of organism or substance becomes so prevalent that it
disrupts the energy and nutrient supply cycles for other parts of the
ecosystem. An imbalance that allows an excess of one element to the
detriment of the others is the main enemy of the system's viability.
Responsible leaders well understand this general law of nature.

Abouleish strives to find the right balance between individuality
and unity, between valuing each individual person and understanding the need for close cooperation to create something of value
together (Abouleish, 2009a, p. 7). There are even two festivals
devoted to each of these poles at SEKEM: in spring, the community
celebrates individuality and in autumn their joint work, as they
commemorate the foundation of the organization. In addition to
finding the right mix between self-assertion and integration,
SEKEM also tries to find the right balance between expansion and
conservation, competition and cooperation, quantity and quality,
and sovereignty and partnership (SEKEM, 2015b).

Maybe the emphasis on balance also stems from Abouleish's own
experience of being immersed in two cultures at the same time. He
has always felt a strong connection to his Islamic faith, in which
balance is also an important value. Since his adolescence, medita-
tion and prayer have played a central role in his life, and the verses
of the Koran have provided him with a constant source of inner
energy. But more interestingly, he has also been strongly exposed to
different religious and cultural traditions. As a child, he grew up in
a Jewish quarter, and had many friends from different religious

backgrounds. During his two decades in Austria, he discovered his love for classical music as well as for the works of the great European philosophers and poets. He was especially fascinated by Goethe and by anthroposophy, a spiritual philosophy originated by Rudolf Steiner. "My inspiration came out of very different cultures: a synthesis between the Islamic world and European spirituality," writes Abouleish in his autobiography, "I moved around freely in these different areas as if in a great garden, picking the fruits of the different trees" (2005, p. 218).

One effect of this emphasis on balance and synthesis is that religious differences are not only respected, but also highly valued at SEKEM. Both a mosque and a Coptic chapel were built on the premises, and Ibrahim Abouleish likes to tell the story of the Coptic children who clean the mosque on Fridays and the Muslim children who decorate the chapel with flowers on Sundays (2005, p. 180).

In addition to the spiritual value of religion, Abouleish also strongly emphasizes our connection to nature and our role as part of a greater whole. He once said he could imagine a new epoch in which "every human being would see himself or herself as part of the world as such and every human being would be deeply connected to the health of nature and take greater care of natural resources" (Karner, 2010, p. 3).

It is those basic human values, having a deep respect for the diversity of cultures, being aware of our responsibility for nature and our fellow human beings, and striving for balance in what we do rather than living a life of excess, which lay the basis for an approach to business that is fully oriented toward the creation of real value.

Responsible leadership as the key to creating real value

Ibrahim Abouleish has planted a blossoming tree full of real value. The organizations that Abouleish built in and around the SEKEM initiative ensure the livelihood of hundreds of farmers and offer high-quality jobs for the local population. They improve the quality of lives of people in a holistic sense, including providing a source of income, better infrastructure, improved hygiene and sanitary conditions, comprehensive education, healthcare, and diverse cultural offerings. SEKEM's organic food, textile, and medicinal products contribute to the health and wellbeing of hundreds of thousands of customers. The environment profits from the sea change from a synthetic fertilizer- and pesticides-addicted form of agriculture to biodynamic farming that builds quality soil instead of destroying it. Contributing to all of these positive effects on individual human beings, society and the environment provides meaning for owners, employees, customers and partners alike, while also being financially profitable. As a powerful contributor to the concept of life improvement, SEKEM exemplifies the creation of *real value*.

No wonder then that Abouleish strikes all the deep roots that we highlight in this book: the main purpose of his enterprise is not making money, but *improving the quality of life*, or, in his own words, "the development of humans in a comprehensive sense" (2005, p. 65). He deliberately decided to take on *leadership responsibility* to turn his vision of a better life for the local population into reality. A *long-term orientation* has been essential in the endeavor to transform the desert into fertile farmland with the help of cow dung and compost. Abouleish knows "the solution to our problems takes a lot of cooperation and time" (Abouleish, 2009a, p. 8). He has taken one step after another – with constant commitment and perseverance – but always with his long-term vision in mind. *Limits recognition* lies at the core of the balance-based values concept that is the heart of the SEKEM culture. And SEKEM is most certainly strongly related to a place, being *locally rooted* in the oasis that Abouleish envisioned and created by digging a well with his own hands in the desert.

Abouleish is also convinced that strong ties, the *lasting relation-ships* that bind people in the economic value chain together, are far more desirable than anonymous trading in which no one really cares for the living and working conditions of others (Abouleish, 2005, p. 124). He prefers full transparency in the value chain, with everyone knowing and agreeing on prices and quality while caring about the conditions under which the goods and services are produced. Even when the market prices go down, farmers can be sure that they will still get the pre-agreed prices from SEKEM. Personal relationships are of utmost importance in this context, particularly with outside partners such as the farmers, who are invited to a personal meeting once per month. The term "economy of love" became a guiding principle for SEKEM. "We consciously want our agricultural business to be based on the principles of love," says Abouleish, "that is, a responsibility towards the earth, the plants and animals and to create trust among people" (Abouleish, 2005, p. 134).

Above all, Abouleish built a remarkable *learning community*. "We strive to learn to work and work to learn," says Abouleish, who sees SEKEM as a "living organization" that is developing in a "never-ending process" (Abouleish, 2005, p. 213). From the beginning, the provision of educational and developmental opportunities has been central to the SEKEM initiative. On every level, from kindergarten to university, Abouleish and his team follow a holistic approach to education as they relentlessly try to integrate artistic and practical work with theoretical learning (Abouleish, 2005, p. 175). "Children should be educated in a way that they do not only absorb things intellectually with their head, but also with their hearts, through artistic exercises," says Abouleish. "They should also be practically active and grasp everything with their hands to also experience everything they hear theoretically" (Abouleish, 2008, p. 10). This is not only true for the children in SEKEM's schools, but also for SEKEM's employees who spend up to 15% of their working time in training and education activities, ranging from the opportunity to learn basic skills such as reading and writing to immersing themselves in artistic activities such as painting, singing, or eurhythmy, in addition to job-related training. SEKEM also provides training and support so that its associated farmers can transfer know-how in the efficient implementation of biodynamic farming (Schrot and Korn, 2004). "Our secret is that we do not put our profits into swimming pools or cast them in concrete in any other way, but fully put them into education," says Abouleish (2009b, p. 56).

Actually, the founder of SEKEM has always himself been an avid learner. During his university days, he went over the lectures of his professors again and again, trying to find out more about their thought processes, constantly asking questions to himself when he did not yet fully make sense of a certain topic. He never memorized like his classmates; instead, he wanted to understand (Abouleish, 2005, p. 42). He also strongly believes that people can change by following concrete examples. Thus, time and time again he personally did exactly the things he wanted others to do – whether it was raking paths, painting walls or treating other people with the greatest respect. He was also sure that people learn from mistakes. In one instance, during the early days of SEKEM, a worker broke the pump for the well. Instead of reprimanding him, Abouleish asked questions – questions about what went wrong and how it could be avoided next time. "As a pedagogue, I was always trying to encourage people to think about what they were doing," he says. "So that they could correct themselves and not ascribe everything to Allah's will" (Abouleish, 2005, p. 79). Real value creation needs a vision to support others in their development, but also the courage to constantly develop oneself.

Ibrahim Abouleish vividly illustrates how responsible leaders mirror the roots of real value creation in their own personality and leadership style. He is a leader who puts the improvement of the quality of life of others ahead of his personal career, takes a long-term view, feels rooted in his homeland despite the decades he spent abroad, builds lasting relationships with his partners, recognizes limits by emphasizing the value of balance, and is always open and eager to learn. This is the kind of leadership that is required for the creation of real value.

A global community of gardeners

Reports on accounting fraud, irresponsible business practices and selfish, greedy managers have steadily eroded trust in business leaders. In three-quarters of the countries surveyed in a global study on trust, CEOs were no longer considered a credible source of information about their own company (Edelman Trust Barometer, 2015). The survey also revealed that business leaders are less trusted than almost any other profession (including financial analysts). That comes close to a declaration of bankruptcy for a societal function that is actually dependent on trust. After all, how can you be an effective leader if no one trusts you in your leadership role?

A team of leadership scholars made an interesting observation. In a study that was conducted in 17 different countries, they found that managers who deliberately considered different stakeholder interests when making decisions (rather than just thinking in terms of maximizing profits for shareholders) were perceived by their subordinates as more visionary leaders. What's more, the subordinates were actually willing to put in extra efforts for such visionary leaders, which, in turn, led to higher performance for their organizations (Sully de Luque *et al.*, 2008). That is quite a remarkable empirical result! Leaders who put the interest of others – or *real value creation* – ahead of pure monetary interests achieve better business results because employees feel more engaged when working for them. Leaders are perceived to be more inspirational and more credible if they show responsibility for others. The study's authors conclude that "[p]rescribing profit maximization as the ultimate controlling rule for less-than-omniscient executives to use in their decision making may not be the best way to improve the value of the firm" (p. 646). Nor, for that matter, would it improve the real value that a firm creates.

Entrepreneurs and managers who put real value creation before profit maximization can be found across continents. In addition to the African example of Ibrahim Abouleish, we will present the approaches of two more leaders from Europe and Asia, demonstrating that responsible leadership knows neither national nor cultural boundaries. We did find a remarkable cluster of responsible leaders in the organic food sector, however. Maybe it is because of their close connection to nature and its cycles and balanced processes? Maybe it is their deep understanding of ecosystems, in which one species cannot exist without the others that makes the difference? Maybe they know better than others that you can only reap fruit over time when you take care of the whole garden? Or maybe it is just a coincidence. Whatever the deeper reason, for some leaders there seems to be a strong connection between the healthy and life-sustaining food that their companies produce and a leadership approach that is oriented toward increasing the quality of life of their employees, customers, and partners.

The "herbs-man in red lederhosen"

Take, for example, Johannes Gutmann, also known as the "herbs-man in red lederhosen" due to the rather unusual standard outfit that he inherited from his grandfather. Gutmann set up an international organic food business in a very small and quiet Austrian village.

Like Abouleish, he uses a widely known symbol of nature, the sun, to brand his company Sonnentor (English translation, "Gate of the Sun"). He founded the company after he was fired by his former employer, who had not even given him the opportunity to try out his innovative ideas to improve the business. "It was the most important learning for me never to act like this as a boss," he says (Reisinger and Brandstätter, 2013).

Gutmann soon convinced three farmers to produce herbs for him: "Their crisis was that they did not have a market, and my crisis was that I did not have work," he recalls.[43] "But minus multiplied by minus equals plus, and so we took the chance to grow in cooperation." Initially selling his products in local farmers' markets, Gutmann soon expanded his business to meet ever-increasing consumer demand, first to domestic organic food stores, later to more than 50 countries around the world. He also set up a thriving chain of Sonnentor stores (some of them via a franchise system) and expanded his product lines from herbs and spices to a broad range of organic food, cosmetics, and related products.

Gutmann sees the creation of jobs in the region rather than making money as his primary entrepreneurial goal. This not only comprises the 350 direct Sonnentor employees in Austria and the neighboring Czech Republic, but also the opportunity for hundreds of farmers to earn their livelihood through supplying his company. "It's about a good life," says Gutmann, "about well-paid quality work, about enabling people to find work near their homes, and about keeping the region alive."

If nothing else, Gutmann's business practices are somewhat unconventional. While others follow planned market rollout strategies and set specific financial goals for their businesses, he just follows opportunities and aims to develop his business "organically" in line with the development of the market. While others use formal market research, he prefers to rely on what customers directly tell him about his products. While others cut costs in the supply chain, he offers his suppliers the highest prices, often at double the market price. While others try to minimize stock levels with a just-in-time approach, he maintains a huge warehouse and buys herbs and spices whenever the right qualities and quantities are available on the market. While others try to get their product listed in the large supermarket chains, he says "no" to any such request from the big retailers, preferring to sell his products in small, specialized organic stores and Sonnentor's own outlets. While others automate their operations wherever they can, Gutmann tries to avoid machines as much as possible. Millions of Sonnentor products are made and packaged by hand every year, creating a lot of additional jobs. Conventional business school wisdom would tell us that such an approach cannot work. Gutmann proves that it can. The company has been very successful financially, with 2014 revenues of over €40 million and sustained growth rates of 10 to 20% per year over more than two decades (wirtschaftsblatt.at, 2015).

Being oriented toward opportunities rather than plans enables Gutmann to sense and capitalize on these opportunities quickly. Listening to customers instead of conducting elaborate market research studies saves time and money and allows him to really understand what his customers need. Offering farmers higher prices creates committed suppliers who are willing to deliver raw materials of the highest possible quality. With his "live and let live" philosophy, Gutmann established mutually beneficial long-term partnerships with the farmers (Sternad, 2015). Besides, treating farmers fairly is also a great sales argument for customers. Including the farmers in additional processing steps such as drying and packaging increases their share of the total value added and decreases

Sonnentor's non-wage labor costs. The huge warehouse reduces the threat of an out-of-stock situation and ensures independence of price fluctuations in the market. Using manual labor instead of machines is another selling point ("hand-made") and allows the entrepreneur to reach his goal of creating more jobs locally. So even if some of Gutmann's decisions may seem unorthodox from a traditional business perspective, they make perfect sense when we look at them through the lens of real value creation.

"We did not grow because I was greedy," says Gutmann. "We grew because I saw possibilities – possibilities to cooperate, and not possibilities of profit maximization." Everything that the company earns is reinvested into the business. There are generally no bonuses for managers in his company, and the spread between the highest- and lowest-paid employees is less than four to one. That includes Gutmann himself, who never pays out dividends and lives off a monthly salary of €2,500 that the company pays for his services as the Managing Director. Gutmann once swore to himself he would never sell his business to anyone just to make money. For him, business is about creating real value for people, not about creating financial wealth for the owner.

Gutmann also shuns all types of pressure situations. For example, he does not like to work with customers who put pressure on him. Neither does he want to put pressure on any of his partners, suppliers, or employees. "In my former role as an employee, I always wanted two things that I never got: appreciation and the right to decide on my own tempo. As a boss, I do not want to impose on others what I do not want for myself," he says in his own interpretation of the Golden Rule. Treating employees with respect and care as human beings is of utmost importance to Gutmann. Everyone working at Sonnentor gets a free, healthy lunch prepared from local organic food every day. Fresh fruits are always available. Sonnentor also established an on-site kindergarten and provides its employees with extensive training and self-development opportunities. Gutmann, who knows and addresses all his employees by their first name, constantly emphasizes the value of fairness and appreciation. "Mistakes may happen. There is no 'bad boss' who runs around yelling at his employees when something does not work optimally," he says (Wirl, 2011). Of course, he then also expects that they will make the necessary corrections. Actually, he sees the approach of trying out new things and correcting them if they do not work as a major competitive advantage: "Many others do not correct. We make corrections on an ongoing basis."

As a result, Sonnentor has extremely low employee turnover and a highly engaged workforce; it receives dozens of unsolicited applications every week. It is an attractive employer, not for high salaries, but for being a place where people have meaningful work and are treated with respect as human beings. Thus, Sonnentor creates real value for its employees. It also does so for farmers and their families, for whom the company has created more than 600 meaningful jobs, many of them for the older generation. "The grandmothers had time, and they were really happy about the fact that they could now do the packaging," explains Gutmann (Reisinger and Brandstätter, 2013). At the same time, Sonnentor also creates deeper, emotional value for its customers. On the one hand, customers know that they support a sustainable business which also cares for their farmers and employees as well as the environment when they buy Sonnentor products. On the other hand, the products themselves, carrying names like "It's all good" tea, "Let me be your guardian angel" chocolate or "True love!" drink, tell stories and speak to the emotional centers of their customers. "People strive for the same, wherever they are – being loved and living a healthy, long life," says Gutmann. In our terminology, we could say that people strive for real value. There are some leaders who understand this better than others. "It is impossible to lead Sonnentor with a big business mindset and spreadsheet-world thinking," says Gutmann, "If you want to move something, you need passion. You cannot just understand our business in a merely calculating, numbers-oriented way" (Sternad, 2015, p. 10).

The "life explorer"

Let us now – after visiting Ibrahim Abouleish in Africa and Johannes Gutmann in Europe – continue our tour around the world to yet another real value-creating leader in the organic food business in Asia.

Helianti Hilman was born and raised in a highland coffee plantation on Java, one of the more than 17,000 islands of Indonesia. "I grew up thinking food is not something you buy," she remembers from her childhood. "If you want vegetables, you pick it from the garden" (Veda, 2014). She studied law at King's College in London and worked as a lawyer, international community development consultant, and serial entrepreneur before establishing the company PT Kampung Kearifan Indonesia (better known for its brand name "Javara," stemming from the local term "Jawara" for "champion") in 2008. She decided to set up Javara after having been exposed to the challenges of small traditional farmers in her country. "I am a life explorer" – that's how Hilman characterizes herself (asianentrepreneur.com, 2015). And when she explored the life of Indonesian smallholders, she found out that they were seriously threatened by the standardized mass-market agriculture that demanded ever more investment in industrial seeds, fertilizers, and chemical pest control. "Farmers were trapped into a capitalization of their profession," she says (whiteboardjournal, 2013). Their subsistence was at stake, along with the country's rich food biodiversity. Hilman decided that she would be the one to take responsibility for defending against these threats, thereby remaining loyal to a core value of her family:

"The reason I became a social entrepreneur was because my parents taught me whatever we do has to benefit others, not our own selfish needs," says Hilman (Veda, 2014).

As in the case of other enterprises that are oriented toward the creation of real value, making a profit has never been Javara's primary goal, although the for-profit company has quickly turned into the largest producer of certified organic products in the country. Hilman set up Javara to protect the diversity of Indonesian food products through opening domestic and international marketing channels, thus providing decent income opportunities for small farmers, whom she pays 50 to 100% up front for their produce. "My main purpose is to sustain indigenous wisdom of holistic farming," says Hilman. She also wants to "save farming as a profession," as she calls it (Ajani, 2013), through supporting smallholders in creating and marketing premium artisanal products. She took a closer look than many others and saw value in the variety of food that local farmers produced with their unique skills and relentless passion. She also saw the deeper significance of food that was grown with a spiritual respect for nature, whether in the form of walking barefoot on the soil, choosing planting times according to the constellation of stars, or considering the importance of the farmers' mood for the thriving of their plants (livingalifeincolour.com, 2013; whiteboardjournal, 2013). At the same time, she recognized that farmers lacked a way to make these treasures available to a wider market, and decided that it was up to her to help them with the marketing of their products.

In the beginning, it was not easy for Hilman to turn her ideas into reality. She started with a lack of knowledge and experience in the food industry, no access to the relevant market, and insufficient capital. She learned to gradually build trust, however, mainly through creating high-quality prototype products in appealing packaging and through telling stories. She told stories about the farmers and the values behind the product, and explained how Javara helped in both creating real value for these farmers and in protecting Indonesia's indigenous food diversity. "Effective story telling comes from genuine intention, transparency and traceability," says Hilman.[44] The stories added deeper, emotional value to her business, and attracted supply chain partners, customers, and investors, as well as other institutions and expert volunteers who offered their help, thus strengthening Javara's organizational capacity.

Today, Javara sources more than 700 products in its portfolio from thousands of small farmers and dozens of artisans from all parts of the country. The brand is now widely known for the many different indigenous, freshly milled varieties of rice that it offers. Other popular products include, for example, raw single blossom honey, coconut oil, sea salt from Bali, organic cashews from the island of Flores, and vegetable noodles. Javara set up marketing and distribution structures that cover supermarkets, hotels, and high-end restaurants in Indonesia, but also developed relationships with overseas partners in almost 20 countries in Europe, Asia, and North America. Up from around 10% in 2011, Javara exported almost 80% of its products in 2014. Thus, Javara has become what Hilman calls "an enabling factor to facilitate champion community-based products from across the archipelago to access the global markets."

But Javara's founder soon realized that the farmers needed a lot more than just market access. They also needed someone to help them create products that meet the requirements of their customers and the quality standards of the global market, and to obtain the financial means and technical tools to make this possible. Consequently, Hilman and her team also engaged in assisting small-holders in many different ways, such as organizing technology transfer and training as well as quality and food safety controls.

Javara also supports farmers with product innovations, sets up production systems, arranges organic certification, and creates financing opportunities so that smallholders can invest in their farms. Hilman's overall aim is to help farmers increase their capacity to create high-quality food products based on their local traditions. For example, she encourages farmers to increase biodiversity on their farms and rotate crops on a seasonal basis instead of engaging in monoculture, knowing that diversity is a way to higher resilience. She does not impose her ideas on others, however. "Farmers come with their own problems and then we find the solutions together," is how she explains her partnership-oriented approach (whiteboardjournal, 2013).

As a learning community, Javara strives to educate not only her partners, but also consumers. Whether through seminars or food workshops, Hilman always tries to raise people's awareness of quality food. Javara's product packaging informs food buyers about the place of origin as well as the farmers and artisans who create the products, making customers more aware of the real value creation process behind the food that they buy. In a new initiative, Hilman also aims to provide a unique learning platform for young people who want to establish themselves as entrepreneurs in the food business. "They can work as intrapreneurs for us for no more than three years to gain knowledge, networks, and experience," says Hilman. "Yet, we are also preparing them to become entrepreneurs that in the future can be part of Javara's supply chain partners." This strategy can help Javara to attract young talent with an entrepreneurial spirit while at the same time also strengthening its overall supply chain ecosystem.

Sharing knowledge, learning, developing – it's not a one-way street at Javara. Hilman is deeply convinced that "Javara would not exist without the valuable lessons we learn from the farmers. These farmers do not only teach us the beauty of the spiritualism in our food system. There are also many product innovations that we derived from their local wisdom and the tradition that they still keep alive."

This spirit of equitable collaboration not only manifests itself in the mutual openness and willingness to learn from each other, but also in the pricing system. Javara – like SEKEM – emphasizes full transparency all along the value chain. Prices are not imposed on farmers, but jointly agreed upon. Hilman explains that "when we decide on the price, we sit down and discuss with the farmers. We ask them how we should value their products according to various aspects such as production cost." She sees this approach also as a "way to build up pride" (whiteboardjournal, 2013). In a similar vein, Hilman encourages farmers to see themselves as local "farm entrepreneurs," providing them with ideas and the means to reach a much higher level of added value and therefore a sustainable source of income. Helping farmers and artisans to set up local processing businesses also enables Javara to maintain a lean and efficient organization with only 53 employees. It's a clear win-win situation, for Javara's business as well as for the farmers and local artisans who get the very real possibility to earn a living. It is Hilman's goal to open these opportunities to as many people as possible: "We never decline any farmers," she says, "because it's our policy to help farmers who meet our criteria" (whiteboardjournal, 2013).

Helianti Hilman clearly makes a difference with her business – for the thousands of farmers and their families whose livelihood she helps to sustain, for society, through keeping local traditions and food diversity alive, and for the consumers, who enjoy access to healthy, authentic food and the pleasure of supporting local smallholders and artisans. Hilman has taken the lead, and has assumed the responsibility to serve others. She has found her own way to create real value with her business.

The qualities of responsible leaders

Our three examples of responsible leaders from the organic food sector, Helianti Hilman, Johannes Gutmann and Ibrahim Abouleish, have much in common. They all share a vision that transcends the self, and a clear idea of how they can improve the quality of life of others and create real value. Whether it is Abouleish's holistic initiative that simultaneously focuses on individual, organizational, and societal development, Gutmann's mission to create meaningful, high-quality jobs in a remote, rural area, or Hilman's goal to protect indigenous food diversity and enable small farmers to live a decent life from the fruits of their land – they all set a primary purpose for their businesses that goes far beyond making money.

Responsible leaders also have the courage and commitment to turn their vision into reality, to give up their comfortable lives, and to fight for a cause even under adverse conditions. Gutmann was frozen out of the town where he originally started his business. People regarded him as a strange person and even filed commercial lawsuits against him. He reacted by relocating his business to a remote village, which began to flourish as a consequence. Hilman faced considerable logistical and infrastructural challenges since Javara's partner farms are located in remote areas on the Indonesian islands. Still, she found a way to offer the smallholders' products to the world market, thus ensuring the livelihood of her partners. And Abouleish was confronted with strong opposition from seemingly overpowering adversaries such as the government, the military, and religious leaders, which he managed to overcome through persuading them of the righteousness of his cause. Despite many reasons for these leaders to give up on their visions, they persisted, found innovative solutions to their problems, and convinced others to support them. Their energy for creating real value is much stronger than the forces opposing them.

One particular characteristic that enables these leaders to over-come difficult situations is their relentless capacity to learn. Gutmann never stops trying to figure things out and make corrections if neces-sary, Hilman constantly tries to learn from the farmers with whom she works, and Abouleish considers his own willingness and ability to learn as one of his major strengths (Abouleish, 2005, p. 62).

In addition to having a clear vision and possessing such qualities as courage, persistence, and a strong learning orientation, all three leaders distinguish themselves with an approach to business that is characterized by a strong cooperative spirit. They understand the needs of their employees, customers, and partners all along the value chain, and authentically care for their wellbeing. They want to find the right balance between the needs of all those who are affected by the business instead of giving one person or group pre-cedence over the other. And they always strive to establish mutually beneficial long-term partnerships and personal relationships rather than just making arms-length deals. To make this possible, they carefully select the right people with whom to work. When Gutmann recruits new employees, he looks at least as closely at their values and social competence as at their skills or professional background. The list of qualities that Hilman is looking for includes "sharing the same vision and mission, being passionate in contributing to the cause in their role, integrity in implementing the values, discipline in complying to the standard, and social skills that will smooth the collaboration and coordination internally as well as with part-ners and buyers." Responsible leaders are looking for *real people* rather than machines who match certain predefined professional qualifications. The same is true for Abouleish, who valued charac-ter higher than intellectual abilities when he selected teachers for SEKEM's schools (Abouleish, 2005, p. 178).

In a sense, these responsible leaders are also "teachers" them-selves. They see their role as not only to run a business, but also to help others develop. One of the most powerful tools that they use for that purpose is storytelling. These leaders tell their stories over and over again, to reach both the minds and hearts of people. In essence, their stories are about individuals who want to make a positive impact on the lives of others. Like most good stories they do not follow a straight line, but include challenges and obstacles that need to be overcome. These again offer learning experiences. Our responsible leaders' stories have a strong emotional value, as they are both personal and deeply human.

Being learners and teachers at the same time, responsible leaders also know that the ability to learn is very dependent on the capacity to perceive. They see opportunities to create real value where others only see problems, and they find such opportunities both outside as well as inside themselves. "Everywhere's a desert," says Abouleish. "There is a physical desert and a desert inside ourselves" (Abouleish, 2008, p. 11). Very few people are able to transform a physical desert into a blooming garden like the founder of SEKEM. But we can each address our inner desert, Abouleish is convinced, if we just ask ourselves a simple question: "Where can we plant 'trees' in the sense of creating something new in ourselves?" (Abouleish, 2008, p. 11).

In brief: leadership responsibility

- Enterprises that create real value result from the work of responsible leaders who find meaning in their lives in contributing to the improvement of the quality of life of others. Through creating real value for others, they also create deeper, emotional value for themselves.

- Responsible leaders are guided by a vision, by a clear picture of what a better future could look like. They then persistently follow their vision, even in the face of obstacles and adversity.

- Responsible leaders take a cooperative approach to business. They want to ensure that all stakeholders can benefit from the activities of their business, and try to find the right balance in everything they do.

- Responsible leaders nurture the roots of the tree of real value. They put life improvement before profit maximization, think long term, build lasting relationships, recognize limits, and are strongly attached to a place.

- Responsible leaders establish their organizations as learning communities, as they themselves have an intense learning orientation. They constantly seek to educate themselves and develop others, and they are never afraid of learning through trying out, even if that means that they risk failure and may need to make corrections.

- When responsible leaders make decisions, they tend to choose the alternative that maximizes real value, not the one with the highest financial return.

8

Conclusion: business for a better life

Money is human happiness in the abstract;
therefore, whoever is not capable of enjoying such
   happiness in the concrete,
attaches his whole heart to it.

Arthur Schopenhauer

(1851, p. 477. Trans. by the authors)

In this book, we have visited exceptional people who have turned the businesses that they own or manage into positive forces that improve the lives of all. To name just a few, Count Anton Wolfgang von Faber-Castell, with his dogged campaign to preserve the arts of handwriting and drawing even while creating a modern, carbon negative and socially responsible company; Tarlach de Blacam, who tapped into the deep well of the local craft tradition to establish a knitwear company that sells globally while providing quality jobs and a distinct identity for the inhabitants of a remote, rocky Irish-speaking island off Ireland's wild Atlantic coast; Andrea Illy, who followed in the footsteps of his forebears to bring a unique blend of quality coffee, culture, and beauty to our world while at the same time improving the living standards of hundreds of small coffee growers; Susanne Henkel, who believes that continuous growth is not only unnecessary, but often counterproductive, and whose company has proven that a recognition of environmental, human, and social limits can be not only liberating, but also sustainably profitable; Helianti Hilman, who contributes to the protection of holistic farming and food diversity in Indonesia and provides local farmers and artisans with a sustainable possibility to earn a living; Ernst Kronawitter, who proved that a financial institution can achieve success without putting undue pressure on employees to generate sales of financial products; or Ibrahim Abouleish, whose simple decision to dig a well transformed a barren stretch of desert land into a thriving learning community.

What they all have in common is their belief that what we do in life – including or even especially in our business lives – can and should have a positive impact on others. This does not mean that they are "do-gooders" who have built nonprofit organizations whose sole purpose is to support a particular social cause. Quite the contrary; they run highly profitable enterprises. But in doing so, they have chosen a rather unconventional path. Their understanding of the *real* role of profits is nuanced and expansive: profits are necessary to ensure the survival of the enterprise and a foundation for investments into the future. Profits are certainly not neglected, for that would be suicide, but they are not the end-all and be-all. The leaders who we portrayed see their enterprises as vehicles for value creation, not just in a narrowly monetary sense, but in the form of *real value*; they produce goods and services in a way that enables others – and themselves – to live a better life.

Having a positive impact on others as a guiding principle is a fundamentally different approach to business; it is light years away from the "business is business" philosophy with its myopic focus on generating as much cash and profit as possible. It requires a new way of thinking, a different way of looking at the world. From a *real value* perspective, businesses are not sharks that battle and bite in the bloody "red ocean" of hyper competition (Kim and Mauborgne, 2004). They should not be celebrating layoffs as efficiency gains. They should not be in search of every loophole that allows them to shunt profits to offshore tax havens, to the detriment of their own place (if they even see themselves as part of one). And by no means should they favor cash over humanity. Rather than following the widespread pseudo-evolutionary notion that the basic precept in business is "follow your self-interest," these leaders understand that it is our capacity for cooperation, more than for competition, that is behind humanity's ability to survive, and thrive.

After all, we are all born helpless. Without the nurturing, sheltering, and protection provided to us by the older generation, we simply could not survive. "It takes a tribe to raise a human," wrote Yuval Noah Harari (2014, p11), arguing that our ability to cooperate in order to overcome obstacles was the major factor that allowed us, a physically weak species, to rise above all other animals to the top of the food chain. Social cooperation rather than competition is the real key to our success. Showing trust, care, and concern for the wellbeing and the quality of life of others – including strangers – is a fundamental precondition for humankind to survive and thrive. Why do we often seem to forget this when we do business? Are we simply schizophrenic? Can we flick the caring switch off when we arrive at the office, and switch it on again when we come home to our families? Is business, after all, just business? Is the old saw about business ethics being an oxymoron really true? This kind of duality seems to us to be unnatural, if not immoral. If we, as individuals, are interested in living a good life and achieving our true potential, then the enterprises in which we work have an obligation to help us do that. Ever-intensifying competition and the relentless pursuit of profit, with no holds barred and no quarter given, are not the way forward. Instead, we need to do business in a way that benefits others and provides meaning for ourselves.

That's the beauty of businesses that create *real value*: Not only do they dig deeper by developing emotional benefits for customers, opportunities for their employees to learn and thrive, mutually beneficial relationships for their partners, and sustainable profits for their owners. They also (not to put too fine a point on it) simply make their owners and managers happier. Researchers have found evidence that people who find meaning in their lives through contributing to the wellbeing of others also achieve higher levels of wellbeing for themselves (Peterson et al., 2005; Post, 2005; Weinstein and Ryan, 2010). Even Robert K. Shiller (2012, p. 208), the Nobel Prize winner in economics for his work on analyzing asset prices and one hardly given to utopian fantasies – agrees that "[a]ltruistic acts in a social context are an effective antidepressant. Showy houses and luxury cars do not bring happiness. Individual fulfillment depends on a sense of meaning and purpose, and society should act so as to encourage individual actions that reinforce such meaning."

Our concern for the welfare of others should certainly not be confined to philanthropy. If caring for each other is a basic condition for human survival, then it should be a condition for business survival as well! Care for our fellows and for the place in which we live (whether at the level of our local community or the planet itself) is as much the business of business as earning a respectable profit. Business is not a separate universe, but an integral part of our endeavor to live a good and meaningful life. As a life of meaning has very little relationship to conventional measures of financial "success," we feel that it is about time to rethink the way in which we define business success.

A different yardstick for business success

How do we measure the success of any business enterprise and those who lead and manage it? The dominant view – strongly influenced by the doctrine of shareholder primacy – is that increasing the wealth of shareholders through profit maximization and an increased share price should be the one and only objective of a business. But this can lead to a destructive short-termism and even the most strident advocates of the shareholder value maxim, such as Michael C. Jensen, admit that blindly following a short-term profit maximization principle "is a sure way to destroy value" (Jensen, 2001, p. 309). Consequently, a new tenet has emerged that: "managers should make all decisions so as to increase the total *long-run* [our emphasis] market value of the firm" (Jensen, 2001, p. 299). However, although the time horizon may have changed, the ultimate goal – making money and nothing but making money – has not. Jensen actually asserts that a firm can only have *one single* objective – maximizing monetary value – arguing mathematically that it is "logically impossible to maximize in more than one dimension at the same time unless the dimensions are monotone transformations of one another." He concludes that "multiple objectives is no objective" (2001, p. 301) and dismisses leaders who actively try to balance the needs of different stakeholder groups as "self-interested managers" who "destroy firm-value" as they "pursue their own interests at the expense of society and the firm's financial claimants." (2001, p. 305). At base, this is really not so different from Milton Friedman's well-known argument in which he claimed that managers who pursued any goal other than profit were "unwitting puppets of the intellectual forces that have been undermining the basis of a free society these past decades" (Friedman, 1970).

Let us pause for a moment and pose this question: Do the people and enterprises portrayed in this book really destroy value as they follow a deeper purpose than just making money? Do they really work "at the expense of society" as they care for the wellbeing of their non-shareholder stakeholders? Are those who try to balance the interests of different stakeholders really the ones who are in thrall to their own narrow "self-interests"? Such questions border on the ludicrous.

Of course, our answers to these questions depend on how we define value. If we believe that the essential, fundamental value is monetary value – and that the lure of money drives every type of productive (or "valuable") behavior – as some advocates of the shareholder value paradigm would have us believe – then (money) value maximization might really be the narrow "objective function" that Jensen postulates. As such, it would naturally be the only measure of managerial success. But if we focus on a definition of *real value* that goes well beyond the narrow conceptualization of monetary value, then the picture that emerges is very different. If we understand that relatively few of the elements of a good quality of life – such as living in an intact natural environment, having rich and authentic social interactions in authentic communities, finding meaning in one's life – can actually be monetized, then the idea of money value maximization as the only legitimate goal of a business is simply untenable. Even Michael C. Jensen now accepts that "being a person of integrity, being committed to something bigger than oneself [and] being authentic are each necessary (but not sufficient) for maximum performance" – for both individuals and organizations (Jensen and Erhard, 2011).

Businesses are a means for the provision of goods and services. They need to make profits – at least over time – to be sustainable. But beyond that, there is no natural (or man-made) law that precludes them from following a deeper purpose. They can choose to attempt to maximize social welfare under the constraint that profit needs to stay within a certain range, they can put weights on monetary versus non-monetary objectives, or can try to combine the two in a synergistic way, as in the examples that we visited in the previous chapters. It is a conscious decision that owners and managers need to take together, not a God-given precept that gives money-making (or shareholder value) overarching preference. Why should striving for a balance between profitability (the life-sustaining "blood" of an enterprise) and creating real value (the "heart" of an enterprise) not be a legitimate managerial goal, and one for which managers should be held accountable? What use is blood if no heart beats?

We can hear the skeptics asking, but aren't profits and market value the hard currency, the tangible "yardstick" by which managers can and should be measured while the deeper, emotional side of value must remain elusive and vague, and thus more or less unmanageable? Shouldn't we focus on that which we can count, and stay away from that which is dense, complicated, and tricky? Let's keep it simple and clear, they say! This is a common argument of those who would have us believe that profits and share prices have always been the end-all and be-all and in fact the only objective measure of business success. However, commercial activity and business enterprises were much in evidence long before the invention of double-entry accounting by Fra Luca Pacioli in Florence in 1494. Before then, of course, it was impossible to calculate profits in the way we do now. And the oldest book about the stock exchange business – a work by José de la Vega with the prophetic title *Confusion of Confusions* – was published only in 1688. The New York Stock Exchange itself was founded in 1792, so clearly stock prices as the "ultimate yardstick" have not existed forever either.

Just as those yardsticks were developed over time, through societal dialogue and in response to contemporary conditions and needs, we also have the capacity to develop new yardsticks for tomorrow's businesses. And we must. The roots of real value creation described in this book can be a starting point. We can assess managerial long-term orientation with a focus on non-financial leading indicators rather than quarterly results; we can assess relationship-orientation with the average retention rates of suppliers, customers, or employees; we can assess limits recognition with social and environmental performance indicators that are already used in corporate sustainability reports; we can assess the extent to which an enterprise is a learning community with the time that employees spend in learning activities. We can indeed quantify outcomes in real value terms: for example, the number of quality jobs that are created in a certain region, the degree to which employees find their work meaningful, or customers' perceptions of the emotional value that they get from the products or services of the firm. These are just a few examples, and by no means exhaustive. And admittedly, all measures, including these, are likely to be imperfect. But these examples suggest that we can find ways to assess both the input factors and outcomes of real value creation – but only if we really want to. Even more important than the hard currency of numbers is the ability, and the desire, to begin an honest dialogue on the real value that firms create – or fail to create. What we really need is a new way of talking about business.

A new narrative

"A new narrative is emerging in society," says R. Edward Freeman, who is widely renowned for his pioneering work on stakeholder theory. At a recent conference in Hamburg he argued that the old story was that business was all about money, but now "the new narrative of business is purpose and passion" (Freeman, 2016). He is so right, and it is long overdue. We need a new narrative about business at both the level of the individual firm, and at the societal level. It is time for the economy (and its businesses) to work for society, rather than the other way around.

This new narrative can, and should, change the way in which we see our economic system. Our current economic system is dominated by a narrative called the "neo-liberal paradigm." According to this paradigm everyone – people and enterprises alike – should be free to follow their individual economic advantage unimpeded by interference from the state. People who selfishly strive for profit-making and wealth accumulation, so the narrative goes, will also benefit society as they fuel economic growth and create jobs for others, thus laying the groundwork for a more affluent society. In this trickle-down school of thought, human beings are more or less reduced to their role as maximizers of economic self-interest. They reflect the quintessential "economic man" beloved of economists. One of the major proponents of neo-liberalism, Nobel laureate Gary S. Becker, "the most important social scientist in the past 50 years" according to a *New York Times* commentator (Wolfers, 2014), set the tone, arguing that "the economic approach provides a valuable unified framework for understanding *all* human behavior" (Becker, 1976, p. 14).

Let us think about this once again. Are we human beings really self-interest maximizers in *all* that we do? Are we really willing to buy this argument? Do we really believe that there is no friendship without calculation, no love without an economic hidden agenda, and no helping hand without a potential personal benefit in the back of our minds? Is such a society, dominated and delineated by calculating egoists and money value, really the sort of place where we would want to live?

"There is no alternative" was the standard answer of former British Prime Minister Margaret Thatcher to criticisms of economic liberalism and the free market system. She was not called "the iron lady" for nothing; on this, as in other matters, she could not be moved. Her answer reflects a black and white world where the "iron law" of free market economics cannot be questioned. Indeed, it is still the standard answer of many of today's neo-liberal evangelists. But this is not only dissembling; it is simply not true. There are alternatives, and no lack of successful examples of firms, and leaders, marching to a very different drumbeat.

At the level of the individual firm, the enterprises portrayed in this book offer a strong testimonial that we do not have to blindly follow the mantra of profit maximization; there are alternative ways of determining, and achieving, business success. On a societal level, as Peter A. Hall and David Soskice convincingly explain in their book *Varieties of Capitalism* (2001, p. 8) there are at least two very distinct types of political economies: *liberal market economies*, which are built on the basic principles of neo-liberalism, and alternative forms of capitalism, *coordinated market economies*, which exhibit important differences. In coordinated market economies, collaborative behavior and non-market coordination mechanisms such as strong relational ties between firms and active partnerships between owners, the management, and employees on both the firm and industry level, are of critical importance. These economies are usually more highly developed welfare states (Hall and Soskice, 2001, p. 50). Despite their considerable institutional and social differences, there is no indication that coordinated market economies such as Germany are economically systematically worse off than liberal market economies like the UK. The existence of highly successful coordinated market economies clearly shows that there *are* alternatives if we just begin to write, and live by, a different narrative. Indeed, such behavior is mirrored in the activities of many of the firms highlighted in this book. Of course, we can choose to passionately accept the narrative that self-interest and free markets rule. But with equal justification, and maybe with an even higher likelihood of creating an inclusive, prospering society, we could also follow the story of eco-social market economies – that we need to find a good balance between economic, social, and environmental goals. We choose the latter. It may not be an easier path, but it is a nobler and more rewarding one.

If different forms of capitalism already exist – based on different narratives and the dominant ideas that hold sway in particular cultures and societies – why can't we also think about a variety of capitalism with a stronger emphasis on creating real value? When we can place real value creation rather than yesterday's stock market prices into the context of serious societal discussion, we will have removed the first few bricks in the imposing wall of the dominant *money value paradigm.*

There will never be alternatives – as long as we do not admit the existence of real alternatives! Economic historian Deirdre McCloskey has extensively studied how the modern capitalist system took off and sparked the unprecedented economic growth of the last few centuries. Her conclusion is that neither purely "materialist" explanations like capital accumulation or an increase of trade, nor the exploitation of one human group by another in the form of imperialism or slavery were the main driving forces. The real "engine of growth," she says, was a new "rhetoric." She argues that prosperity in the modern age is attributable to the rise and dissemination of bourgeois culture, virtues, and *ideas* – in particular a "rhetoric" – a new narrative – that protected and supported innovators (McCloskey, 2010). Ideas and stories changed the world. Clearly, new ways of talking about things can effect real change. Our stories and myths can change the course of history (Harari, 2014, p. 35).

As John Maynard Keynes so wisely wrote: "Practical men who believe themselves to be quite exempt from any intellectual influence, are usually the slaves of some defunct economist. Madmen in authority, who hear voices in the air, are distilling their frenzy from some academic scribbler of a few years back" (Keynes, 1936, pp.

383-384). We "academic scribblers" and business practitioners have the power to decide whether we want to tell a story of business as a profit-making engine in which selfish individuals strive to maximize their individual money value, and the rest get the crumbs from the table, or if we want to tell a different story – the story of business as a vehicle for improving our quality of life and the wellbeing of society. Who are our heroes? The wolves of Wall Street or the responsible entrepreneurs who follow a deeper purpose? Who gets media attention and the most political support – the untethered, opportunistic investment bankers and derivatives dealers or the creators of *real value* who respect the limits of both people and the environment? Do we want to educate our future leaders as well-oiled self-interest-seeking machines or as responsible, holistic, long-term thinkers who pursue profit along with the common good? It is up to us to decide. We can create an alternative – if we just start thinking and talking about it. Indeed, the enterprises in this book are already "walking the walk." We will need to quicken our pace to catch up with them.

In brief: business for a better life

- We need to practice business in a way that benefits others and provides meaning for ourselves. This is a fundamental tenet for those who believe businesses should be engaged in *real value* creation.

- Those who defend the dominant "shareholder value" paradigm claim that there are no alternatives – but they are deeply, fundamentally, and demonstrably wrong.

- Different forms of capitalism already exist, and they work. We *can* envision a variety of capitalism that supports a strong emphasis on the creation of real value.

- To practice business a new way, and to create real value, we must begin to tell a different story.

- Stories matter, and change begins with ideas. It is time for a new narrative of business, a narrative of *real value creation*.

Endnotes

1 Dan Ariely quotes from the documentary *Real Value* by Jesse Borkowski (2014).

2 See oxforddictionaries.com/definition/value.

3 Ibid.

4 See, for example, Nocera, 2012, *Forbes*, 2014, and Meyerson, 2014.

5 *Financial Times* (2015); a similar statement, "profit is as important as the air for breathing, but it would be sad if we just conducted business to make profits, as it would be sad if we just lived to breathe" was made by the former President of the Board of Deutsche Bank AG, Hermann Josef Abs (Abs, 1976, p. 91).

6 Personal email communication of the authors with Ulrik Nehammer, February 10, 2015.

7 Pink (2006). Just as a caveat, we would like to point out that modern neuroscience regards the distinction between "left-brained" and "right-brained" learners as a "neuromyth" that over-simplifies the hemispheric specialization of the brain (Goswami, 2006).

8 From the speech that Count Anton Wolfgang von Faber-Castell gave at the ceremonial act for the 250th anniversary of Faber-Castell, provided to the authors in a personal communication with Faber-Castell AG on August 20 2015.

9 This unpublished quote of Count Anton Wolfgang von Faber-Castell was provided to the authors in a personal communication with Faber-Castell AG on August 20 2015.

10 From the speech that Count Anton Wolfgang von Faber-Castell gave at the ceremonial act for the 250th anniversary of Faber-Castell, provided to the authors in a personal communication with Faber-Castell AG on August 20 2015.

11 Ibid.

12 With kind permission of and acknowledgement to the Bertrand Russell Peace Foundation and the publisher Routledge.

13 The slogan of Mondragón Corporation is "Humanity at Work."

14 Ulgor is taken from the first letter of the last names of the five founders.

15 All the data in this paragraph is based on Mondragón Corporation (2015b).

16 The Rochdale Pioneers were unemployed weavers who founded the first consumer cooperative and first articulated their principles of cooperation; these principles form the core of the cooperative philosophy today as exemplified in the principles of the ICA (www.ica.coop).

17 Personal communication with R. North, July 14 2014.

18 Copyright © 1983 by Wendell Berry, from *Standing by Words*. Reprinted by permission of Counterpoint.

19 Personal communication with T. de Blacam, March 12 2012. This quotation is also referenced in Bradley and Kennelly (2013).

20 Ibid.

21 See inismeain.com (n.d.).

22 Personal communication with T. de Blacam, November 9 2011. This quotation is also referenced in Bradley and Kennelly (2013).

23 Author Tim Robinson wrote a best-selling book about the largest of the Aran Islands (Árainn) entitled *Stones of Aran* (1995).

24 Attribution to Orwell found in esquire.co.uk (2013).

25 Plunkett's famous slogan for his cooperative movement in Ireland, which was most successful in the dairy sector, was "better farming, better business, better living."

26 See www.pubs.coop

27 © Libreria Editrice Vaticana for all citations of Pope Francis. Reprinted with permission.

28 The anchor point of this movement is the work of Jackson (2011).

29 R. Daelmans, unpublished interview with Kristina Erlacher, May 12, 2015.

30 R. Daelmans, unpublished interview with Kristina Erlacher, May 12, 2015.

31 R. Daelmans, unpublished interview with Kristina Erlacher, May 12, 2015.

32 *Parade Magazine*, September 8 1996, p. 5, quoted from MoreThanMoney (2002).

33 This quote and all uncited Andrea Illy quotes in this chapter are taken from a personal interview with Andrea Illy that one of the authors conducted at illycaffè's headquarters in Trieste (Italy) on October 13 2015.

34 Personal communication with M. Elsas, 2011.

35 Ibid.

36 Personal communication with M. Elsas, 2014.

37 Personal communication with M. Elsas, 2014

38 Personal communication with M. Elsas, 2011.

39 Personal communication with M. Elsas, 2011.

40 The following comparisons of the bureaucratic model and a learning community in this paragraph are based on Sugarman (2000).

41 Yeats attributes this quote to an "old play."

42 Abouleish (2005, p. 80). This quote and all other quotes from *SEKEM: A Sustainable Community in the Egyptian Desert* are reproduced by kind permission of Floris Books, Edinburgh. © 2005 Ibrahim Abouleish.

43 This statement and all other uncited statements by Johannes Gutmann originate from a personal interview with the founder of Sonnentor with one of the authors of this book on September 10 2013.

44 This statement and all other uncited statements by Helianti Hilman originate from a personal communication of the founder of Javara with one of the authors of this book on July 24 2015.

References

Aaker, D.A. (1996). *Building Strong Brands*. New York, NY: Free Press.

Abouleish, I. (2005). *SEKEM: A Sustainable Community in the Egyptian Desert*. Edinburgh: Floris Books.

Abouleish, I. (2008). SEKEM: Nachhaltige Entwicklung. A dialogue at the University of Graz, January 18, 2008. Transcript by Mario Diethart. Graz: RCE.

Abouleish, I. (2009a). Wie können Europa und Ägypten für nachhaltige Entwicklung zusammen arbeiten? Speech at the Technical University of Graz, August 20, 2009. Transcript by Mario Diethart. Graz: RCE.

Abouleish, I. (2009b). Wer den Weg der sozialen Dreigliederung nicht kennt, der sucht im Dunkeln. *Drei: Zeitschrift für Anthrosophie in Wissenschaft, Kunst und sozialem Leben*, 11, 55-60.

Abs, H.J. (1976). *Lebensfragen der Wirtschaft*. Duesseldorf/Vienna: Econ.

Ajani, D. (2013). Javara: Treasuring food biodiversity. *The Jakarta Post*. Retrieved from: http://www.thejakartapost.com/news/2013/05/26/javara-treasuring-food-biodiversity.html

Allen, D. (2012). Darina Allen's blog. Retrieved from: http://darinasblog.cooking-isfun.ie/2012/07/collecting-sea-urchins-on-inis-mean.html

Alperovitz, G., & Hanna, T.M. (2013). Mondragón and the system problem. Retrieved from: http://www.truth-out.org/news/item/19704-mondragon-and-the-system-problem

Anderson, R. (2009, February). TED Talk: The business logic of sustainability. Retrieved from: http://www.ted.com/talks/ray_anderson_on_the_business_logic_of_sustainability?language=en

Anderson, R.C., & White, R. (2009). *Confessions of a Radical Industrialist: Profits, People, Purpose – Doing Business by Respecting the Earth*. New York, NY: St. Martin's Press.

Argyle, M. (2001). *The Psychology of Happiness* (2nd edn). London: Routledge.

asianentrepreneur.com (2015). Helianti Hilman, founder of Javara. http://www.asianentrepreneur.org/helianti-hilman-founder-of-javara/. Published 18 March 2015, accessed July 16, 2015

Balch, O. (2015, April 20). Garden cities: Can green spaces bring health and happiness. *The Guardian*. Retrieved from: http://www.theguardian.com/sustainable-business/2015/apr/20/garden-cities-can-green-spaces-bring-health-and-happiness

bankingclub.de (2015). "Mitarbeiter brauchen mehr als nur materielle Anreize". Retrieved from: https://www.bankingclub.de/news/view/mitarbeiter-brauchen-mehr-als-nur-materielle-anreize

Becker, G.S. (1976). *The Economic Approach to Human Behavior*. Chicago: The University of Chicago Press.

Berkshire Hathaway (1989). Chairman's letter to the shareholders 1988. Retrieved from: http://www.berkshirehathaway.com/letters/1988.html

Berkshire Hathaway (1990). Chairman's letter to the shareholders 1989. Retrieved from: http://www.berkshirehathaway.com/letters/1989.html

Berkshire Hathaway (1991). Chairman's letter to the shareholders 1990. Retrieved from: http://www.berkshirehathaway.com/letters/1990.html

Berkshire Hathaway (2001). Chairman's letter to the shareholders 2000. Retrieved from: http://www.berkshirehathaway.com/2000ar/2000letter.html

Berkshire Hathaway (2003). Chairman's letter to the shareholders 2002. Retrieved from: http://www.berkshirehathaway.com/letters/2002pdf.pdf

Berkshire Hathaway (2011). Chairman's letter to the shareholders 2010. Retrieved from: http://www.berkshirehathaway.com/letters/2010ltr.pdf

Berkshire Hathaway (2015). Chairman's letter to the shareholders 2014. Retrieved from: http://www.berkshirehathaway.com/letters/2014ltr.pdf

Berry, W.E. (2011). *Standing By Words*. Berkeley, CA: Counterpoint Press.

Berry, W. (2012, 23 April). It all turns on affection. 41st Jefferson Lecture, The National Endowment for the Humanities, John F. Kennedy Center for the Performing Arts, Washington, D.C. Retrieved from: http://events.tvworldwide.com/Events/NEH2012JeffersonLecture.aspx?VID=events/neh/120423_NEH_Jefferson_Lecture_KennedyCtr.flv&Cap=events/neh/120423_NEH_Jefferson_Lecture_KennedyCtr.xml

Birch, S. (2014, 18 July). How community shops are beating big business. *The Guardian*. Retrieved from: https://www.theguardian.com/sustainable-business/social-enterprise-blog/community-shops-big-business

Block, The (2013, 26 September). Gem of the Aran Islands: A talk with Tarlach de Blacam of Inis Meáin, *The Block*. Retrieved from: http://clothiers65.rssing. com/chan-15451005/all_p1.html

Böhler, N. (2010). Reinhold Geiger: Monsieur L'Occitane (D. Sternad, J.J. Kennelly & F. Bradley, Trans.). *Vorarlberger Nachrichten*, p. D6.

Borkowski, J. (2014). *Real Value* (Documentary). Copyright 2014 Nothing Underground.

boss-magazin.de (2009). Auch in schwierigen Zeiten zuversichtlich. Retrieved from: http://www.bossticker.de/bitverlag/boss/index.asp?ogr=boss&item=82 83&step=99999&start=1&rb=artikel&ur=suche&titel=

Boyle, G., & Bradley, F. (2005). The undergraduate as an engaged explorer. Retrieved from: http://repec.maynoothuniversity.ie/mayecw-files/N1600905. pdf

Bradley, F. (2011). Creativity: Does place matter? *London Review of Education*, 10(2), 145-157.

Bradley, F.D., & Kennelly, J.J. (2013). *The Irish Edge*. Dublin: The Orpen Press.

Brattleboro Reformer (2008). Old vs. new. Retrieved from: http://www.reformer. com/ci_8051027

Braun, G. (2013). Die Selbstverpflichtung der Firma Faber-Castell zum Erhalt der Biodiversität. Presentation at the Fachtagung "Business and Biodiversity", November 28 2013, Vienna, Austria.

Brochet, F. (2001). La dégustation: Etude des représentations des objets chimiques dans le champ de la conscience. Paris: Academie Amorim. Retrieved from: http://www.academie-amorim.com/documents/brochet.pdf

Buck, T. (2015, 3 August). A fine balance between solidarity and survival. *The Financial Times*. Retrieved from: http://www.ft.com/intl/cms/s/0/26740e3e-2aee-11e5-acfb-cbd2e1c81cca.html#axzz3lYPYoD32

Bündnis 90/Die Grünen Baden Württemberg (2010). Nachhaltigkeit. Na dann Prost. *Grüne Blätter*, 3, 7.

Burlingham, B. (2005). *Small Giants: Companies that Choose to be Great Instead of Big*. New York, NY: Portfolio.

Burlington Free Press (2012). John Replongle. Retrieved from: http://archive.burlingtonfreepress.com/article/20120628/BUSINESS08/306280010/John-Replogle

Business Insider (2014, 28 February). Tim Cook erupts after shareholder asks him to focus only on profit. Retrieved from: http://www.businessinsider.com/ tim-cook-versus-a-conservative-think-tank-2014-2?IR=T

Canals, L.J. (2010). Rethinking the firm's mission and purpose. *European Management Review*, 7(4), 195-204.

Capra, F. (2002). *The Hidden Connections*. London: HarperCollins Publishers.

CBS News (2003). The mensch of Malden Mills. Retrieved from: http://www. cbsnews.com/news/the-mensch-of-malden-mills

Chalmers, N. (2012, November). My business life: Count Anton Wolfgang von Faber Castell. *Director Magazine.* http://www.director.co.uk/MAGA-ZINE/2012/11_November/MBL_Count%20Anton%20Wolfgang%20von%20Faber-Castell_66_03.html

Chang, V., Hoyt, D., Carrol, G., & Rao, H. (2010a). Illycafè and Gruppo Illy (A): Expanding beyond Gourmet Coffee. Stanford Graduate School of Business, Case no. SM-188A.

Chang, V., Carroll, G., & Rao, H. (2010b). Gruppo Illy SpA (B): Universita del Caffè. Stanford Graduate School of Business Teaching Case no. SM-188 B.

chcany.org (2015). Cooperative Home Care Associates. Retrieved from: http://www.chcany.org

CNN (2011). How one small bank keeps its staff among the happiest in Europe. Retrieved from: http://edition.cnn.com/2011/09/30/business/gargiulo-route-to-the-top-middelfart-sparekasse

cnn.com (2012). Germany's Mittelstand businesses. Retrieved from: http://edition.cnn.com/2012/05/24/business/german-economy-mittelstand/index.html

Cohen, R. (2015, 6 August). Incurable American excess. *The New York Times.* Retrieved from: http://www.nytimes.com/2015/08/07/opinion/roger-cohen-incurable-american-excess.html?_r=0

Cook, K. (2014). In pursuit of a circular economy: Market-leading product and service innovation at Desso. Sustainable Brands Case Study. San Francisco, CA: Sustainable Life Media Inc.

Co-operatives UK (2011). Bob Cannell: Doing it the hard way? Retrieved from: http://www.uk.coop/newsroom/bob-cannell-doing-it-hard-way

Corti, S. (2013, 7 February). Andrea Illy: Nie mehr als halbvoll (D. Sternad, J.J. Kennelly & F. Bradley, Trans.). *Der Standard.* Retrieved from: http://derstandard.at/1358305737149/Andrea-Illy-Nie-mehr-als-halbvoll

Crawford, M. (2015). *The World Beyond Your Head: On Becoming an Individual in an Age of Distraction.* New York, NY: Farrar, Straus & Giroux.

cremamagazin.de (n.d.). Interview mit Andrea Illy. Retrieved from: http://www.cremagazin.de/illy

Cunningham, L.A. (ed.) (2014). *The Essays of Warren Buffett: Lessons for Investors and Managers* (4th edn.). Hoboken, NJ: Wiley.

Daly, H. (1973). The steady-state economy: Toward a political economy of biophysical equilibrium and moral growth. In H. Daly, (ed.). *Toward a Steady-State Economy* (pp. 149-174). San Francisco, CA: Freeman.

Dawson, M. (2015). German Retail Blog: Mr. Illy talks Expresso and illy-caffè. Retrieved from: http://www.german-retail-blog.com/topic/past-blogs/Coffee-talk-with-Illycaffs-Mr-Illy-319

de Gues, A. (2002). *The Living Company: Habits for Survival in a Turbulent Business Environment*. Boston, MA: Harvard Business School Press.

Department for Communities and Local Government, & Marcus Jones MP – United Kingdom (2016). New £3.6 million programme to help communities take control of their local pub [Press release]. Retrieved from: https://www.gov.uk/government/news/new-36-million-programme-to-help-communities-take-control-of-their-local-pub

Derbyshire, D. (2013, 23 June). Wine tasting: It's junk science. *The Guardian*. Retrieved from: http://www.theguardian.com/lifeandstyle/2013/jun/23/wine-tasting-junk-science-analysis

Desso (2015a). Business concept. Retrieved from: http://www.desso.com/about/business-concept

Desso (2015b). Health & wellbeing. Retrieved from: http://www.desso-business-carpets.com/about/health-wellbeing

Dierig, C. (2013, 9 March). "Wir brauchen Konsolidierung in der Bier-Branche." *Die Welt*. Retrieved from: http://www.welt.de/wirtschaft/article114287494/Wir-brauchen-Konsolidierung-in-der-Bier-Branche.html

Dohner, M. (2014). Graf von Faber-Castell: "Im Zweifelsfall gelten Werte, nicht Adelstitel". Retrieved from: http://www.aargauerzeitung.ch/panorama/vermischtes/graf-von-faber-castell-im-zweifelsfall-gelten-werte-nicht-adelstitel-127773946

Dolan, P., Peasgood, T., & White, M. (2008). Do we really know what makes us happy? A review of the economic literature on the factors associated with subjective well-being. *Journal of Economic Psychology*, 29(1), 94-122.

Dougherty, C. (2009, July 11). A happy family of 8,000, but for how long? *The New York Times*. Retrieved from: http://www.nytimes.com/2009/07/12/business/global/12german.html

ebdaegypt.com (2015). Welcome to EBDA. Retrieved from: http://www.ebdaegypt.org/node/325. Accessed July 20, 2015.

Eccles, R.G., Miller Perkins, K., & Serafeim, G. (2012). How to become a sustainable company. *Sloan Management Review*, 53(4), 43-50.

Ecoheart (2013). Tapping Deganawidah's Wisdom: An Interview with "Seventh Generation" Cofounder Jeffrey Hollender. Retrieved from: http://www.eco-hearth.com/eco-zine/eco-heroes/1404-tapping-deganawidahs-wisdom-interview-seventh-generation-cofounder-jeffrey-hollender.html

Economist, The (2013, 2 February). The Nordic countries: Politicians right and left could learn from the Nordic countries. Retrieved from: http://www.

economist.com/news/leaders/21571136-politicians-both-right-and-left-could-learn-nordic-countries-next-supermodel

Economist, The (2014a, 14 June). Second wind: Some traditional businesses are thriving in an age of disruptive innovation. Retrieved from: http://www.economist.com/news/business/21604156-some-traditional-businesses-are-thriving-age-disruptive-innovation-second-wind

Economist, The (2014b, July 12). German lessons: Many countries want a Mittelstand like Germany's. It is not so easy to copy. Retrieved from: http://www.economist.com/news/business/21606834-many-countries-want-mittelstand-germanys-it-not-so-easy-copy-german-lessons

Edelman Trust Barometer (2015). Global results. Retrieved from: http://www.edelman.com/2015-edelman-trust-barometer-2/trust-and-innovation-edelman-trust-barometer/global-results. Accessed July 14, 2015.

El Mohandes, Y. (2008, 4 December). "Ich hätte mir vor 30 Jahren nicht vorstellen können, je eine Gesichtscreme zu benützen." (D. Sternad, J.J. Kennelly & F. Bradley, Trans). Retrieved from: http://wirtschaftsblatt.at/home/1081428/index

Equal Exchange (2015). History of Equal Exchange. Retrieved from: http://equalexchange.coop/story

esquire.co.uk (2013). Is this the end of the great English pub? Retrieved from: http://www.esquire.co.uk/culture/article/4289/great-british-pub-is-dying

EU (2012). Small companies create 85% of new jobs. Retrieved from: http://europa.eu/rapid/press-release_IP-12-20_en.htm

EU (2015a). Entrepreneurship and small and medium-sized enterprises (SMEs). Retrieved from: http://ec.europa.eu/growth/smes/index_en.htm

EU (2015b). Facts and figures about the EU's small and medium enterprise (SME). Retrieved from: http://ec.europa.eu/enterprise/policies/sme/facts-figures-analysis/index_en.htm. Accessed 21 July 2015.

Ewing, J. (2013, 3 December). Hands-on Bavarian count presides over a pencil-making empire. *The New York Times*. Retrieved from: http://www.nytimes.com/2013/12/04/business/international/hands-on-bavarian-count-presides-over-a-pencil-making-empire.html

EY (2013). Built to last: Family businesses lead the way to sustainable growth. London: EY Family Business Service.

EY (2014). EY Family Business Yearbook 2014. London: EY Family Business Service.

Faber-Castell (2011). Official ceremony at the Frankenhalle. *Faber-Castell Topics*. Stein: Faber-Castell.

Faber-Castell, Count A.-W. (2014 a). People make brands. *Faber-Castell Newsletter for Employees and Friends*, 2, pp. 1-3.

Faber-Castell (2014 b). Our green conscience. *Faber-Castell Newsletter for Employees and Friends*, 1, pp. 1-2.

Faber-Castell (2015 a). Unternehmensgrundsätze. Retrieved from: http://www.faber-castell.at/unternehmen/unternehmensgrunds%C3%A4tze

Faber-Castell, Count A.-W. (2015 b). Nachhaltigkeit. Retrieved from: http://www.faber-castell.at/unternehmen/nachhaltigkeit

Faber-Castell, Cosmetics (2015). Tradition and progress. Retrieved from: http://www.fc-cosmetics.com/Company

Fairtrade Foundation (2012). Fairtrade and coffee. Retrieved from: http://www.fairtrade.net/fileadmin/user_upload/content/2009/resources/2012_Fairtrade_and_coffee_Briefing.pdf

faz.net (2006a). Ich über mich: A. W. von Faber-Castell. Retrieved from: http://www.faz.net/aktuell/beruf-chance/mein-weg-ich-ueber-mich-a-w-graf-von-faber-castell-1384164.html

faz.net (2006b). Der spätberufene Graf. Retrieved from: http://www.faz.net/aktuell/beruf-chance/mein-weg/a-w-graf-von-faber-castel-der-spaetberufene-graf-14619.html

Fernández, J.R. (2015). *Mondragón: 1956-2014*. Retrieved from: http://www.Mondragon-corporation.com/wp-content/themes/Mondragon/docs/History-MONDRAGON-1956-2014.pdf

Financial Times (2009, 12 March). Welch condemns share price focus. Retrieved from: http://www.ft.com/intl/cms/s/0/294ff1f2-0f27-11de-ba10-0000779fd2ac.html#axzz3bi3z3l4J

Financial Times (2015, 12 May). Good corporations should drive the economy. Retrieved from: http://www.ft.com/intl/cms/s/0/06f681ca-f887-11e4-beoo-00144feab7de.html#axzz3bi3z3l4J

Flanders, L. (2014). How America's largest worker owned co-ops lift people out of poverty. Retrieved from: http://www.yesmagazine.org/issues/the-end-of-poverty/how-america-s-largest-worker-owned-co-op-lifts-people-out-of-poverty

Fondazione Ernesto Illy (2015). Ernesto Illy. Retrieved from: http://www.fondazi-onernestoilly.org/fondazioneEilly/ENG/AboutUs-ErnestoIlly2.htm. Accessed 30 October 2015.

Forbes (2008). The world's billionaires. Retrieved from: http://www.forbes.com/2008/03/05/richest-people-billionaires-billionaires08-cx_lk_0305billie_land.html

Forbes (2014, 14 October). The unanticipated risks of maximizing shareholder value. Retrieved from: http://www.forbes.com/sites/stevedenning/2014/10/14/the-unanticipated-risks-of-maximizing-shareholder-value

Frankl, V.E. (2001). *Der Mensch vor der Frage nach dem Sinn* (13th edn). Munich: Piper Verlag. [English edition: Frankl, V.E. (2004). *Man's Search for Meaning*. London: Rider.]

Freeman, R.E. (1984). *Strategic Management: A Stakeholder Approach*. Boston, MA: Pitman.

Freeman, R.E., Harrison, J.S., Wicks, A.C., Parmar, B.L., & de Colle, S. (2010). *Stakeholder Theory: The State of the Art*. Cambridge: Cambridge University Press.

Freeman, R.E. (2016, May 25). Statement in the panel discussion "The Research-Practice Gap." GRONEN Research Conference 2016, Hamburg, Germany.

Fresco, J. (1974). Interview with Larry King. Retrieved from: https://www.youtube.com/watch?v=n2p8uydG3cs

Friedman, M. (1970, 13 September). The social responsibility of business is to increase its profits. *New York Times Magazine*, p. SM17.

Gardener's World (2013). BBC *Gardener's World* Magazine happiness report. Retrieved from: http://www.gardenersworld.com/downloads/PDFs/happiness-survey-results.pdf

Gasser, C. (2009). Ab neunzig arbeite ich halbtags. *Weltwoche*, 33. Retrieved from: http://www.weltwoche.ch/ausgaben/2009-33/artikel-2009-33-ab-neunzig-arbei.html

Gladwin, T.N., & Berdish, D. (2010, 8 February). MBAs unprepared for a morally complex future. *The Financial Times*. Retrieved from: http://www.ft.com/intl/cms/s/0/df5c80e2-1452-11df-8847-00144feab49a.html#axzz3rdtWBi8w

Gladwin, T.N., Kennelly, J.J., & Krause, T. (1995). Shifting paradigms for sustainable development: Implications for management theory and research. *Academy of Management Review*, 20(4), 874-907.

Godfrey, P.C. (2005). The relationship between corporate philanthrophy and shareholder wealth: A risk management perspective. *Academy of Management Review*, 30(4), 777-798.

Gogoi, P. (2008). Church groups espouse fair trade. *Bloomberg Business*. Retrieved from: http://www.bloomberg.com/bw/stories/2008-06-18/church-groups-espouse-fair-tradebusinessweek-business-news-stock-market-and-financial-advice

Goswami, U. (2006). Neuroscience and education: From research to practice? *Nature Reviews Neuroscience*, 7(5), 406-413.

Gordon, M.J., & Rosenthal, J.S. (2003). Capitalism's growth imperative. *Cambridge Journal of Economics*, 27(1), 25-48.

Graham, J. R., Harvey, C.R., & Rajgopal, S. (2006). Value destruction and financial reporting decisions. *Financial Analysts Journal*, 62(6), 27-39.

greatplacetowork.dk (2013). 11 år blandt Europas Bedste Arbejdspladser. Retrieved from: http://www.greatplacetowork.dk/publikationer-a-events/blog-a-nyheder/684-middelfart-sparekasse-11-ar-blandt-europas-bedste-arbejdspladser. Accessed August 11 2015.

Grinyer, J., Russell, A., & Collison, D. (1998). Evidence of managerial short-termism in the UK. *British Journal of Management*, 9(1), 13-22.

Gulati, R., Huffman, S., & Neilson, G.L. (2002). The barista principle: Starbucks and the rise of relational capital. *Strategy + Business*, 28.

haerle.de (2009). Brauerei Clemens Härle: seit 01. Januar zu 100 Prozent klimaneutral. Retrieved from: https://www.haerle.de/aktuelles.38.html

Haidt, J. (2006). *The Happiness Hypothesis: Finding Modern Truth in Ancient Wisdom*. New York: Basic Books.

Hall, P.A., & Soskice, D. (Eds.) (2001). *Varieties of Capitalism: The Institutional Foundations of Comparative Advantage*. Oxford: Oxford University Press.

Harari, Y.N. (2014). *Sapiens: A Brief History of Humankind*. London: Vintage Books.

Härle, G. (2014). Liebe Leserin, lieber Leser. *Härle Zeit*, November, 2.

Hart, S.L., & London, T. (2005). Developing native capability. *Stanford Social Innovation Review*, Summer, 28-33.

Havel, V. (1992, 1 March). The end of the modern era. *The New York Times*. Retrieved from: http://www.nytimes.com/1992/03/01/opinion/the-end-of-the-modern-era.html?pagewanted=all

Hawken, P., Lovins, A.B., & Lovins, L.H. (1999). *Natural Capitalism: The Next Industrial Revolution*. London: Earthscan Publications.

Heath, A. (2014, 10 December). The real reasons for the tragic demise of the British pub industry. *The Daily Telegraph*. Retrieved from: http://www.telegraph.co.uk/finance/newsbysector/retailandconsumer/11283995/The-real-reasons-for-the-tragic-demise-of-the-British-pub-industry.html

Henkel, S. (2012). Langlebig- und Reparaturfähig – Wichtige verkannte Bausteine. Presentation at the *Jahrestagung von IÖW und VÖW*, March 8-9 2012, Berlin.

Henrich, A. (2009). Admont-Wirtschaftsdirektor Neuner: "Es geht auch anders". Retrieved from: http://www.wiwo.de/unternehmen/interview-admont-wirtschaftsdirektor-neuner-es-geht-auch-anders-seite-2/5525220-2.html

Heracleous, L. & Lan, L.L. (2010). The myth of shareholder capitalism. *Harvard Business Review*, 88(4), 24.

Hevesi, D. (2008, 8 February). Ernesto Illy, chairman of coffee company, is dead at 82. *The New York Times*. Retrieved from: http://www.nytimes.com/2008/02/06/world/europe/06illy.html

Hofer, G. (2014, 5 October). Wir sind Täter, keine Opfer. *Die Presse*, p. 19.

Höfler, K. (2009, 13 August). Abt Bruno Hubl: "Nur schneller Gewinn – das kann es nicht sein." Retrieved from: http://diepresse.com/home/politik/innenpolitik/502019/Abt-Hubl_Nur-schneller-Gewinn-das-kann-es-nicht-sein

Honeyman, R. (2014). *The B Corp Handbook: How to Use Business as a Force for Good*. Oakland, CA: Berrett Koehler.

Illy, A. (2015). *A Coffee Dream*. Torino: Codice Edizioni.

Imbroscio, D.L., Williamson T., & Alperovitz, G. (2003). Local policy responses to globalization: Place-based ownership models of economic enterprise. *The Policy Studies Journal*, 31(1), 31-52.

inismeain.com (n.d.). Elemental eating. Retrieved from: http://inismeain.com/restaurant

Interface (2015a). Interface's history. Retrieved from: http://www.interfaceglobal.com/Company/History.aspx. Accessed August 10 2015.

Interface (2015b). Company. Retrieved from: http://www.interfaceglobal.com/company.aspx. Accessed August 28 2015.

Interface UK (2014). Interface Europe reaches sustainability milestones, achieving 90% carbon reduction. Retrieved from: http://www.interfaceflor.co.uk/web/about_us/media_centre_landing_page/press_releases/press-Interface-Europe-reaches-sustainability-milestones-achieving-90-carbon-reduction-. Published February 5 2014, accessed August 25 2015.

International Cooperative Alliance (2012). Top 300 co-operatives generate USD 2 trillion. Retrieved from: http://ica.coop/en/media/news/top-300-co-operatives-generate-usd-2-trillion

iöw (2015). Wir sind so frei: Elf Unternehmen lösen sich vom Wachstumspfad. Retrieved from: http://www.ioew.de/fileadmin/user_upload/BILDER_und_Downloaddateien/Publikationen/2015/Wir_sind_so_frei_-_Elf_Postwachstumspioniere.pdf

Irish Examiner (2014). Future hots up for island knitwear firm as profits rise. Retrieved from: http://www.irishexaminer.com/business/future-hots-up-for-island-knitwear-firm-as-profits-rise-258312.html

Irish Times (2008, 28 June). Bia blasta. Retrieved from: http://www.aran-isles.com/inis-meain.php

Irish Times (2010, 5 June). Top tables. Retrieved from: http://www.irishtimes.com/life-and-style/food-and-drink/restaurant-reviews/top-tables-1.674522

Jackson, T. (2011). *Prosperity Without Growth: Economics for a Finite Planet*. New York, NY: Earthscan.

Jensen, K. (2014). Trust: A fragile but wealth-building commodity. *Forbes*. Retrieved from: http://www.forbes.com/sites/keldjensen/2014/06/22/trust-a-fragile-but-wealth-building-commodity. Accessed August 10, 2015.

Jensen, M.C. (2001). Value maximization, stakeholder theory, and the corporate objective function. *European Financial Management*, 7(3), 297-317.

Jensen, M.C., & Erhard, W. (2011). A "value-free" approach to values. *Harvard Business School NOM Unit Working Paper* No. 11-010. http://papers.ssrn.com/sol3/papers.cfm?abstract_id=1640302, published April 11, 2011. Accessed June 24, 2016.

Jowett, B. (1999). *The Essential Plato*. New York, NY: Quality Paperback Club.

Kallis, G. (2011). In defence of degrowth. *Ecological Economics*, 70(5), 873-880.

Karner, G. (2010, July). Sustainable development is the only way for mankind and nature to survive. *SEKEM Insight*, 3.

Kasmir, S. (1996). *The Myth of Mondragón: Cooperatives, Politics, and Working-Class Life in a Basque Town*. Albany, NY: State University of New York Press.

Keats, J. (1919). To a Nightingale. In A. Quiller-Couch, *The Oxford Book of English Verse: 1250–1900* (pp. 630-644). Oxford: Clarendon.

Keynes, J.M. (1936). *The General Theory of Employment, Interest and Money*. London: Macmillan (repr. 2007).

Kiatpongsan, S., & Norton, M.I. (2014). How much (more) should CEOs make? A universal desire for more equal pay. *Perspectives on Psychological Science*, 9(6), 587-593.

Kim, W.C., & Mauborgne, R. (2004). Blue ocean strategy. *Harvard Business Review*, 82(10), 76-84.

Kjerulf, A. (2014). 5 simple office policies that make Danish workers way more happy than Americans. Retrieved from: http://www.fastcoexist.com/3029110/5-simple-office-policies-that-make-danish-workers-way-more-happy-than-americans

Kotler, P., Kartajaya, H., & Setiawan, I. (2010). *Marketing 3.0: From Products to Customers to the Human Spirit*. Hoboken, NJ: Wiley.

Kronawitter, E. (2013a). *Führen ohne Druck: Erfolgreiches Bankgeschäft ohne Zielvorgaben und vertriebsabhängige Vergütungen*. Wiesbaden: Springer Gabler.

Kronawitter, E. (2013b). Führen ohne Druck. *Bankinformation – Das Fachmagazin der Volksbanken Raiffeisenbanken*, May, 50-53.

Kump, A. (2012). Am Boden bleiben. *Adoro – Your Admonter Magazine*, 2, pp. 10-17.

Lafuente, J.L., & Freundlich, F. (2012). The Mondragón cooperative experience: Humanity at work. Retrieved from: http://www.managementexchange.com/story/Mondragón-cooperative-experience-humanity-work

Lander, N. (2011, 21 October). Fresh and wild. *The Financial Times*. Retrieved from: http://www.ft.com/cms/s/2/2ef67046-f9de-11e0-9c26-00144feab49a.html

Lawless, G., & Reynolds, A. (2004). Worker cooperatives: Case studies, key criteria & best practices. University of Wisconsin Center for Cooperatives Staff Paper (3).

Laurence, L. (2009). Desso beats goals with nine cradle to cradle carpets. Retrieved from: http://www.sustainablebrands.com/news_and_views/articles/desso-beats-goals-nine-cradle-cradle-carpets

Lester, R.K., & Piore, M.J. (2004). *Innovation – The Missing Dimension*. Boston, MA: Harvard University Press.

Lewitan, L. (2013, 21 February1). Kaffee in der DNA (D. Sternad, J.J. Kennelly & F. Bradley, Trans.). *Zeit Online*. Retrieved from: http://www.zeit.de/2013/09/Rettung-Andrea-Illy-Kaffee

Lindeman, E.C. (1926). To discover the meaning of experience. *Survey*, 55, 545-546.

Linley, P.A., Maltby, J., Wood, A.M., Osborne, G., & Hurling, R. (2009). Measuring happiness: The higher order factor structure of subjective and psychological well-being measures. *Personality and Individual Differences*, 47(8), 878-884.

livingalifeincolour.com (2013, October 27). Show me a proud farmer. Retrieved from: http://www.livingalifeincolour.com/show-me-a-proud-farmer. Accessed July 16, 2015.

Logue, J., & Yates, J. (2005). Productivity in cooperatives and worker-owned enterprises: Ownership and participation make a difference! Paper prepared as a background paper for the *World Employment Report 2004–05*. Geneva: Employment Sector, International Labour Office.

Ludden, J. (2012). Home help aides: In demand, yet paid little. *National Public Radio*. Retrieved from: http://www.npr.org/2012/10/16/162808677/home-health-aides-in-demand-yet-paid-little

Markevich, A. (2009). The evolution of sustainability. *Sloan Management Review*, 51(1), 13-14.

McCloskey, D. (2010). *Bourgeois Dignity: Why Economics Can't Explain the Modern World*. Chicago: University of Chicago Press.

McDonough, W., & Braungart, M. (2002). *Cradle to Cradle: Remaking the Way We Make Things*. New York, NY: North Point Press.

McKenna, J., & McKenna S. (2008). *The Bridgestone 100 Best Restaurants in Ireland 2009*. Durrus: Estragon Press.

McKinsey (2013). Focusing capital on the long term. Retrieved from: http://www.mckinsey.com/insights/leading_in_the_21st_century/focusing_capital_on_the_long_term

McQuillan, D. (2011, 4 September). Inis Meáin. *Financial Times*. Retrieved from: http://howtospendit.ft.com/style/6010-inis-mein

McWilliams, D. (2015, August 17). The cashed up new collectives. *Irish Independent*. Retrieved from: http://www.davidmcwilliams.ie/2015/08/17

Meyerson, H. (2014, 11 February). Harold Meyerson: The myth of maximizing shareholder value. *The Washington Post*. Retrieved from: http://www.washingtonpost.com/opinions/harold-meyerson-the-myth-of-maximizing-shareholder-value/2014/02/11/00cdfb14-9336-11e3-84e1-27626c5ef5fb_story.html

Mintzberg, H. (2004). *Managers, Not MBAs*. London: Financial Times Prentice Hall.

Monbiot, G. (2015, 31 March). "Wealth creators" are robbing our most productive people. *The Guardian*. Retrieved from: http://www.theguardian.com/commentisfree/2015/mar/31/wealth-creators-klepto-rewards-bosses

Mondragón Corporation (2015a). The "MONDRAGON of the Future" project is at the analysis by co-operative stages. Retrieved from: http://www.mondragon-corporation.com/eng/the-mondragon-of-the-future-project-is-at-the-analysis-by-co-operatives-stage

Mondragón Corporation (2015b). Home page. Retrieved from: http://www.mondragon-corporation.com/eng

Mondragón Corporation (2015c). Our principles. Retrieved from: http://www.mondragon-corporation.com/eng/co-operative-experience/our-principles

MoralHeroes (2015). Aaron Feuerstein. Retrieved from: http://moralheroes.org/aaron-feuerstein

MoreThanMoney (2002). After the fire. *MoreThanMoney*, 31(Fall/Winter), 16-17.

Mount, I. (2013, 27 November). Defiant Spanish workers stage lock-in, resist layoffs. *Fortune*. Retrieved from: http://fortune.com/2013/11/27/defiant-spanish-workers-stage-lock-in-resist-layoffs

Neßhöver, C. (2013). Das Grauen der deutschen Brauer. Retrieved from: http://www.manager-magazin.de/unternehmen/artikel/bier-ruin-deutscher-brauer-schwieriger-biermarkt-a-940119.html

Nevins, J.L., Bearden, W.O., & Money, B. (2006). Ethical values and long-term orientation. *Journal of Business Ethics*, 71(3), pp. 261-274.

Niko (2015). Middelfart Sparkekasse: Unique lighting for unique building. Retrieved from: http://www.niko.eu/enus/niko/realisations/subprojectdetail/Middelfart

Nocera, J. (2012, 10 August). Down with shareholder value. *The New York Times.* Retrieved from: http://www.nytimes.com/2012/08/11/opinion/nocera-down-with-shareholder-value.html?_r=0

oikocredit (2014, May 27). Vom "verrückten Ägypter" zum alternativen Nobelpreis. Retrieved from: http://www.oikocredit.at/k/n1042/news/view/79958/2314/vom-verruckten-agypter-zum-alternativen-nobelpreis.html. Accessed July 13, 2015.

Old Crown Pub (2015). The Old Crown. Retrieved from: http://www.theoldcrownpub.co.uk/history. Accessed March 19, 2015.

OSB (2015). The Rule of Benedict. Retrieved from: http://www.osb.org/rb/text/rbemjo1.html

Oxford Rural Community Council (2013). Saving the village pub. Retrieved from: http://www.oxonrcc.org.uk/Content/Sites/oxonrcc-org-uk/Documents/Saving%20the%20Village%20Pub.pdf

Paarlberg, R. (2015). *The United States of Excess: Gluttony and the Dark Side of American Exceptionalism.* New York, NY: Oxford University Press.

Paech, N. (2012). *Liberation from Excess.* Munich: Oekom Verlag.

Palmisano, S. (2014). Managing investors. *Harvard Business Review*, 92(6), pp. 80-85.

Pegolotti, F.B. (1766). *Della Decima e Delle Altre Gravezze, Vol. 3 (Contenente La Pratica della Mercatura).* Lisbon and Lucca: Giuseppe Bouchard Librajo.

Pencavel, J., Pistaferri, L., & Schivardi, F. (2006). Wages, employment, and capital in capitalist and worker-owned firms. *Industrial and Labor Relations Review*, 60(1), 23-44.

Perrini, F., & Russo, A. (2008). illycaffè: Value creation through responsible supplier relationships. *Journal of Business Ethics Education*, 5, 139-170.

Peterson, C., Park, N., & Seligman, M.E. (2005). Orientations to happiness and life satisfaction: The full life versus the empty life. *Journal of Happiness Studies*, 6(1), 25-41.

phinational.org (2015). Survey: Home care worker turnover topped 60 percent in 2014. Retrieved from: http://phinational.org/blogs/survey-home-care-worker-turnover-topped-60-percent-2014

Pink, D.H. (2006). *A Whole New Mind: Why Right-Brainers Will Rule the Future.* New York: Riverhead Books.

Pirsig, R.M. (1974). *Zen and the Art of Motorcycle Maintenance.* New York, NY: Random House.

Plato (n.d.). *The Republic* (B. Jowett, Trans.). Retrieved from: http://classics.mit.edu/Plato/republic.3.ii.html

Plunkett Foundation (n.d. a). New support launched to help communities save local pub as a cooperative. Retrieved from: http://www.plunkett.co.uk/news-andmedia/news-item.cfm/newsid/674. Accessed March 18 2015.

Plunkett Foundation (n.d. b). Co-operative Pubs: What are they and is it right for my community. http://www.open4community.info/bradford1/documents/bradford/Co-operative_Pubs.pdf. Accessed March 18, 2015.

Plunkett Foundation (2014). *Cooperative Pubs 2014: A Better Way of Business.* Woodstock: The Plunkett Foundation.

Pope Francis (2015). *Encyclical Letter Laudato Si' of the Holy Father Francis on Care for our Common Home.* Vatican City: Vatican Press.

Porter, M.E. & Kramer, M.R. (2011). Creating shared value. *Harvard Business Review*, 89(1/2), 62-77.

Post, S.G. (2005). Altruism, happiness, and health: It's good to be good. *International Journal of Behavioral Medicine*, 12(2), 66-77.

Prahalad, C.K., & Hammond, A. (2002). Serving the world's poor, profitably. *Harvard Business Review*, 80(9), 48-57.

Pretty, J. (2004). How nature contributes to mental and physical health. *Spirituality and Health International*, 5(2), 68-78.

PYMNTS.com (2013). Fireside chat with Warren Buffett. Retrieved from: http://www.pymnts.com/uncategorized/2013/warren-buffett-video

Raiffeisenbank Ichenhausen (2015). Raiffeisenbank Ichenhausen "Die etwas andere Bank" Warum? Retrieved from: https://www.rb-ichenhausen.de/wir-fuer-sie/ueber-uns/leitbild.html

Ready, D. (2002). How storytelling builds next-generation leaders. *Sloan Management Review*, 43(4), 63-69.

Reich, R. (1991). Who is them? *Harvard Business Review*, 69(2), 77-88.

Reisinger, R.M., & Brandstätter, C. (2013, June 24). Erfolg ist so einfach. Interview with Johannes Gutmann. Retrieved from: http://www.lebensart.at/erfolgist-so-einfach. Accessed July 15, 2015.

Relph, E. (2009). A pragmatic sense of place. *Environmental and Architectural Phenomenology*, 20(3), 24-31.

Rieder, C.H., Miller, C., & Sturgeon, J.M. (2012, 9 December). Too few good jobs? Make bad jobs better. *The Huffington Post*. Retrieved from: http://www.huffingtonpost.com/corinne-h-rieder/make-bad-jobs-better_b_1953051.html

Roberts, C. (2014, 28 August). Suma: the natural food wholesaler run by workers on equal pay. *The Guardian*. Retrieved from: https://www.theguardian.com/sustainable-business/2014/aug/28/suma-the-natural-food-wholesaler-run-by-workers-on-equal-pay

Roberts, P.W., & Dowling, G.R. (2002). Corporate reputation and sustained superior financial performance. *Strategic Management Journal*, 23, 1077-1093.

Robinson, T. (1995). *Stones of Aran: Labyrinth*. London: Penguin.

Roosevelt, F.D. (1912). Speech at the People's Forum in Troy, New York (March 3, 1912). Retrieved from: https://ir.library.oregonstate.edu/xmlui/bitstream/handle/1957/9445/FDR_and_Con_1911_1945_vol_1.pdf?sequence=1

Rose, J.M. (2007). Corporate directors and social responsibility: Ethics versus shareholder value. *Journal of Business Ethics*, 73(3), 319-331.

Ruhling, N.A. (2011). Be the change. *Lifestyles Magazine*, Fall 2011, pp. 126-131.

Russell, B. (2009). *Human Society in Ethics and Politics*. London: Routledge.

Sanders, L. (2012, 13 January). Are the Green Bay Packers the worst stock in America? *The Wall Street Journal*. Retrieved from: http://blogs.wsj.com/totalreturn/2012/01/13/are-the-green-bay-packers-the-worst-stock-in-america

Saskatchewan Co-operative Association (2015). Co-op facts and figures. Retrieved from: http://www.sask.coop/facts_and_figures.html#How_many_coops

SBE Council (2015). Small business facts & data. Retrieved from: http://www.sbecouncil.org/about-us/facts-and-data

Schieffer, A., & Lessem, R. (2014). *Integral Development: Realising the Transformative Potential of Individuals, Organisations and Societies*. Farnham: Gower Publishing.

Schopenhauer, G. (1851). *Parerga and Paralipomena: Kleine philosophische Schriften*, Volume 1. Berlin: A.W. Hahn.

Schrot & Korn (2004). Interview with Helmy Abouleish. Schrot & Korn, issue 4. Retrieved from: http://schrotundkorn.de/lebenumwelt/lesen/200404b2.html. Accessed July 10, 2015.

Schumacher, E.F. (1973). *Small is Beautiful: A Study of Economics As If People Mattered*. New York, NY: Harper & Row.

Schumann, H. (2010, June 5). Die Grenzüberschreitung. *Der Tagesspiegel*. Retrieved from: http://www.tagesspiegel.de/wirtschaft/mythos-wachstum-die-grenzueberschreitung/1851786.html

Schweitzer, A. (1998). *The Primeval Forest*. Baltimore: The Johns Hopkins University Press.

Seelos, C., & Mair, J. (2007). SEKEM: Liberating a vision, an artistic approach to entrepreneurship. *IESE Business School Case Study* no. DG-1466-E0-304-072.

Sehgal, K. (2015). *Coined: The Rich Life of Money and How Its History Has Shaped Us*. London: John Murray.

SEKEM (2014, June 5). Weltumwelttag 2014: Kein "Business as Usual" – Geschäft und Nachhaltigkeit müssen Hand in Hand gehen. SEKEM Group Press Release.

SEKEM (2015a). The idea of sustainable development and giving back to the community. Retrieved from: http://www.SEKEM.com/aboutus.html. Accessed July 13, 2015.

SEKEM (2015b). The vision of sustainable development in the desert ... became reality. Retrieved from: http://www.SEKEM.com/vision.html. Accessed July 13, 2015.

Senge, P., Scharmer, C.O., Jaworski, J., & Flowers, B.S. (2004). *Presence: Human Purpose and the Field of the Future.* New York: Doubleday.

Seventh Generation (2014). A Generation of Good: 2013 Corporate Consciousness Report. Burlington, VT: Seventh Generation.

Shiller, R.J. (2012). *Finance and the Good Society.* Princeton, NJ: Princeton University Press.

Smith, A. (1904). *An Inquiry into the Nature and Causes of the Wealth of Nations* (5th edn). Edited by Edwin Cannan. Originally published in 1776. Retrieved from: http://www.econlib.org/library/Smith/smWN1.html#I.2.2

Snyder, G. (1995). *The Rediscovery of Turtle Island in a Place in Space.* Washington, DC: Counterpoint.

Stahl, G., & Sully de Luque, M. (2014). Antecedents of responsible leader behavior: A research synthesis, conceptual framework, and agenda for future research. *Academy of Management Perspectives*, 28(3), 235-254.

Stamp, S. (2014). Expansion um jeden Preis? Retrieved from: ttp://www.neueshandeln.de/blogazin/expansion-um-jeden-preis

St. Augustine (1843). *The Confessions of St. Augustine* (E.B. Pusey, Trans). Oxford: John Henry Parker.

Stein, N. (2002, 9 December). Crisis in a coffee cup. The price of beans has crashed. Growers around the world are starving. And the quality of your morning cup is worse. So why is everyone blaming Vietnam? *Fortune.* Retrieved from: http://archive.fortune.com/magazines/fortune/fortune_archive/2002/12/09/333463/index.htm

Sternad, D. (2013). Managerial long-term responsibility in family-controlled firms. *Management*, 8(2), pp. 93-107.

Sternad, D. (2015). Organic growth at Sonnentor. Ivey Publishing case nr. 9B15M031. London, Ontario: Ivey Publishing.

Sternad, D. (2016). *Long-term orientation in the Benedictine monastery of Admont.* London, ON: Ivey Publishing, 12. Available from Ivey Publishing, product no. 9B16M045.

Stieber, B. (2013). Weniger bringt mehr. *enorm: Wirtschaft für die Menschen*, 5, 42-45.

Stout, L.A. (2013, April 13). The shareholder value myth. *The European Financial Review.* Retrieved from: http://www.europeanfinancialreview.com/?p=883.

Sugarman, B. (2000). *A Learning-Based Approach to Leading Change.* Arlington, VA: The PricewaterhouseCoopers Endowment for the Business of Government.

Sully de Luque, M., Washburn, N.T., Waldman, D.A., & House, R.J. (2008). Unrequited profit: How stakeholder and economic values relate to subordinates perceptions of leadership and firm performance. *Administrative Science Quarterly,* 53(4), 626-654.

Suma (2010). Suma shortlisted for another Grocer Gold Award. Retrieved from: http://www.suma.coop/2010/04/suma-shortlisted-for-a-second-grocer-gold-award

Suma (2015). Home. Retrieved from: http://www.suma.coop

Sunday Business Post (2012, 8 January). Smart men of Aran. *Agenda Magazine.*

Sweeney, G. (Ed.) (2001). *Innovation, Economic Progress and the Quality of Life.* Cheltenham, UK: Edward Elgar.

swp.de (2012). Reparieren statt produzieren. Retrieved from: http://www.swp.de/ulm/nachrichten/wirtschaft/Reparieren-statt-produzieren;art4325,1535859

taz.de (2015). "Es gibt Alternativen zur Wachstumsstrategie". Retrieved from: http://www.taz.de/1/archiv/digitaz/artikel/?ressort=wu&dig=2015%2F02%2F23%2Fa0046&cHash=faf6e1d8e67429c493b9cfccd897fc2b

The Right Livelihood Award (2013, March). SEKEM/Ibrahim Abouleish (Egypt). Retrieved from: http://www.rightlivelihood.org/SEKEM.html. Accessed July 9, 2015.

thinkprogress.org (2015). Court ruling grants home care minimum wage, overtime protection. Retrieved from: http://thinkprogress.org/economy/2015/08/21/3693967/appeals-court-home-care-minimum-wage

Tracy, A. (2014, 20 March). Seth Godin on what marketers are getting wrong. *Inc. com.* Retrieved from: http://www.inc.com/abigail-tracy/seth-godin-marketing-is-not-about-paying-for-attention.html

Trumpf (2015). Company principles. Retrieved from: http://www.trumpf.com/en/company/company-principles.html

UNCTAD (2012). World investment report 2012: Towards a new generation of investment policies. Retrieved from: http://unctad.org/en/PublicationChapters/diaeia2012a4_en.pdf

Unterberger, G. (2008). 15 Jahre Wirtschaftsführung im Stift Admont. *PAX – Magazin des Benediktinerstiftes Admont,* 1, pp. 20-23.

Value (2015). In *Oxford Dictionaries.* Retrieved from: http://www.oxforddictionaries.com/definition/english/value

Van Gogh (1883). Letter to Anthon van Rappard, 15 June 1883. Retrieved from: http://vangoghletters.org/vg/letters/let354/letter.html

Veda, T. (2014, September 2). Helanti Hilman: Preserving Indonesia's indigenous culinary riches. Retrieved from: https://titaniaveda.wordpress.com/2014/09/02/the-woman-behind-javara. Accessed 17 July 2015.

Voltaire (1918). *Candide*. New York: Boni and Liveright. Available at http://www.gutenberg.org/files/19942/19942-h/19942-h.htm. Published November 27, 2006, accessed July 13, 2015.

Weinstein, N., & Ryan, R.M. (2010). When helping helps: Autonomous motivation for prosocial behavior and its influence on well-being for the helper and recipient. *Journal of Personality and Social Psychology*, 98(2), 222-244.

Weiser, S., & Stone, O. (1987). *Wall Street*. Retrieved from: http://www.americanrhetoric.com/MovieSpeeches/moviespeechwallstreet.html

whiteboardjournal (2013, August 28). The wealth of indigenous Indonesia with Helianti Hilman. Retrieved from: http://www.whiteboardjournal.com/interview/10552/the-wealth-of-indigenous-indonesia-with-helianti-hilman. Accessed 16 July 2015.

Wilde, O. (1894). *A Woman of No Importance*. Retrieved from: http://www.gutenberg.org/files/854/854-h/854-h.html

Williams, R.C. (2007). *The Cooperative Movement: Globalization from Below*. Aldershot: Ashgate Publishing Ltd.

Wirl, C. (2011). Tausche Audi Quattro gegen 2,5 Tonnen Anis. Interview with Johannes Gutmann. Retrieved from: http://www.magazintraining.com/2011/07/10/hr-interview-052011. Accessed August 29, 2013.

Wirtschaftsblatt.at (2015, June 11). Sonnentor wächst weiter kräftig. Retrieved from: http://wirtschaftsblatt.at/home/nachrichten/oesterreich/niederoesterreich/4752823/Sonnentor-waechst-weiter-kraeftig. Accessed July 29, 2015.

Wolfers, J. (2014, May 5). How Gary Becker transformed the social sciences. *The New York Times*. http://www.nytimes.com/2014/05/06/upshot/how-gary-becker-transformed-the-social-sciences.html?_r=0. Accessed June 7, 2016.

Yeats, W.B. (1916). *Responsibilities and Other Poems*. New York: The Macmillan Company.

Zamagni, S., & Zamagni, V. (2010). *Cooperative Enterprise: Facing the Challenge of Globalization*. Cheltenham: Edward Elgar.

About the authors

Dr. Dietmar Sternad is Professor of International Management and the Program Director of the "International Business Management" master's program at Carinthia University of Applied Sciences (Austria), where he teaches several management and leadership-related subjects in both full-time and executive programs. He  holds degrees from the universities of Graz and Klagenfurt (Austria), the Open University (GB), and IEDC Bled School of Management (Slovenia). In his prior managerial career, he was the Managing Director and Publisher of one of Austria's leading trade book publishing groups and the CEO of Slovenia's highest-circulation daily newspaper. He has also lectured at universities and business schools in Belgium, France, Italy, Poland, and Slovenia, is an alumnus of the IMTA (CEEMAN) and GloColl (Harvard Business School) management teachers' programs and received several national and international awards for creating case-based teaching materials (e.g. from the Academy of Management or from Emerald/CEEMAN) and

Photo: Helge Bauer/FH Kärnten

for teaching excellence (he was the first management professor ever to receive the *Austrian State Prize for Teaching Excellence*). Sternad has authored and edited several books and published in a range of scientific journals. His current research interests focus on responsible business and management practices and strategies of qualitative enterprise growth.

Dr. James J. Kennelly is Professor of International Business and the Courtney and Steven Ross Chair in Interdisciplinary Studies at Skidmore College, Saratoga Springs, New York. He has also taught at NYU's Stern School of Business and at Aalto University (Finland). In his first career he held managerial positions in accounting and  finance for multinational enterprises including Bristol-Myers Squibb and N.V. Philips. He holds an MBA and Ph.D. from the Stern School of Business at NYU in International Business and Management. Kennelly has published in the *Academy of Management Review, Sustainable Development, Case Research Journal, Organization and Environment, New Hibernia Review, Studies*, and other journals. His book *The Kerry Way: A History of the Kerry Group* was published by the Oak Tree Press in 2001. He has co-authored three books with Finbarr Bradley: *Gombeens at the Gate: Renewing the Rising through Ideals, Character and Place* (Teacht Anair, 2016), *The Irish Edge: How Enterprises Compete on Authenticity and Place* (Orpen Press, 2013), and *Capitalising on Culture, Competing on Difference: Innovation, Learning and Sense of Place in a Globalising Ireland* (Blackhall Publishing, 2008). His current research interests center on indigenous, place-based enterprises as necessary components of a sustainable economy and society.

Dr. Finbarr Bradley teaches at the Michael Smurfit Graduate Business School, University College Dublin. He worked as an engineer with GE in Ireland, U.S.A., and Korea. He was a professor of finance at Dublin City University where he also set up and was director of its Irish-medium center, *Fiontar*. He was a professor in the Economics Department at  Maynooth University and visiting professor at the University of Michigan, Fordham University, and Aalto University. He previously co-authored three books with James Kennelly, *Gombeens at the Gate: Renewing the Rising through Ideals, Character and Place* (Teacht Aniar, 2016), *The Irish Edge: How Enterprises Compete on Authenticity and Place* (Orpen Press, 2013), and *Capitalising on Culture, Competing on Difference: Innovation, Learning and Sense of Place in a Globalising Ireland* (Blackhall Publishing, 2008). He wrote the Irish-language book *Meol Gaelach, Aigne Nuálaíoch* (Coiscéim, 2011) and co-edited a book of essays from the 2009 MacGill Summer School, *Ireland's Economic Crisis: Time to Act* (Carysfort Press, 2009). Finbarr Bradley graduated with an electrical engineering degree from University College Cork, has an MBA from Syracuse University, New York and a Ph.D. from the Stern School of Business, New York University (NYU).

Photo: Máire Uí Mhaicín/Foras na Gaeilge